Business Companion:
SPANISH

TIM DOBBINS
PAUL WESTBROOK

Translation and culture notes by
CARLOS VEGA

Edited by
ZVJEZDANA VRZIĆ

LIVING LANGUAGE®
A Random House Company

Available from LIVING LANGUAGE

IN THE KNOW. This cross-cultural guide makes it simple for business people and their families to adapt successfully to their new surroundings, whether it's for a long-term relocation or just for a short business trip. Learn how to give toasts, speeches, and presentations while steering clear of potentially embarrassing or offensive gaffes in the office, at a meeting, or in social situations. This guide supplies essential background information on each country and its culture, with information on business environments, company structures, work attire, women in business, meetings, communication, and everyday life. The package also includes an audio CD to help the reader master basic social expressions. Guides are available for China, Germany, and Mexico & Central America.

ULTIMATE COURSES. The comprehensive program covers conversation, grammar, reading, writing, and culture. Each of the 40 lessons begins with a dialogue and includes explanations of grammar and usage, vocabulary, and notes on customs and culture. Unique to this course are two sets of recordings: four hours in the target language for use with the manual, and four bilingual recordings ideal for learning on the go. Basic–Intermediate. French, German, Inglés, Italian, Japanese, Russian, Spanish, Portuguese, and Chinese.

ULTIMATE ADVANCED COURSES. Sequels to the Basic–Intermediate program, these courses include sections on business vocabulary and etiquette in addition to the dialogue-based lessons. Advanced. French, German, Inglés, Italian, Japanese, Russian, and Spanish.

COMPLETE BASIC COURSES (Level 1). The original, best-selling Living Language program developed by U.S. government experts in 1946, revised and updated in 1993, includes three hours of recordings on cassette or compact disc, a manual, and a two-way, 20,000-word dictionary. Featuring a proven speed-learning method, the course progresses from words to phrases to complete sentences and dialogues. Recordings are done entirely in the target language. Beginner–Intermediate. French, German, Inglés, Italian, Japanese, Portuguese, Russian, and Spanish.

LIVING LANGUAGE® SKILL BUILDER: VERBS. This course teaches more than 150 conjugations through practical phrases and dialogues. The set includes four 60-minute bilingual cassettes and a 384-page text with 40 dialogues, exercises, and verb charts. Intermediate. French, German, Italian, and Spanish.

Books also available separately.

Living Language® publications are available at special discounts for bulk purchases for sales promotions or premiums, as well as for fund-raising or educational use. Special editions can be created in large quantities for special needs. For more information, write to: Special Sales Manager, Living Language, 280 Park Ave., New York, NY 10017.

At bookstores everywhere. You can also reach us on the Web at:
www.livinglanguage.com

To my sons, Matt and John Dobbins, for continuously reminding me to not take myself too seriously. To my parents, Christine and Peter, for letting me spend my most joyous years of childhood in the Spanish culture of Quito, Ecuador. To my brother, Dan, for his unconditional support of my vision to help others communicate beyond their differences. And finally, for his editorial contribution, to Christopher Warnasch, who has never, until now, had a book dedicated to him. *Pax Domini.*

—*Tim Dobbins*

To business men and women around the globe who are practicing the noblest of professions: business.

—*Paul Westbrook*

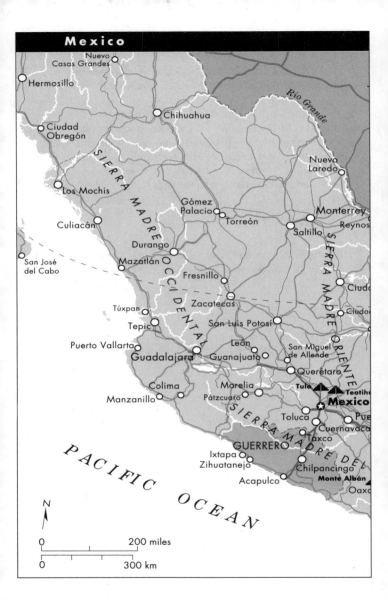

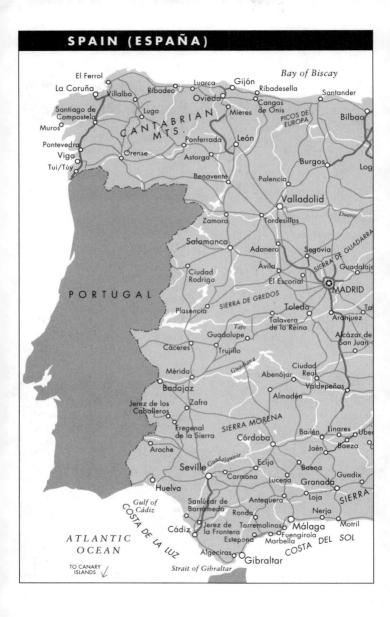

SPAIN (ESPAÑA)

Bay of Biscay

El Ferrol
La Coruña
Villalba
Ribadeo
Luarca
Gijón
Ribadesella
Santander
Santiago de Compostela
Oviedo
Cangas de Onís
PICOS DE EUROPA
Bilbao
Muros
Lugo
Mieres
CANTABRIAN MTS.
Pontevedra
Orense
Ponferrada
León
Burgos
Log
Vigo
Astorga
Tui/Túy
Benavente
Palencia
Valladolid
Zamora
Tordesillas
Duero
Salamanca
Adanero
Segovia
SIERRA DE GUADARRA
Ciudad Rodrigo
Ávila
Guadalaja
El Escorial
MADRID
PORTUGAL
SIERRA DE GREDOS
Toledo
Plasencia
Ta
Talavera de la Reina
Aranjuez
Tajo
Guadalupe
Alcázar de San Juan
Cáceres
Trujillo
Guadiana
Mérida
Abenójar
Ciudad Real
Badajoz
Valdepeñas
Jerez de los Caballeros
Zafra
Almadén
Fregenal de la Sierra
SIERRA MORENA
Córdoba
Bailén
Linares
Ube
Aroche
Jaén
Baeza
Seville
Guadalquivir
Écija
Baena
Huelva
Carmona
Lucena
Granada
Guadix
Antequera
Loja
SIERRA
Gulf of Cádiz
Sanlúcar de Barrameda
Ronda
Nerja
COSTA DE LA LUZ
Cádiz
Jerez de la Frontera
Torremolinos
Málaga
Motril
ATLANTIC OCEAN
Estepona
Fuengirola
Marbella
COSTA DEL SOL
Algeciras
Gibraltar
TO CANARY ISLANDS
Strait of Gibraltar

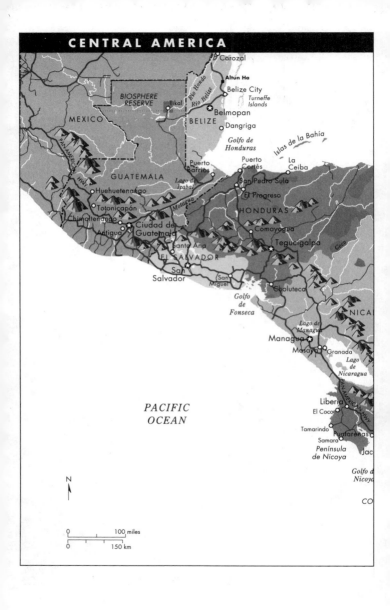

CENTRAL AMERICA

Corozal

Altún Ha

Belize City

Turneffe
Islands

Río Hondo

BIOSPHERE
RESERVE

Río Belize

Tikal

MEXICO

Belmopan

BELIZE

Dangriga

Golfo de
Honduras

Islas de la Bahía

Puerto
Cortés

Puerto
Barrios

La
Ceiba

GUATEMALA

San Pedro Sula

Lago de
Izabal

El Progreso

Huehuetenango

Motagua

HONDURAS

Totonicapán

Chimaltenango

Ciudad de
Guatemala

Comayagua

Antigua

Tegucigalpa

Coco

Santa Ana

EL SALVADOR

San
Salvador

San
Miguel

Choluteca

Golfo
de
Fonseca

NICA

Lago de
Managua

Managua

Granada

Masaya

Lago
de
Nicaragua

PACIFIC
OCEAN

Liberia

El Coco

Tamarindo

Puntarenas

Samara

Península
de Nicoya

Jac

Golfo d
Nicoya

N

CO

0   100 miles

0   150 km

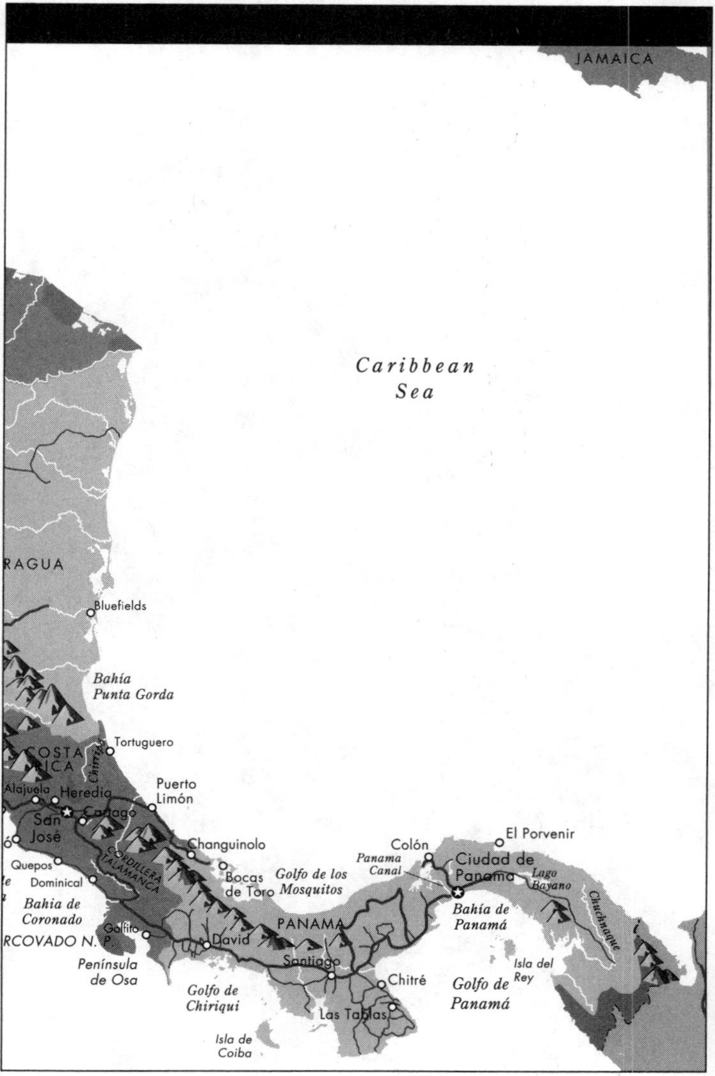
JAMAICA
Caribbean
Sea
RAGUA
Bluefields
Bahía
Punta Gorda
Tortuguero
COSTA
RICA
Chirripó
Puerto
Limón
Alajuela
Heredia
San
José
Cartago
CORDILLERA
TALAMANCA
Quepos
Dominical
Bahia de
Coronado
Golfito
RCOVADO N. P.
Península
de Osa
Changuinolo
Bocas
de Toro
Golfo de los
Mosquitos
PANAMA
David
Santiago
Chitré
Las Tablas
Golfo de
Chiriqui
Isla de
Coiba
Colón
Panama
Canal
El Porvenir
Ciudad de
Panamá
Lago
Bayano
Chuchnaque
Bahía de
Panamá
Isla del
Rey
Golfo de
Panamá

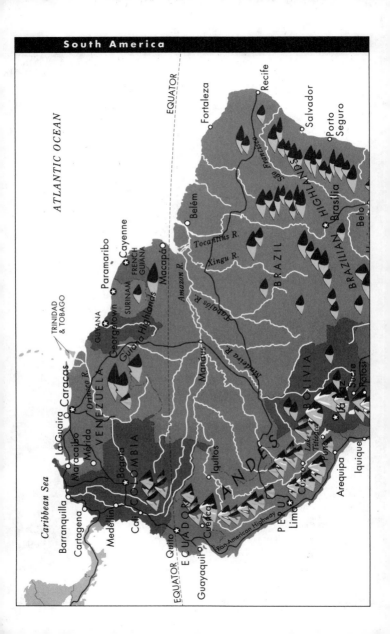

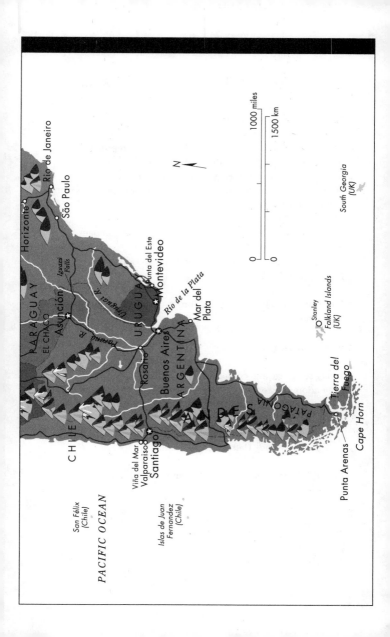

Maps © 1998, 2000, Fodor's Travel Publications.

Published by Living Language, A Random House Company,
New York, New York.
Living Language is a member of the Random House
Information Group.

Random House, Inc. New York, Toronto, London, Sydney,
Auckland

www.livinglanguage.com

Manufactured in the United States.

Designed by Wendy Halitzer.

Library of Congress Cataloging-in-Publication Data available.

ISBN 0-609-80628-9

10   9   8   7   6   5   4   3   2   1

First Paperback Edition

ACKNOWLEDGMENTS

Thanks to the Living Language staff: Lisa Alpert, Elizabeth Bennett, Christopher Warnasch, Suzanne McGrew, Helen Tang, Elyse Tomasello, Fernando Galeano, Marina Padakis, Pat Ehresmann, and Wendy Halitzer. Thanks also to David Salas Mezquita.

AUTHOR INFORMATION

Timothy Dobbins, M Div., is a communications and strategic alignment specialist. As President of Leadership Technologies, Inc./Cultural Architects™.com, he provides advice, direction, and conflict management skills. An Episcopal priest, he was educated in the United States and Jerusalem, and had studied at the C.G. Jung Institute in Zurich. He lives in Philadelphia and New York City.

Paul Westbrook has a broad business background, and has worked for major corporations and business consulting firms. He is now running his own financial and retirement firm, WestBrook Financial Advisers, in Ridgewood, New Jersey. He is the author of *Word Smart for Business* and *Math Smart for Business*, both published by Random House.

CONTENTS

2 Getting Involved

3 Getting Out

4 Getting Around

5 Getting Businessized

6 Reference

Appendix A:
Measurements 205

Appendix B:
Useful Addresses, Telephone Numbers,
and Web Sites 209

Appendix C:
Religious and National Holidays
in Spanish-speaking Countries 215

Appendix D:
Grammar Summary and Verb Charts 217

Glossary of Industry-Specific Terms

General Glossary

Index

Acknowledgments

Preface

It can be said that business is the basis of human relationship. The opportunity to interact with people beyond our own "hometown experience" is both a growing necessity and a challenging adventure. Business never stops. Journeying from one country to another becomes easier every day. *Business Companion* is written for people in the global marketplace of today's world.

But, you don't need to cross borders to experience the people and culture of other lands. In today's global marketplace, business is conducted without borders. The telecommunications revolution allows the businessperson to travel to distant lands measured not in miles but in megahertz.

Do business in Hong Kong, Mexico City and Berlin, without ever leaving your desk! Of course, a great deal of global business is conducted in English. Yet, these interactions are enhanced and strengthened by the strategic use of key words and phrases in the others' native tongue, and placed in letters, conversations and over the Internet.

The primary aim of this book, then, is to provide you with the tools to put language to work for you, even if you don't have the time for a traditional language course. Whether you travel to work in foreign lands by plane, train, ship, telephone, or computer, this book will increase your business self-confidence and help you develop the power of using a foreign language. After all, communicating on a global level will only continue to be essential in the workplace of the 21st century.

The second, and subtler purpose of this book is to offer you proven and effective ways to communicate the keywords and phrases themselves. This aim has to do with enhancing your global communication skills. Whenever business leaders ask me to help them and their companies create, shape, and sustain a new organizational culture, I try to help them use the talents, insights and creative energy of their employees. In guiding this collective leadership effort, I am amazed at how broad and deep the desire is for learning one of the core competencies of global business today: key words and phrases in a foreign language. Developing your foreign language skills and practicing them in the context of the scenarios in this book, will improve your chances for business success.

To assume that English is the only language necessary for successful business interactions is to limit yourself to fewer growth possibilities and maybe even to offend potential clients or associates. In fact, speaking the words and phrases of another language is only part of the equation to more effective communication.

Just as important is your understanding of them when they are used in dialogue. When you begin to read, mark, learn, and "inwardly digest" the material in this book, you will be seen as a person willing to expand your communication horizons beyond what's comfortable. You will reveal an intellectual curiosity that will gain the respect of your business partners and your colleagues. Now, let's go to work!

—*Tim Dobbins*

ORGANIZATION
OF THE PHRASEBOOK

Even if your Spanish is only rudimentary, and you don't have the time (or will?) to immerse yourself in yet another general Spanish course, this phrasebook is here to help you get by and get ahead in doing business in Spanish-speaking countries in spite of it. While it provides you with basic phrases and expressions you need to make an appointment or introduce yourself in a meeting, it also contains a wealth of very specific business-related terminology and phrases that you would have hard time finding even in a dictionary.

The book can be used either as a reference, where you will look up things of special interest, or as a continuous read, containing interesting commentary on doing business abroad and helpful cultural information in addition to abundant language material.

Before you start, here's how we organized it:

Pronunciation Chart

In order to avoid including cumbersome pronunciation transcriptions throughout the book, we give this guide to Spanish spelling and pronunciation, which will help you pronounce any Spanish word without stumbling.

Chapters 1–6

The chapters provide over a thousand phrases and sentences to be used when on the telephone, in a negotiating meeting, at the dinner table with your business associate, or when settling down in your office abroad. They also provide you with language basics, such as numbers, emergency expressions or days of the week.

Dialogues

Each chapter has several dialogues recreating a variety of

business situations to help you experience the language as it is really used.

Key Words

Here, we provide lists of the key terms you will need to remember from each section or subsection. In order to make them easy to locate, we put them into shaded boxes, with a key icon in the top right corner.

Culture Notes

Culture notes are interspersed throughout the chapters, and provide you with fascinating and useful information about business related behavior abroad. Their location in the text is marked by a globe icon.

Appendices

If you feel that things have been missed in the chapters, appendices are here to prove you wrong. They provide such useful information as measurements used in the country of your interest, holidays celebrated, or interesting web sites. Appendix D also provides a grammar summary.

Glossary of Industry-Specific Terms

This section contains a very thorough glossary of the terminology used in a wide range of different industries.

General Glossary

Both English-Spanish and Spanish-English, the glossary lists both basic vocabulary words and much specific business terminology used in the six chapters of the book.

CD

If you acquired our package including the CD, you will be able to listen to the recordings of more than 500 phrases from the book. You can just listen, or listen and repeat during a pause provided between the recordings. All the words, phrases, and sentences recorded come from Chapters 1–6 and appear in **boldfaced type.**

PRONUNCIATION CHARTS AND ALPHABET

1. *The Vowels*

Spanish Sound	Approximate Sound in English	Example
a	(f<u>a</u>ther)	*España*
e	(b<u>e</u>d)	*señor*
i	(f<u>ee</u>)	*día*
o	(t<u>a</u>ll)	*hotel*
u	(r<u>u</u>le)	*mucho*
y	(f<u>ee</u>t)	*y* (only a vowel when standing alone)

2. *The Dipthongs*

Spanish Sound	Approximate Sound in English	Example
ai/ay	(<u>ai</u>sle)	*bailar*
		hay
au	(n<u>ow</u>)	*auto*
ei	(m<u>ay</u>)	*peine*
ia	(<u>ya</u>rn)	*gracias*
io	(<u>yo</u>del)	*adiós*
iu	(<u>you</u>)	*ciudad*
oi/oy	(<u>oy</u>)	*oigo*
		estoy
ua	(q<u>ua</u>druped)	*cuando*
ue	(<u>we</u>t)	*bueno*
ui/uy	(L<u>oui</u>s)	*cuidado*
		muy

3. *THE CONSONANTS*

The letters *k* and *w* appear in Spanish in foreign words like *kilowatt, kilometer*. In some Spanish speaking countries, the *k* is spelled with the Spanish equivalent, *qu: quilómetro*. The *w* in Spanish sounds like an English *v: kilowatt*.

Spanish Sound	Approximate Sound in English	Example
l/m/n/p/s/t	similar to corresponding English consonants	
b	*b* (<u>b</u>oy), at the beginning of a word or after a consonant	*bueno, mambo*
	like *v* (<u>v</u>ain) but softer, allowing air to pass between lips	*cabeza*
c (before e/i)	*s* (<u>c</u>ertain) in Latin America	*cena*
	th (<u>th</u>ink) in Spain	
c (before a/o/u)	*k* (<u>c</u>atch)	*como*
cc	*x* (ta<u>x</u>) in Latin America	*lección*
	k+th (big+<u>th</u>ing) in Spain	
ch	*ch* (<u>ch</u>urch)	*mucho*
d	like *th* (<u>th</u>e) but softer allowing air to pass between the lips.	*verdad*
g (before i/e)	*h* (<u>h</u>e)	*gente*
g (before a/o/u)	*g* (<u>g</u>o)	*ganar*
h	always silent	*hasta*
j	*h* (<u>h</u>e)	*jefe*
ll	*y* (<u>y</u>et) in Latin America	*pollo*
	lli (mi<u>lli</u>on) in Spain	
ñ	*ny* (ca<u>ny</u>on)	*caña*
qu	*k* (<u>k</u>ite)	*que*
r	*r* (<u>thr</u>ow), but trilled	*pero*
r (in word-initial position)	*r* rolled, double trill	*rosa*

rr	*r* rolled, double trill	*carro*
v	*v* (<u>v</u>ote), but softer, allowing air to pass between lips.	*viernes*
x	*x* (ta<u>x</u>)	*taxi*
y	*y* (<u>y</u>et)	*yo*
z	*s**	*zona*
	same as c* (before e/i)	

4. *THE ALPHABET*

Letter	Name	Letter	Name	Letter	Name
a	a	**j**	jota	**r**	ere
b	be	**k**	ka	**rr**	erre
c	c	**l**	ele	**s**	ese
ch	che	**ll**	elle	**t**	te
d	de	**m**	eme	**u**	u
e	e	**n**	ene	**v**	ve/uve
f	efe	**ñ**	eñe	**w**	doble ve/ uve doble
g	ge	**o**	o	**x**	equis
h	hache	**p**	pe	**y**	i griega
i	i	**q**	cu	**z**	zeta

1 GETTING STARTED

Business is global, business is fast-paced, and business is high-tech. There is an energy and urgency underlying our activities and communications.

High-tech tools give instant access to clients and associates. Finding the right way to communicate is the key to success in business as much as it is in our private lives. Learning the following greetings, introductions, or openers will go a long way. When you say "Hello!" to someone in her native language, you show your willingness to make an effort in her tongue and you also make a great first impression.

We cover a bunch of subjects that all help you get started in doing overseas business successfully. Here is a list of sections in this chapter:

Saying Hello
Introducing Oneself and
   Getting Names Right
Introducing Others
Thank You and Please
Small Talk
Presenting Your Business and
   Department
Telephone: Making a Call
Telephone: Getting Through
Telephone: Why You Are Calling
Setting the Time for the
   Appointment or Meeting
Talking to Machines: Voice Mail
   and Answering Machines
Telling Time and Giving Dates
Business Letters
E-mail and Internet

So let's start with the basics—the opener, the ice-breaker, the hand offered in greeting.

SAYING HELLO

"Cómo saludar."
SR. SMITH: *Hola, soy el Sr. Smith.*
SR. SÁNCHEZ: *Soy el Sr. Sánchez. Le esperaba a las diez.* *
SR. SMITH: *Sí, siento llegar tarde. El taxista no sabía la dirección.*
SR. SÁNCHEZ: *Está bien. Pase y tome asiento.*

"Saying Hello."
MR. SMITH: *Hello, my name is Mr. Smith.*
MR. SÁNCHEZ: *My name is Mr. Sánchez. I was expecting you at 10.*
MR. SMITH: *Yes. I'm sorry to be late. The taxi didn't know how to find you.*
MR. SÁNCHEZ: *Well, come in and have a seat.*

Key Words	
Good-bye	*Adiós*
Hello	*Hola*
Introduce oneself/ someone (to)	*Presentarse uno mismo/ presentar a alguien (a)*
Name	*Nombre*
It's nice to meet you	*(Mucho) Gusto en conocerle/ Encantado (de concerle)*
Repeat (to)	*Repetir*
Thank you	*Gracias*
You're welcome	*De nada*

---

*Throughout the book, Spanish numbers occurring in the text will be written out as words to indicate their pronunciation.

2

Good morning/afternoon/ evening/night.	**Buenos días/buenas tardes/ buenas noches.**
Good-bye.	**Adiós.**
Hello.	**Hola.**
See you soon/later.	Hasta **pronto/luego.**
See you tomorrow/next week/next year.	Hasta **mañana/**la semana próxima/el año próximo.
It's a pleasure to see you again.	(Mucho) **Gusto en volverle a ver./**Encantado de volverle a ver.
It's great to see you again.	**Me alegra mucho volverle a ver.**
How are you?	**¿Cómo está?**
It's a pleasure to finally meet you.	Es un placer conocernos finalmente.
I'm glad to meet you in person. (We've spoken on the phone so many times.)	**Me alegra mucho conocerle en persona. (Hemos hablado por teléfono tantas veces.)**
Hi! How are you doing?	**¡Hola! ¿Cómo le va?**
I'm honored to be here.	**Me honra estar aquí.**
I'm so glad to be here.	Me alegra mucho estar aquí.

Like people in the United States, people in Spanish-speaking countries shake hands when they are introduced to each other. However, handshakes usually last longer and are firmer in the Spanish-speaking world. When getting a handshake, especially from a man, expect a jolt, and don't be afraid to correspond.

Then, there is also the *abrazo*, meaning "embrace" or "hug," a very distinctive and widely used social custom intended to show great affection and friendship to another person, usually between two men. It is really an outburst of true inner emotions responding to a happy, festive occasion, such as a wedding or birthday, or, among business people, a successful conclusion of a business deal.

INTRODUCING ONESELF AND GETTING NAMES RIGHT

Names are important for a business relationship. Get them right! Since a person's name is critically important to that person, if you get it wrong it can mean an unsuccessful business connection.

If a person's name seems long or difficult, ask what they prefer to be called. Use whatever name they say. If they want to use their full name, then it's up to you to learn it. It's part of doing business abroad. No one said it was going to be easy. At the same time, you should know that English names can be just as difficult for your foreign contacts, so be as patient and flexible as you would expect others to be.

My name is . . .	**Me llamo . . .**
I am . . .	**Soy . . .**
What is your name?	**¿Cómo se llama?**
You are?	**¿Usted es?**
Can you please repeat your name/it?	**¿Puede repetir su nombre?**
Can you please write it/ your name down for me?	**¿Me lo podría escribir?/¿Me podría escribir su nombre?**
How do you spell that?	**¿Cómo se deletrea eso?**
Do you have a nickname/ a shorter version of your name?	**¿Tiene usted un apodo ó un nombre abreviado?**
My name is . . . But everyone calls me . . .	**Me llamo . . . Pero todos me llaman . . .**
My name is . . . But I like to be called . . .	**Me llamo . . . Pero prefiero que me llamen . . .**

4

My name is spelled . . .	Así se escribe mi nombre . . .
My title/position is . . .	Mi título/ cargo es . . .
How do you do!	¿Cómo (le) va?
It's a pleasure to meet you. I am . . .	(Mucho) gusto en conocerle.
It's nice to meet you. I'm . . .	**Encantado de conocerle.** Soy . . .
So, we finally meet.	Bueno, finalmente nos conocemos.
Please call me.	**Sírvase llamarme.**
(Please) keep in touch.	**(Por favor) mantengámonos en contacto.**

In modern Spanish, the use of *Don* and *Doña* (always preceding the person's first name, e.g. *Doña Isabella*) is fast diminishing. However, when dealing with older people of rank (a president, a vice president, or other executives), it should be used. This also applies to grandparents and the parents of a business associate. With regard to the use of the polite pronoun *usted*, also expressed by the use of the third person singular of all verbs (e.g. *trabajar>trabaja; comer>come; escribir>escribe*), the rule of thumb is to wait to be told by your listener what form of address he or she would prefer. Once you are both into the conversation, the person you're speaking to may say: "*Tuteémonos.*" What he or she is suggesting is to drop *usted* and use the pronoun *tú*, or the second person singular of all verbs (e.g. *trabajar> trabajas; comer> comes; escribir> escribes*). In other words, start the conversation with *Usted*, and wait for the signal to switch over.

INTRODUCING OTHERS

Juan, may I introduce you to . . .	Juan, le presento a . . .
I'd like to introduce you to . . .	**Me gustaría presentarle a . . .**
Ms. Pérez, this is . . .	Srta. Pérez, le presento a . . .
Have you met Mateo?	**¿Ha conocido a Mateo?**
It's important for you to meet . . .	Es importante que conozca usted a . . .
You should meet . . .	**(Usted) debería conocer a . . .**

THANK YOU AND PLEASE

Thank you (very much).	(Muchas) **gracias.**
You're welcome.	**De nada.**
Please.	**Por favor.**
Excuse me.	**Perdón.**
Sorry.	**Lo siento.**
I'm so sorry.	**Lo siento mucho.**
It doesn't matter.	**No importa.**
That's fine./Okay.	**Está bien./Vale.**
Here you are./Here you go.	**Aquí tiene (usted)./Tenga la amabilidad de tomar esto./Tenga.**

SMALL TALK

When you make even a stumbling attempt at small talk, you show that you're willing to put yourself out there and make an effort. You don't need to be perfect; you just need to show you'll take the lead and try your best to make a great first impression.

We Americans are a chatty bunch of people. People in other cultures do not feel as pressed to engage in small talk and keep the conversation going when there is not much to be said. So don't get impatient or offended if there are moments when people don't have anything to say to you. Learning to communi-

6

cate in other languages and cultures is like learning to dance—relax and let the music lead you.

 Generally speaking, in the United States, we try to shy away from talking about or discussing such topics as politics and religion, that may have the potential of ending up in controversy, especially in a business setting. In broad terms, however, Spaniards and Latin Americans don't see it that way, and you may find yourself challenged to get into a conversation of substance at the least expected moment. If this should happen, follow it along, but be careful in voicing your personal opinion.

"Conversación menuda ó casual"

SR. BUSTAMANTE: *¿Qué tal el vuelo?*
SRTA. JACKSON: *Un poco de turbulencia, aunque la comida estaba buena.*
SR. BUSTAMANTE: *Claro que no tan buena como la de restaurante.*
SRTA. JACKSON: *¿Ha comido usted aquí alguna vez?*

"Small Talk"

MR. BUSTAMANTE: *How was your flight?*
MS. JACKSON: *It was somewhat turbulent. But surprisingly the food was good.*
MR. BUSTAMANTE: *Probably not as good as in this restaurant.*
MS. JACKSON: *Have you eaten here before?*

Key Words

English	Inglés
How do you say . . . ?	¿Cómo se dice . . . ?
Language	Idioma

Today	Hoy
Tomorrow	Mañana
Weather	Tiempo

How are you?	¿Cómo está?
So, how have you been?	Bien, ¿cómo ha estado?
How are you feeling this morning?	¿Cómo se siente esta mañana?

Very well. Thank you. And you? — **Muy bien. Gracias. ¿Y usted?**

It's very hot/cold today.	**Hoy hace mucho calor/frío.**
What beautiful weather/lousy weather.	**Qué tiempo más bonito/más malo.**
It's supposed to rain/to snow/to be nice tomorrow.	**Se supone que** lloverá/nevorá/**hará buen tiempo mañana.**
Is it always this hot here?	¿Hace siempre tanto calor aquí?

I'm looking forward to working with you.	**Espero trabajar con usted pronto.**
I am looking forward to our time together.	Espero que estemos juntos pronto.
Me too.	**Yo también.**

| I'd like to keep in touch with you. | Quisiera mantenerme en contacto con usted. |
| I'll give you a call when I get back (to my office). | **Lo llamaré cuando regrese** (a mi oficina). |

| I want to try using your language. | **Quisiera hablar su idioma.** |
| Please be patient with me. | **Por favor, tenga paciencia conmigo.** |

| Unfortunately, I speak only English. | **Desgraciadamente, sólo hablo inglés.** |

| I'd like to learn (some words in) your language. | Quisiera aprender (algunas palabras) en su idioma. |

Can you teach me some words in your language?	¿Puede enseñarme algunas palabras en su idioma?
Of course, it will be my pleasure.	Desde luego. Con mucho gusto.
How do you say . . . ?	¿Cómo se dice . . . ?
Can you say that again?	¿Puede repetirlo?
Repeat, please.	Repita, por favor.
How do you write that?	¿Cómo se escribe eso?

On Weather

The best small talk? Yes, the weather. When in doubt, talking about the weather is the safest subject. It's non-political, non-religious, and non-business.

"El tiempo"

SRTA. JACKSON: *Indudablemente que el tiempo ha cambiado.*

SR. BUSTAMANTE: *Así es. Ayer, estaba el cielo despejado, pero ahora llueve a cántaros.*

SRTA. JACKSON: *¿Estamos en tiempo de lluvia?*

SR. BUSTAMANTE: *Realmente no. Es sólo un día lluvioso.*

"The Weather"

MS. JACKSON: *The weather sure has changed.*

MR. BUSTAMANTE: *Yes. Yesterday it was clear, but now it's raining very hard.*

MS. JACKSON: *Is this the season for rain?*

MR. BUSTAMANTE: *Not really. It's just a rainy day.*

Key Words

Clear	Despejado
Cold	Frío
Cool	Fresco

9

Hot	Caliente
Rain/rainy	Lluvia/lluvioso
Snow	Nieve
Windy	Ventoso
Temperature	Temperatura
Warm	Cálido
Weather	Tiempo

What's the temperature?*	¿Cuál es la temperatura?
It's 15 degrees Celsius.	Hace quince grados centígrados.
What's the average temperature this time of year?	¿Cuál es la temperatura media en esta época del año?
What's the weather report?	¿Qué dice el informe del tiempo?
What's the forecast for tomorrow?	¿Cuál es el pronóstico para mañana?
It's going to stay nice.	Seguirá haciendo buen tiempo.
It's going to be cloudy.	Estará nublado.
It should be sunny.	Debe hacer sol.
The forecast is for warm weather.	Se espera un tiempo cálido.
We're going to have . . .	Vamos a tener . . .
fine weather.	tiempo excelente.
good weather.	buen tiempo.
hot weather.	tiempo caluroso.
bad weather.	mal tiempo.
Will it . . .	
rain?	¿Lloverá?
snow?	¿Nevará?

*Please refer to Appendix A for the conversion table between Celsius and Fahrenheit.

10

How are the road conditions between . . . and . . . ?	¿Cómo están las carreteras entre . . . y . . . ?
It's very foggy.	**Hay mucha niebla.**
The roads are slippery.	**Las carreteras están resbalosas.**
The roads have been plowed.	Han limpiado las carreteras.

PRESENTING YOUR BUSINESS AND DEPARTMENT

Following the initial greetings and introductions, you may wish to identify your company, organization, or group, as well as your position in it. Never take for granted that others know your role.

The name of my company is . . .	**El nombre de mi compañía es . . .**
I/We specialize in . . .	**Yo me especializo/nos especializamos en . . .**
My department is . . .	**Mi departamento es . . .**
I am with . . .	Estoy con . . .
I work with . . .	**Trabajo con . . .**
I'm . . .	**Soy . . .**
president of . . .	**presidente de . . .**
vice president of . . .	vicepresidente de . . .
in charge of operations.	a cargo de operaciones.
the chief financial officer.	el director de finanzas.
the treasurer.	el tesorero.
the general counsel.	el asesor legal.
a director.	un director.
a manager.	un gerente.
the leader of our team.	el dirigente de nuestro equipo.

I'm . . .	Estoy . . .
in administration.	en administración.
in customer service.	en servicios al cliente.
in finance.	en finanzas.
in human resources.	en personal./en recursos humanos.
in the legal department.	en el departamento legal.
in marketing.	en marketing.
in production.	en producción.
in sales.	en ventas.

In the United States, the word *director* can mean a member of the board of directors, or another, lower level of management. Commonly, a director usually reports to a vice president and has managers reporting to him or her. However, in other countries, the word *director* or *managing director* refers to one of the highest levels of management, equivalent to a president in some organizations in the United States.

Business Cards

If you are offering your business card, be careful to follow the appropriate cultural norms of the country in which you are doing business. In general, never force a card on a potential client. Ask if you may give him or her one. It is also good etiquette, and natural, to ask for one of his or her cards.

Don't stuff it into your pocket immediately! Don't write a restaurant's telephone number on the back of it (at least not in front of the person). Be sure to actually take a look at it and note what's on it—to some people it really matters! Then, put it away in a careful manner.

One last point. You may be passing out more business cards than you do at home, so bring plenty.

"Una reunión en la oficina"

SRTA. JOHNSON: *Srta. Rodríguez, aquí tiene mi tarjeta. Verá que mi número de teléfono es 495–3771 [quatro nueve cinco tres siete siete uno], y que también incluye mi dirección electrónica.* ¿Me puede dar una de sus tarjetas?*

SRTA. RODRÍGUEZ: *Por supuesto. Aquí la tiene.*

SRTA. JOHNSON: *O, veo que usted trabaja en la oficina de Cajamarca, y que incluye su dirección electrónica.*

"A Meeting at the Office"

MS. JOHNSON: *Ms. Rodríguez, this is my card. You will see that my phone number is 495–3771. My e-mail address is also included. May I have one of your cards?*

MS. RODRÍGUEZ: *Sure. Here you go.*

MS. JOHNSON: *I see that you work out of the Cajamarca office. It also includes your e-mail address.*

Here is my business card.	**Aquí tiene mi tarjeta de presentación.**
You will see that our telephone number is . . .	**Verá que nuestro número telefónico es . . .**
Our address is . . .	Nuestra dirección es . . .
Our E-mail is . . .	Nuestra dirección electrónica es . . .
May I have one of your business cards?	**¿Me puede dar su tarjeta?**
Do you have a business card?	¿Tiene usted una tarjeta de presentación?

---

*The last four digits of the telephone number can also be grouped into two digit numbers, and pronounced as 37–71.

Your company has very nice business cards.	**Me gustan las tarjetas de su compañía.**
Your card looks very professional.	Sus tarjetas tienen un aspecto muy profesional.
Your logo is very nice.	Me gusta su logotipo.
Could you pronounce your name for me?	**¿Puede pronunciarme su nombre?**
Could you repeat your name?	¿Puede repetir su nombre?
Could you repeat the name of your firm?	¿Puede repetir el nombre de su empresa?

 In Spanish-speaking countries, people usually have two last names: the father's name is followed by the mother's name, as in Carlos Rodríguez Bustamante. When you address the person, however, you do not say *Sr. Rodríguez Bustamante.* Whether in conversation or in correspondence, *Sr. Rodríguez* will suffice. With women, it works pretty much in the same way, except that a married woman's last name is composed of her maiden name and her husband's last name, as in *Sra. Isabella Suárez de Cepeda. De Cepeda* means "(the wife) of Cepeda."

TELEPHONE: MAKING A CALL

When you're trying to be understood in another language, using a telephone is not as simple as picking up the receiver. Here are the vocabulary and phrases you need to make this common business activity a success.

"En el teléfono"
SR. SINCLAIR: *¿Puede repetir el número, por favor?*
OPERADORA: *El número es 775–4964 [siete siete cinco cuatro nueve seis cuatro]. Permítame pasarle la llamada.*
SR. SINCLAIR: *Gracias.*

"On the Phone"

MR. SINCLAIR: *Would you repeat that number, please?*

OPERATOR: *The number is 775–4964. Let me transfer you now.*

MR. SINCLAIR: *Thank you.*

Key Words

Answer (to)	Contestar
Answering machine	Grabador/Contestador (automático)
Be on hold (to)	Esperar contestación
Busy	Ocupado/Comunica
Call (to)	Llamar
Calling card	Tarjeta telefónica
Cell phone	Teléfono celular/Teléfono móvil
Dial (to)	Marcar
Extension	Extensión
Hang up (to)	Colgar
Line	Linea
Local call	Llamada interurbana
Long distance call	Llamada de larga distancia
Message	Mensaje
Number	Número
Operator	Operador/a
Put on hold (to)	Mantenerse en la línea
Telephone	Teléfono
Transfer (to)	Transferir
Voice mail	Contestador

I'd like to place a call.	**Quisiera hacer una llamada.**
How can I make a phone call?	**¿Cómo puedo hacer una llamada?**
Where can I make a phone call?	**¿Dónde puedo hacer una llamada?**

Is there a telephone booth here?	¿Hay una cabina telefónica aquí?
How much does a local call cost?	¿Cuánto cuesta una llamada local?
How can I use my calling card on this phone?	¿Cómo puedo usar mi tarjeta telefónica?
How can I make a local call?	¿Cómo puedo hacer una llamada interurbana?
How can I make a long distance call?	¿Cómo puedo hacer una llamada de larga distancia?
How can I make a conference call?	¿Cómo puedo hacer una llamada de conferencia?
How do I get an outside line?	¿Qué tengo que hacer para llamar afuera?
How can I call the United States?	¿Cómo puedo llamar a los Estados Unidos?

Please . . .	Por favor . . .
call this number.	llámeme a este número.
dial this number.	marque este número.
forward this call to . . .	pase esta llamada a . . .
get an operator.	consígame una operadora./póngame con una operadora.
redial this number.	vuelva a marcar este número.
transfer this call.	transfiera esta llamada.

I need to call . . .	Necesito llamar a . . .
I would like to leave a message for . . .	Quisiera dejar un mensaje a . . .
No one is answering.	No contesta nadie.
Please hang up.	Cuelgue, por favor.
My party hung up.	La persona con la que estaba hablando me colgó.

I was put on hold.	**Me dijeron que esperara.**
Please put me on speaker.	**Por favor, pase mi llamada al altavoz.**
I have you on speaker.	Ya lo tengo en el altavoz.
How do I redial?	¿Cómo puedo volver a llamar?
How do I forward/transfer this call?	¿Cómo puedo transferir esta llamada?
I'd like to check my voice mail.	**Quisiera revisar mi contestador.**
How do I make a recording?	¿Cómo puedo grabar la llamada?

Do you have a/an . . .	**¿Tiene usted . . .**
answering machine?	un contestador automático?
calling card?	una tarjeta telefónica?
direct line?	**una línea directa?**
switchboard?	una centralita?
telephone directory?	una guía telefónica?
contact list?	una lista de contactos?

I would like to buy a/an . . .	**Quisiera comprar . . .**
car phone.	un teléfono de automóvil.
cellular phone.	un teléfono celular./un teléfono móvil.
portable phone.	**un teléfono portátil.**
video phone.	un teléfono con video./un videoteléfono.

Does your office have . . .	**¿Tiene . . .**
e-mail capability?	**correo electrónico?**
Internet?	Internet?
Web access?	acceso al Internet en su oficina?

The line is busy.	**La línea está ocupada./Está** comunicando.

We have a bad connection.   Hay problemas con la
                             conexión.
We got cut off.   **Nos cortaron la
                             comunicación.**

TELEPHONE: GETTING THROUGH

"Cómo darse a entender"
SR. LÓPEZ: *Hola. Le habla el Sr. López.*
SR. SMITH: *Quisiera hablar con el Sr. Delgado.*
SR. LÓPEZ: *Manténgase en la línea, por
favor . . . Lo siento, pero el Sr. Delgado no está.
¿Quiere dejarle un mensaje?*
SR. SMITH: *Sí. Dígale al Sr. Delgado que llame al
Sr. Smith al hotel Hilton, número 555–1197
[cinco cinco cinco uno uno nueve siete]. El
número de mi habitación es el quinientos veinte y
tres.*
SR. LÓPEZ: *Le daré el mensaje.*

"Getting Through"
MR. LÓPEZ: *Hello. This is Mr. López speaking.*
MR. SMITH: *I would like to speak to Mr. Delgado.*
MR. LÓPEZ: *Please hold . . . I'm sorry, but Mr. Del-
gado is not here. May I take a message?*
MR. SMITH: *Yes. Please tell him to call Mr. Smith
at the Hilton Hotel, number 555–1197. My room
number is 523.*
MR. LÓPEZ: *I will give him this message.*

Hello?   ¿Hola?
This is . . . calling/   Soy/habla . . .
  speaking.

18

I'd like to speak to . . .	Quisiera hablar con . . .
Could I speak to . . . ?	¿Puedo hablar con . . . ?
Do I have the office of . . . ?	¿Es la oficina de . . . ?
Could you connect me with . . . ?	¿Puede pasarme con . . . ?
Extension . . . please.	Extensión . . . por favor.
Please put me through to . . .	Por favor, páseme a . . .
I don't mind holding.	No me importa esperar.
Is . . . available?	¿Se puede poner . . . ?
Is . . . in the office?	¿Está . . . en la oficina?
When do you expect . . . to return?	¿Cuándo volverá . . . ?
He/she is busy/not available right now.	Está ocupado./No está disponible ahora.
He/she is not at his desk.	No está en su mesa.
He/she is in a meeting.	Está en una reunión.
He/she is out to lunch.	Salió a almorzar.
He/she is out of town/ away from the office.	Está de viaje/fuera de la oficina.
Yes, I understand.	Sí, entiendo.
I'm sorry, I did not understand.	Lo siento, no le entendí.
Could you repeat that?	¿Puede repetir eso?
Okay.	Está bien.
Could you repeat your name?	¿Puede repetir su nombre?
Could I ask you to spell that please?	Por favor, ¿cómo se deletrea eso?

Just as in the United States, there are certain rules about addressing women in Spanish-speaking countries. There are three possible forms

19

of address, *Sra.*, *Srta.*, and *Sa.*,* roughly corre-sponding to the English *Mrs.*, *Miss*, and *Ms.*; it can be tricky to decide which one to use. In general, do not venture to use any of the terms without a certain knowledge of fact. Before jumping onto shaky ground, ask a friend or an associate.

TELEPHONE: WHY YOU ARE CALLING

I'm calling to follow up with/on . . .	Llamo para continuar nuestra sobre . . .
I am calling to arrange an appointment with . . .	Llamo para concertar una cita con . . .
The reason for my call is . . .	La razón de mi llamada es . . .
I'm calling at the request of . . .	Llamo a petición de . . .
I'm calling to tell you . . .	Le llamo para decirle . . .
This call is in reference to . . .	Esta llamada es en referencia a . . .
. . . asked me to call him/her this morning.	. . . me pidió que le llamara esta mañana.
I'm returning your call.	Le estoy devolviendo la llamada . . .
You may remember . . .	Quizás usted recuerde . . .
Who's calling?	¿De parte de quién?
Hold the line.	Manténgase en la línea.
You have a call on line 1.	Le llaman por la línea uno.
You have the wrong number.	Tiene el número equivocado.

---

* The term *Sa.* is still very rarely used in everyday life. In general, the term *Srta.* is used whenever an American would use *Ms.* This practice has also been adopted in this book.

SETTING THE TIME FOR THE APPOINTMENT OR MEETING

In most Latin cultures, people, even in business, have a different orientation to time from what you're used to. While things are slowly changing everywhere with business becoming more global, it is still possible for business people to be late without causing offense. (At the same time, visitors should always be on time.) Therefore, avoid scheduling multiple meetings in one day.

"Cómo fijar una cita"

SRTA. JACKSON: *Nos gustaría comenzar la reunión a las diez.*

SR. BENÍTEZ: *¿Podríamos comenzar más temprano, a eso de las nueve y media?*

SRTA. JACKSON: *Está bien. Estaremos en su oficina unos minutos antes de las nueve y media*

SR. BENÍTEZ: *Nos vemos entonces.*

"Setting the Appointment"

MS. JACKSON: *We would like to start the meeting at 10.*

MR. BENÍTEZ: *Could we start earlier, say 9:30?*

MS. JACKSON: *Fine. We'll be in your office a few minutes before 9:30.*

MR. BENÍTEZ: *See you then.*

Key Words

Appointment	*Cita*
Beginning/End	*Comienzo/Fin*
Calendar	*Calendario*
Cancel an appointment (to)	*Cancelar una cita*

Day	Día
Earlier	Más temprano
Later	Más tarde
Make an appointment (to)	Hacer una cita
Meeting	Reunión
Okay	Está bien
Schedule	Horario
Start	Inicio
Time	Hora
Week	Semana

Time

I'd like to meet with you tomorrow.	Me gustaría reunirme con usted mañana.
Would next week be okay?	¿Va bien la semana próxima?
How does Thursday/next week look?	¿Qué le parece el jueves/la semana próxima?
Does he/she have room on her calendar for . . . ?	¿Está libre el . . . ?
It's important to meet soon.	Es importante que nos reunamos pronto.
I can't meet next week.	No puedo la semana próxima.
I'm not available/ busy tomorrow.	No estoy libre/ocupado mañana.
At what time will the meeting begin?	¿A qué hora comenzará la reunión?
What time do we begin?	¿A qué hora comenzamos?
When will the meeting be over?	¿Cuándo se terminará la reunión?
When do we finish?	¿A qué hora se termina?
Tomorrow is fine/excellent.	Mañana va bien/excelente.

Setting the Place and Asking for Directions

Where shall we meet?	**¿Dónde nos reunimos?**
Do you wish to meet in my office?	**¿Nos vemos en mi oficina?**
Shall I come to your office?	¿Desea que vaya yo a su oficina?
Where is your office/hotel?	**¿Dónde se encuentra su oficina/hotel?**
Could you fax me a map, please?	**Por favor, ¿me puede enviar un mapa por fax?**
Please wait while I get a pencil and some paper.	**Por favor, permítame buscar un lápiz y papel.**
Do you need directions to my office?	¿Necesita que le indique cómo llegar a mi oficina?
I will meet you in my office/the lobby of the hotel.	**Le esperaré en mi oficina/ en el vestíbulo del hotel.**
Where is the hotel?	¿Dónde se encuentra el hotel?

Completing the Conversation

Thank you very much for your assistance.	**Gracias por su ayuda.**
It's been a pleasure/great to talk to you.	**Ha sido un placer/gran placer hablar con usted.**
I'm very glad we were able to talk.	Me alegra que hayamos hablado.
I can't believe we finally connected!	¡Me parece increíble que al fin nos hayamos reunido!
I look forward to the meeting.	**Quedo a la espera de la reunión.**
I look forward to hearing from/talking to you again.	Espero saber de usted pronto/ nuevamente hablar con usted.
Take care, and I hope to see you soon.	Cuídese, y espero verle pronto.

Other Helpful Phrases While on the Telephone

Yes, I understand.	**Sí, entiendo.**
I'm sorry. I did not understand you.	**Lo siento. No le entendí.**
Could you please repeat that/your name?	**Por favor, ¿puede repetir eso/su nombre?**
Could you please spell your/the name for me?	Por favor, ¿puede deletrear su/el nombre?
All right/Okay.	**Está bien. /Vale.**
Sure.	**Claro.**
May I read the number back to you?	¿Puedo repetirle el número?
Could you please speak louder?	**¿Puede hablar más alto, por favor?**
This is a bad line. Let me call you back.	**Tenemos una mala conexión. Le volveré a llamar.**

TALKING TO MACHINES: VOICE MAIL AND ANSWERING MACHINES

When leaving a message on an answering machine, remember to speak slowly and repeat important information, such as telephone numbers, names, and specific times.

"Cómo dejar un mensaje"

SR. JONES: *Sr. Sánchez, soy el Sr. Jones de la compañía Amalgamated. Estoy en el hotel Hilton. El teléfono de aquí es el 324–2965 [tres dos cuatro dos nueve seis cinco]. Me gustaría encontrarme con usted para cenar, a las ocho de la noche, tal como acordamos. ¿Puede recogerme en el hotel? Le repito que estoy en el Hilton, cuyo número es 324–2965. Por favor, dígame si puede recogerme a las ocho.*

"Leaving a Message"

MR. JONES: *Mr. Sánchez, this is Mr. Jones of Amalgamated. I'm staying at the Hilton Hotel. The telephone here is 324–2965. I would like to meet you for dinner at 8 P.M. as we had talked about. Could you pick me up at the hotel? Again, I'm at the Hilton, telephone number 324–2965. Let me know if you can pick me up at 8.*

Key Words

Answering machine	Contestador (telefonico)
Leave a message (to)	Dejar un mensaje
Message	Mensaje
Press (to)	Apretar
Take a message (to)	Tomar un mensaje
Voice mail	Contestador/Correo de voz

I would like to leave a message.	**Me gustaría dejar un mensaje.**
Could you take a message?	**¿Puede tomar un mensaje?**
Could you transfer me to his voice mail?	**¿Puede transferirme a su contestador?**
Please tell . . . I will call later/at a later date.	Por favor, diga a . . . que llamaré más tarde/otrodía.
Please tell . . . to give me a call as soon as possible.	Por favor, diga a . . . que me llame lo antes posible.
I will call back again later.	**Volveré a llamarle después.**
May I ask who is calling?	**¿De parte de quién, por favor?**
Would you like to leave a message?	**¿Desea dejar un mensaje?**
Would you like to leave your name and number?	¿Desea dejar su nombre y número?

25

Please hold while I try that extension.	Por favor, espere mientras le paso con esa extensión.
Is there anything you would like me to tell . . . ?	¿Desea que diga algo a . . . ?
This is. . . . I'm away from my desk.	**Le habla. . . . No estoy en mi escritorio en este momento.**
You have reached . . .	Se ha comunicado usted con . . .
I'm away from the office until . . .	**Estoy fuera de la oficina hasta . . .**
I'm on vacation until . . .	Estoy de vacaciones hasta . . .
I'm on the other line.	**Estoy en la otra línea.**
Please call back after 9 A.M. on Monday, June 1.	Por favor, vuelve llamar el lunes, primero de junio, a las nueve de la mañana.*
Please leave a message.	**Por favor, deje un mensaje.**
Leave a message after the tone.	Deje un mensaje después del tono.
Please leave your name, number, and a brief message, and I will call you back.	Por favor, deje su nombre, número, y un breve mensaje, y le llamaré.
If you wish to speak to my assistant, please dial extension . . .	**Si desea hablar con mi ayudante, por favor marque la extensión . . .**
To return to an operator, please press 0 now.	Para volver a la operadora, apriete el cero ahora.
To return to the main menu, please press 4.	Para regresar al menú principal, apriete el cuatro, por favor.
To leave a message, press # now.	Para dejar un mensaje, apriete cuadradito ahora.

---

* Please refer to the section Telling Time in Chapter 6 for additional ways of expressing time.

To speak to an operator, press # now.	Para hablar con la operadora, apriete cuadradito ahora.
To return to the main menu, press # now.	Para regresar al menú principal, apriete cuadradito ahora.
If you have a touchtone phone, press 1 now.	Si tiene un teléfono de botones, apriete uno ahora.
If you have a rotary phone, please stay on the line.	Si tiene un teléfono de disco, manténgase en la línea.

TELLING TIME AND GIVING DATES

"Cómo decir la hora"

SR. BUSTAMANTE: *¿Qué hora tiene?*
SR. SMITH: *Aquí son las once y media de la mañana. Me parece que ustedes van tres horas adelantados.*
SR. BUSTAMANTE: *Sí. Aquí son las dos y media de la tarde. En estos momentos estoy ocupado. ¿Podría llamarme en una hora?*
SR. SMITH: *Cómo no. Le volveré a llamar en una hora, a las tres y media de la tarde, hora de ustedes.*

"Telling Time"

MR. BUSTAMANTE: *What time do you have?*
MR. SMITH: *It is 11:30 A.M. here. I believe you are three hours ahead of us.*
MR. BUSTAMANTE: *Yes. It is 2:30 P.M. here. I'm busy right now. Could you call in one hour?*
MR. SMITH: *Yes, I'll call you back in one hour, at 3:30 P.M. your time.*

| What time is it? | ¿Qué hora es? |
| It's 10:30 A.M. | Son las diez y media/diez y treinta de la mañana. |

27

What day is it?	¿Qué día es?
It's Monday.	Hoy es lunes.
What month is it?	¿En qué mes estamos?
It's November.	Estamos en noviembre.
What year is it?	¿En qué año estamos?
It's the year 2000.	Estamos en el año dos mil.
It's morning.	Es la mañana.
It's noon.	Es el mediodía.
It's afternoon.	Es la tarde.
It's evening.	Es la noche.
It's midnight.	Es medianoche.
Five minutes/two hours ago.	Hace cinco minutos/dos horas.
In twenty minutes/a half hour/an hour.	En veinte minutos/en media hora/en una hora.
What time do we begin?	¿A qué hora comenzamos?
When is the meeting over?	¿Cuándo se termina la reunión?

BUSINESS LETTERS

No, the business letter is not a relic of the pre-Internet era. A well-written letter on your company's letterhead is still an effective means of communication.

The business letter is also effective as a follow-up thank you note. People appreciate receiving even a short personalized business note. It says you care. It tends to build relationships, the bedrock of success in business or in any walk of life.

There is an art to writing a business letter. The first rule, however, is to express yourself as clearly as possible. The second rule is to write well. Use proper grammar and sentence structure. There is no excuse for misspellings with computerized spell-checking. The third and most crucial rule is to write persuasively. That's the most important type of business letter. In business, non-profit, or governmental agencies, you are often trying to win people over to do something, or to take action. Here's how to begin . . .

The Greeting

Dear . . .	Estimado/a/os/as . . .
Mr./Mrs./Ms. . . .	Sr./Sra./Srta. . . .
Sir(s)/Madam(s)	Señor(es)/Señora(s)
Doctor/Dr. . . .	Doctor/Dr. . . .
Professor . . .	Profesor . . .
Dear Mr. Bustamante:	Estimado Sr. Bustamante:
Dear Ms. Hernández:	Estimada Srta. Hernández:

Stating the Purpose

This should be done right up front. Don't beat around the bush.

I am writing . . .	Me dirijo a usted para . . .
to accept . . .	aceptar . . .
to ask . . .	pedirle . . .
to answer . . .	contestar . . .
to apologize . . .	pedir disculpas . . .
to confirm . . .	confirmar . . .
to commend/ congratulate . . .	felicitarle . . .
to inform . . .	informarle . . .
to provide . . .	proporcionarle . . .
to recommend . . .	recomendarle . . .
to reject . . .	rehusar . . .
to request . . .	pedirle . . .
to submit . . .	presentarle . . .
to thank you . . .	agradecerle . . .

You may wish to start more informally.

In connection with . . .	Conforme a . . .
In regard to . . .	De acuerdo con . . .
In response to . . .	En contestación a . . .
Instead of calling . . .	En vez de llamar . . .
On behalf of . . .	En nombre de . . .
With reference to . . .	En referencia a . . .

You may wish to organize your letter with bullets:

• This is the first point.

• This is the second point.

Or, perhaps, numbers:

1. This is the first point.

2. This is the second point.

Other Important Phrases

The purpose of this letter is . . .	El propósito de la presente es . . .
The mission of our business/organization is . . .	La misión de nuestra empresa/organización es . . .
Our strategic goals include . . .	Nuestros objetivos estratégicos incluyen . . .
The quality assurance team wishes to present its report on . . .	Nuestro equipo de garantía de calidad desea presentar su informe sobre . . .
It has come to our attention that . . .	Se nos ha informado que . . .
We regret to inform you . . .	Sentimos informarle que . . .
Could you please provide me/us with . . . ?	Por favor, ¿puede proporcionarme/ proporcionarnos . . . ?

Unfortunately we cannot accept/agree/complete . . .	Desgraciadamente, no podemos aceptar/ concordar/completar . . .
In consultation with . . .	En consulta con . . .
In reviewing your proposal . . .	Al estudiar su propuesta . . .
In going over the contract, I/we discovered . . .	Al revisar el contrato, noté/notamos . . .
While reviewing the financial statements . . .	Al revisar el estado financiero . . .
It is my/our pleasure to accept/reject your proposal.	Me/nos place aceptar/rehusar su propuesta.
Would you contact us at your earliest convenience?	¿Puede comunicarse con nosotros tan pronto le sea posible?
Enclosed is . . .	Le adjunto . . .
Enclosed please find . . .	Adjunto encontrará . . .

The Closing

Thank you for your attention to this matter.	Gracias por su atención a este asunto.
I look forward to hearing from you.	Espero saber de usted próximamente.
Please let me know if I can provide further information.	Por favor, dígame si necesita más información.
Please contact me at the following telephone number or e-mail address.	Por favor, comuníquese conmigo al siguiente número telefónico o dirección electrónica.
I look forward to receiving . . .	Espero pronto recibir . . .
your response to this letter.	su respuesta a la presente.

your/the proposal(s).	su/la/las propuesta(s).
the contract.	el contrato.
your evaluation.	su evaluación.
your call.	su llamada.
your order.	su pedido.
the samples.	las muestras.
the corrected statements.	los informes corregidos.
additional information.	información adicional.

Salutations

Sincerely,	Sinceramente,
Signed,	Firmado,
Yours truly,	Atentamente,
Yours sincerely,	Sinceramente,
Best wishes,	Con mis mejores deseos,
With affection,	Con afecto,

----

15 de octubre del 2001

Sr. José Chevez
Corporación ABC
Calle Lagunas No. 422
12345 México, D.F., México

Estimado Sr. Chevez:

Gracias por las adiciones hechas al contrato propuesto, las cuales nos parecen muy acertadas. Se lo enviaremos terminado para que lo firme en un par de días.

En caso de tener alguna pregunta, sírvase comunicármelo.

Sinceramente,

Jennifer Smith

October 15, 2001

Mr. Jose Chevez
ABC Corporation
422 Calle Lagunas
Mexico City, Mexico 12345

Dear Mr. Chevez,

Thank you for the additions to the proposed contract.
We agree that this will improve the contract. We will
be sending the final version of the contract to you for
your signature in a couple of days.

If you have any questions, please let me know.

Sincerely,

Jennifer Smith

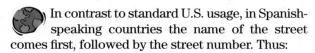 In contrast to standard U.S. usage, in Spanish-
speaking countries the name of the street
comes first, followed by the street number. Thus:

Calle Hermosillo Nº 39

The zip code comes before the name of the city, followed by the name of the country. Thus:

1425 Buenos Aires
Argentina (South America)

In correspondence and when addressing envelopes,
always use the full name of the addressee: first name,
father's last name, mother's last name. Thus:

Rodolfo Rodríguez del Castillo

However, only the last name Rodríguez is used there-
after: *Estimado Sr. Rodríguez* (Dear Mr. Rodríguez).

If the person is a senior executive or simply an elderly person, it is always advisable to use the title *Don* or *Doña* before the name. Thus:

> *Sr. D. Rodolfo Rodríguez del Castillo,* or
> *D. Rodolfo Rodríguez del Castillo*
>
> *Doña Isabel Suárez de Cepeda*

In addressing a woman in a letter, you can either write:

> *Estimada Doña Isabel,* or
> *Estimada Sra. Suárez de Cepeda* (without *Doña**)

E-MAIL AND INTERNET

In a few short years, e-mail and the Internet have gone from curiosities to essential parts of our existence. Here's an important tip if you wish to impress others and get ahead in your organization: Use complete sentences and proper grammar. Don't use e-mail slang, such as GTG, for "got to go." Using the correct language and grammar communicates that you're a professional. And spell-check your messages! Nothing turns off other professionals more than careless errors.

Key Words

Browser	*Navegador*
CD-ROM disk	*Disco de CD-ROM*
Check/download	*Revisar/descargar correo*
e-mail to	*electrónico*

---

* Remember that *Doña* can only be used in front of the person's first name.

Computer disk	*Disco de computadora/Disco de ordenador*
Desktop computer	*Computadora* de mesa/ Ordenador de mesa*
E-mail or *electronic mail*	*Correo electrónico* or *e-mail*
Laptop computer	*Computadora portátil/ Ordenador portátil*
Send/receive e-mail to	*Enviar/recibir correo electrónico*
Server	*Servidor*

More computer talk

Cyberspace	Ciberespacio
Database	Base de datos
Download (to)	Descargar
File	Archivo
Flat-panel display	Pantalla plana
Forward an e-mail	Reenviar correo electrónico
Help	Ayuda
Home page	Página inicial
Hypertext	Hipertexto
Internet	Internet
Link	Enlace
Log on/off	Iniciar/terminar la conexión
Mailing list	Lista de distribución
Mainframe	Marco principal
Modem	Módem
Multimedia	Multimedia
Network	Red
Online service	Servicio en línea
Open a file	Abrir un archivo

---

* In Latin America, the word for computer is *computadora*, while in Spain the word is *ordenador*.

35

Portable	Portátil
Reboot	Reiniciar
Reply to an e-mail	Contestar a un correo electrónico
Search engine	Motor de búsqueda
Search the Internet/Web	Buscar en el Internet/Web
Send a file	Enviar un archivo
Surf (to)	Navegar
Technical support	Asesoramiento técnico
URL	URL
Videoconferencing	Videoconferenciar
Virtual reality	Realidad virtual
Web page/site	Página/espacio Web
World Wide Web	Red mundial

How do I turn the computer on?	¿Cómo enciendo la computadora?
How to I dial up?	¿Cómo marco?
Do I need a password?	¿Necesito una contraseña?
What is the password?	¿Cuál es la contraseña?
Do you have an IBM-compatible computer?	¿Tiene usted una computadora compatible (con IBM)?
Do you have a Mac computer?	¿Tiene usted una computadora Mac?
What word processing software do you use?	¿Qué software de procesamiento de textos usa usted?
What spreadsheet software do you use?	¿Qué software de hoja de cálculo usa usted?
What database software do you use?	¿Qué software de base de datos usa usted?
What presentation software do you use?	¿Qué software de presentación usa usted?

How can I get Word/ WordPerfect on this computer?	¿Cómo puedo obtener Word/WordPerfect en esta computadora?
How can I get Excel/ Lotus 1-2-3 on this computer?	¿Cómo puedo obtener Excel/Lotus 1-2-3 en esta computadora?
How can I get PowerPoint on this computer?	¿Cómo puedo obtener PowerPoint en esta computadora?
How can I get Dbase on this computer?	¿Cómo puedo obtener Dbase en esta computadora?
Do you have Internet capability?	**¿Tiene usted (facilidades de) Internet?**
Do you have e-mail capability?	¿Tiene usted (facilidades de) correo electrónico?
How can I get AOL on this computer?	**¿Cómo puedo obtener AOL en esta computadora?**
How do I . . .	¿Cómo puedo . . .
log on?	iniciar la conexión?
check my e-mail?	mirar mi correo electrónico?
access a Web site?	tener acceso a una página/ un sitio Web?
search the Web?	buscar en el Web?
bookmark a Web site?	marcar un sitio en el Web?
print this page.	imprimir esta página?
print this document.	imprimir este documento?
send an e-mail	enviar un correo electrónico?
send this document to someone?	enviarle a alguien este documento?
forward this message to someone?	reenviar este mensaje a alguien?
attach a file to an e-mail?	adjuntar un archivo a un correo electrónico?

Do I leave the computer on?

How do I turn the computer off?

¿Dejo la computadora encendida?

¿Cómo apago la computadora?

2 GETTING INVOLVED

Conducting business overseas adds an unusual dimension to your work. Not only do you need to transact sales, negotiate contracts, communicate plans, and receive feedback on products and services, but you now need to do it in a foreign place and even in a foreign tongue.

As a general principle, don't assume that your own ways of doing business apply in other countries and cultures. Be cautious until you know the culture you're dealing with, and take an active role in learning about it. For example, in some cultures, it is bad form to be overly assertive, a common U.S. business trait. In the course of this chapter, and indeed, this whole book, we give you tips on how to proceed.

Business Companion, however, is not content just to help you with the language and culture. We also want to remind you of how to handle your business successfully. For instance, in talking about business presentations we not only give you the words *easel*, *slide projector*, and *refreshments*, we provide you with a review of what makes a presentation successful. Thus, we mix language and culture with ideas on how to make your business flourish.

Here are the most common business situations you'll confront in your work that you will learn about in this chapter:

> **The General Business Meeting**
> **The Presentation or Speech**
> **The Sales Call or Meeting**
> **The Negotiating Meeting**
> **The Training Session**

THE GENERAL BUSINESS MEETING

What's the purpose of the meeting? If you're in charge, make it clear. If you're a participant, find out ahead of time, so you can successfully contribute.

If you are leading the meeting, you need to make sure things are organized on two levels: The purpose of the presentation and the details, including announcements, agenda, room arrangements, presentation equipment, and refreshments. Ask yourself: Is there anything else that needs to be on the agenda to make the meeting more successful?

People in Spanish-speaking countries tend to place great importance on long-lasting relationships. Even in business, expect to invest a lot of time to build a pleasant and relaxed relationship with your foreign colleagues if you wish to establish a trustful and solid business *rapport*.

Now, let's go have a meeting!

"En la reunión"

SR. SMITH: *¿Por qué se dejaron fuera de la agenda las fechas límites?*

SRTA. RUBIO: *Buena pregunta. Incluyámoslas para la tarde, cuando concluyamos nuestra charla sobre el informe del comité de grupo de trabajo.*

SR. CASTILLO: *¿Y qué tal si hablamos de ello mañana a primera hora? Es probable que no terminemos el informe del comité hasta pasado la tarde, y no todos los presentes estarán aquí.*

SRTA. RUBIO: *Esa es una mejor idea. Lo hablaremos mañana a primera hora.*

"At the Meeting"

MR. SMITH: *Why were deadlines left out of the agenda?*

MS. RUBIO: *That's a good question. Let's put that in for later this afternoon, after we finish our discussion of the Team Force Committee report.*

MR. CASTILLO: *Why not discuss it first thing tomorrow morning? We may not finish the committee report until late this afternoon and not everyone will be here.*

MS. RUBIO: *That's an even better idea. We'll discuss it first thing tomorrow morning.*

Key Words

Agenda	*Agenda*
Answer	*Respuesta*
Cancel a meeting (to)	*Cancelar una reunión*
Committee	*Comité*
Deadline	*Fecha límite*
Decision	*Decisión*
Discussion	*Charla*
Facilitator	*Facilitador*
Feedback	*Reacción*
Information	*Información*
Have a meeting (to)	*Tener una reunión*
Lead a meeting (to)	*Dirigir una reunión*
Materials	*Materiales*
Meeting	*Reunión*
Participant	*Participante*
Problem solving	*Solución de problemas*
Purpose	*Propósito*
Question	*Pregunta*
Schedule	*Horario*

Schedule a meeting (to)	Fijar una reunión
Set an agenda (to)	Fijar una agenda
Team building	Organización de equipo

Hello.	Hola.
Good morning/afternoon/ evening.	Buenos días/buenas tardes/noches.
Welcome to . . .	**Bienvenido a . . .**
My name is . . .	Me llamo . . .
I am . . .	Soy . . .
I want to introduce . . .	**Deseo presentarle/ presentarles . . .**
myself.	**a mí mismo.**
the participants.	**a los participantes.**
the secretary.	a la secretaria/al secretario.
the administrative assistant.	al/a la ayudante de administración.
the recorder.	al registrador.
Please introduce yourself.	Por favor, preséntese.
Before we begin the meeting, let's introduce ourselves.	**Antes de comenzar la reunión, que se presente cada cual.**
Beginning on my left/right please state your name, company, and position/ title.	**Comenzando por mi** izquierda/**derecha,** **dé su nombre, compañía y cargo**/título.

Agenda: **Team Force Committee**

9:00 A.M.	*Apertura*
9:10 A.M.	*Repaso de la última reunión*
9:20 A.M.	*Discusión sobre la fusión de los dos departamentos administrativos*
	Gestión de los procedimientos
	Nueva gráfica de organización

	Recolocación
10:30 A.M.	*Descanso*
10:45 A.M.	*Sesiones en grupos—Gestión de problemas*
11:45 A.M.	*Informe sobre las sesiones*
12:00	*Almuerzo*
del mediodía	
1:00 P.M.	*Discusión sobre nuevos procedimientos*
4:30 P.M.	*Cierre*

Agenda: **Team Force Committee**

9:00 A.M.	*Opening*
9:10 A.M.	*Review of last meeting*
9:20 A.M.	*Discussion of merging the two administrative departments*
	Handling of procedures
	New organization chart
	Outplacement
10:30 A.M.	*Coffee break*
10:45 A.M.	*Breakout sessions—Handling problems*
11:45 A.M.	*Reporting on the sessions*
12:00 noon	*Lunch*
1:00 P.M.	*Discussion of new procedures*
4:30 P.M.	*Close*

Purpose of Meeting

The purpose of this meeting is . . .	El propósito de esta reunión es . . .
Today's meeting concerns itself with . . .	La reunión de hoy trata sobre . . .
I've been asked to lead this discussion about . . .	Se me ha pedido que dirija esta charla sobre . . .
This morning/afternoon/ evening we'll be discussing . . .	Esta mañana/tarde/noche, hablaremos sobre . . .
I'm sure you all know why we are here.	Estoy seguro que todos saben por qué estamos aquí.
Let's begin by going over the agenda.	Comencemos por la agenda.

Are there any questions about the agenda?	¿Alguien tiene alguna pregunta sobre la agenda?
Yes, I have a question.	**Sí, yo tengo una pregunta.**
Yes, please, what is your question?	**Muy bien, ¿cuál es su pregunta?**
Who determined the agenda?	¿Quién se encargó de determinar la agenda?
I set the agenda.	Yo determiné la agenda.
The agenda was determined by the committee.	El comité determinó la agenda.
The agenda was determined in our last meeting.	**La agenda se determinó en nuestra última reunión.**
Is the agenda complete?	¿Está completa la agenda?
Does everyone have a copy of the agenda?	**¿Cada cual tiene copia de la agenda?**
Does anyone need a copy of the agenda?	¿Quién necesita una copia de la agenda?
Is there anything that needs to be added to the agenda?	**¿Hay algo que deba añadirse a la agenda?**
Has everyone received the materials?	**¿Ha recibido cada cual los materiales?**

Schedule

We will have a coffee break at . . .*	**Habremos un descanso a las . . .**
10:15 A.M.	**diez y quince A.M.**
10:30 A.M.	diez y media de la mañana.
2:30 P.M.	dos y media de la tarde.
3:00 P.M.	tres de la tarde.

---

*For more on how to tell time, refer to section Telling Time in Chapter 6.

Lunch will be served at . . . 12:00 noon.	**Se servirá el almuerzo a las . . . doce del mediodía.**
Lunch will last . . . one hour. one hour-and-a-half.	El almuerzo durará . . . una hora. una hora y media.
The meeting will continue at 2:00 P.M.	**Continuará la reunión a las dos P.M.**
The meeting should be over at . . . 4:30 P.M. 5:00 P.M.	La reunión debe terminar a las . . . cuatro y media de la tarde. cinco de la tarde.
Let's begin. Does anyone have any questions before we begin? Does anyone have a question on the first subject?	**Comencemos.** **¿Alguien tiene alguna pregunta antes de comenzar?** **¿Alguien tiene una pregunta sobre el primer tema?**
Not everyone has spoken. Juan, do you have something to add?	**No todos han hablado.** Juan, ¿tiene usted algo que añadir?
We have not heard from everyone here. Does anyone else have a comment or a question?	No todos los aquí presentes han hablado. **¿Hay alguien que tenga un comentario o una pregunta?**
Can we move on to item number 2? Who will take responsibility for this item? Has everyone spoken on this point?	**¿Podemos pasar al punto número dos?** **¿Quién se hará responsable de este punto?** ¿Han hablado todos sobre este punto?

Do we need to vote on this item?	¿Hay necesidad de votar sobre este punto?
Those in favor, raise your hand.	**Los que estén de acuerdo, levanten la mano.**
Those opposed, raise your hand.	**Los que no estén de acuerdo, levanten la mano.**
The agenda passes.	**Se aprueba la agenda.**
The agenda loses.	**Se desaprueba la agenda.**
The motion passes.	Se aprueba la moción.
The motion fails.	Se desaprueba la moción.
Would you like to discuss this topic at a later meeting?	**¿Prefiere usted hablar de este tema en una reunión posterior?**
Let's table discussion on this matter.	**Hablemos con todos los aquí reunidos sobre este asunto.**

The Closing

Do we need a follow-up meeting?	**¿Debe dársele seguimiento a esta reunión?**
Before we leave, let's set a date for the next meeting.	**Antes de concluir, fijemos una fecha para la próxima reunión.**
Thank you for being here today.	Gracias por su presencia hoy aquí.

THE PRESENTATION OR SPEECH

How can you tell if the content of your presentation or speech is sound? Perhaps the most successful way is to answer this question: Does it tell a logical story? If it does, people will follow you step by step. If not, you will probably confuse your audience and questions will be raised that will sidetrack you.

Give your presentation or speech ahead of time to those you can count on to provide you with constructive comments. When do they ask questions? That's where your thoughts may be unclear. Go over each point and make sure you know the information and can articulate it.

One final thought. Assume that there will always be something wrong about the physical aspects of the presentation or speech: arrangements, handouts, equipment, or refreshments.

"*Cómo hacer una presentación*"
SRTA. OLIVER: *Tenemos la suerte de que esté hoy entre nosotros al Sr. Sánchez de la oficina central. Por favor, dénle la bienvenida.*
SR. SÁNCHEZ: *Gracias por tenerme entre ustedes. Quería visitar su oficina desde hace varios meses y, finalmente, lo pude hacer esta semana.*
¿Quieren hacer preguntas durante mi charla o esperar a terminarla?
SRTA. OLIVER: *Lo puede hacer de una forma u otra.*

"*Giving a Presentation*"
MS. OLIVER: *We are so fortunate to have Mr. Sánchez from our central office here today. Please welcome Mr. Sánchez.*
MR. SÁNCHEZ: *Thank you for having me. I've wanted to come to visit your office for several months, and finally I was able to do so this week. May I take questions during my talk or do you want me to wait until the end?*
MS. OLIVER: *You can do it either way.*

Key Words

Clarification question	Pregunta aclaratoria
Discussion question	Pregunta sobre la charla
Discussion	Charla
Introduction	Introducción
Microphone	Micrófono
Mission	Misión
Point	Punto
Presentation	Presentación
Question	Pregunta
Q&A period	Sesión de preguntas y respuestas
Subject	Tema
Talk	Charla
Topic	Tema
Vision	Visión

Audio Visual Presentation Aids

Here are some common aids you may use.

Audio	Audio
Board	Pizarra
Chalk	Tiza
Chart	Gráfico
Computer	Computadora/Ordenador
Diagram	Diagrama
Easel	Caballete
Extension cord	Extensión eléctrica
Folder	Carpeta
Hand out	Dar
Illustration	Illustración
Marker	Marcador/Rotulador
Microphone	Micrófono

Model	Modelo
Monitor	Monitor
Notepads	Bloc de notas
PowerPoint presentation	Presentación de PowerPoint
Screen	Pantalla
Slide projector	Proyector de diapositivas
Tape recorder	Magnetófono
Television	Televisión
Transparency	Transparencia
Video	Video
Video recorder	Aparato de video
Thank you for having me.	Gracias por tenerme entre ustedes.
I want to thank Juan for that nice introduction.	**Quiero darle las gracias a Juan por tan grata presentación.**
I want to thank Juan for inviting me to tell you about . . .	Quiero darle las gracias a Juan por invitarme a hablarles sobre . . .
I want to thank your organization for having me.	**Quiero darle las gracias a esta organización por tenerme aquí.**
It's an honor to be with you today.	Es para mí un honor estar aquí con ustedes hoy.
It's my pleasure to speak to you today.	**Es un placer para mí hablarles hoy.**
I'm grateful for the opportunity to speak to you.	Agradezco la oportunidad para hablarles.

The Subject

The purpose of this presentation/speech/ talk is . . .	**El propósito de esta presentación**/discurso/ charla **es** . . .

This morning/afternoon/ evening I'm going to talk about . . .	Esta mañana/tarde/noche les voy a hablar sobre . . .
The major point of my presentation/speech/talk is . . .	**El tema principal de mi presentación** discurso/ charla **es** . . .
In this presentation/ speech/talk, I'd like to . . .	En esta presentación/discurso/ charla me gustaría . . .
My topic today is . . .	El tema de hoy es . . .
The subject of my presentation is . . .	El tema de mi presentación es . . .
I'd like to begin by telling you my conclusion.	**Me gustaría comenzar diciéndoles mi conclusión.**
I'd first like to tell you about the concept behind my presentation/ speech/talk.	Primeramente, quisiera hablarles sobre el concepto primordial de mi presentación/discurso/ charla.
Please feel free to interrupt me with any questions.	**Por favor, siéntanse en plena libertad de interrumpirme con preguntas.**

The Major Points

I'd like to begin with a story.	Me gustaría comenzar con una historia.
There are three issues I would like to cover today.	**Hay tres temas que me gustaría abarcar hoy.**
There are three points that I would like to make/cover today.	Hay tres puntos que me gustaría hacer/abarcar hoy.
I want to make several points today.	**Quisiera hacer varios puntos hoy.**
First I want to cover . . .	**En primer lugar, quiero abarcar . . .**

Second I want to discuss . . .	En segundo lugar, quiero hablar sobre . . .
There is a growing need to be aware of . . .	Cada vez se hace más necesario que se amos conscientes de . . .
My/our mission is . . .	Mi/nuestra misión es . . .
My/our vision is . . .	Mi/nuestra visión es . . .
The following . . .	Los/Las siguientes . . .
data	datos
financial figures	cifras financieras
findings	conclusiones
information	información
results	resultados
provide support for my central thesis.	corroboran mi tesis central.
Now, on to the second point.	Ahora, referente a mi segundo punto.
Next, I would like to discuss . . .	Seguidamente, me gustaría hablar sobre . . .
Moving along, let's now consider . . .	Continuando, consideremos ahora . . .
Before I move on, are there any questions?	Antes de continuar, ¿hay alguna pregunta?
I hope you'll understand . . .	Espero que entenderán . . .
You should be able to see . . .	Podrán ver . . .
To support my point, I would like to . . .	Para respaldar mi explicación, quisiera . . .
demonstrate . . .	demostrar . . .
display . . .	exponer . . .
distribute . . .	distribuir . . .
illustrate . . .	ilustrar . . .
provide . . .	proporcionar . . .

| reveal . . . | revelar . . . |
| show . . . | mostrar . . . |

The Summary and Conclusion

| I would like to review my main points/items/ideas now. | Me gustaría repasar ahora mis puntos/temas/ideas principales. |

| Finally, I want to say . . . | Finalmente, quiero decir . . . |
| In summary, I would like to reiterate . . . | En resumen, quisiera reiterar . . . |

In conclusion . . .	En conclusión . . .
This concludes my main points.	Así, termino mis puntos principales.
This ends my remarks.	Así, termino mis comentarios.

| I hope this presentation has convinced you of . . . | Espero que esta presentación les haya convencido de . . . |

| It has been a pleasure talking to you. | Ha sido un placer hablarles. |
| It has been a pleasure being with you today. | Ha sido un placer estar aquí con ustedes hoy. |

| I have enjoyed presenting my . . . | He tenido gran gusto en presentarles a ustedes mi/mis . . . |

activities	actividades.
experience(s)	experiencia(s).
ideas	ideas.
paper	escrito.
thesis	tesis.
theories	teorías.
to you.	

I hope you have . . .	Espero que hayan . . .
enjoyed . . .	disfrutado con . . .
gained insight from . . .	adquirido nuevos enfoques con . . .

gained knowledge from . . .	adquirido nuevos conocimientos con . . .
learned something from . . .	aprendido algo de . . .
my presentation.	**mi presentación.**
Thank you for your attention.	**Gracias por su atención.**

As in the United States, in Spain and Latin America there is a certain dress code in business. At a business meeting or function a man should wear a suit and tie and a woman should wear a dress or a suit. Generally speaking, Spaniards and Latin Americans strive to create a good impression on others and are careful about how they dress and about how they speak and conduct themselves. If they are going to meet you for the first time, or even the second or third, they will try to look their best at whatever cost (literally). They expect you to do the same.

THE SALES CALL OR MEETING

The basis of successful sales is building relationships, that is, establishing the trust that allows for the free flow of information. Selling skills also involve the ability to understand and match customer needs with the features of your product or service.

The crucial element of sales, and the most difficult to learn, is the ability to close—to ink the deal. That's where passion and motivation on your part can make a difference.

"Cómo vender sus productos"
SR. JOHNSON: *Entonces, usted quisiera viente y cinco ó cincuenta de nuestras nuevas bombas, dependiendo de su horario de mantenimiento.*

SR. PELÁEZ: *Bueno, no le he dicho que compraría sus bombas.*

SR. JOHNSON: *¿Qué habría que hacer para que usted las comprase? ¿Precio, entrega, formalidad?*

SR. PELÁEZ: *Mayormente, precio.*

SR. JOHNSON: *Estoy dispuesto a ofrecerle un quince por ciento de descuento si usted compra cincuenta ahora.*

SR. PELÁEZ: *De acuerdo.*

"Selling Your Products"

MR. JOHNSON: *Then, you would like either 25 or 50 of our new pumps depending on your maintenance schedule?*

MR. PELÁEZ: *Well, I haven't said that I would buy your pumps.*

MR. JOHNSON: *What would it take for you to purchase them? Price, delivery, reliability?*

MR. PELÁEZ: *Mainly price.*

MR. JOHNSON: *I am prepared to offer you a 15 percent discount if you buy 50 now.*

MR. PELÁEZ: *We have a deal.*

Key Words

Brochure	*Folleto*
Buy (to)	*Comprar*
Close a deal	*Carrar un trato*
Cold call	*Llamada inesperada*
Deal	*Trato*
Delivery	*Entrega*
Delivery date	*Fecha de entrega*
Discount	*Descuento*

Follow-up	Seguimiento
Option	Opción
Price	Precio
Product	Producto
Quality	Calidad
Quantity	Cantidad
Sell (to)	Vender
Service	Servicio
Shipping	Transporte
Specification(s)	Especificación/
	Especificaciones

My name is . . .	Me llamo . . .
I am from . . . company/ organization . . .	Soy de la compañía/ organización . . .
Here is a brochure on our product/service.	**Aquí tiene un folleto sobre nuestro producto**/servicio.
Here is a folder with information on our firm/ company/organization.	Aquí tiene una carpeta con información sobre nuestra empresa/compañía/ organización.
Here is our company's brochure.	**Aquí tiene el folleto de nuestra compañía.**

Questions to Ask

Is everything working okay?	¿Todo funciona bien?
Would you like to improve your current business?	**¿Quisiera mejorar su negocio actual?**
Would you like to increase your productivity?	**¿Quisiera aumentar su productividad?**

| What problems are you having? | ¿Qué problemas está teniendo? |
| What are your concerns? | ¿Qué le preocupa? |

Your Product or Service

Our product was designed by our engineers with our customers' needs in mind.	Nuestro producto ha sido diseñado teniendo presentes las necesidades de nuestros clientes.
Our product was designed by our experts.	Nuestro producto ha sido diseñado por nuestros expertos.
Our products/services have proven to be highly successful.	Se ha comprobado que nuestros productos/servicios han tenido mucho éxito.
We are able to tailor the product/service to your needs.	Somos capaces de adaptar nuestro producto/servicio a sus necesidades.
We can alter our product/service to your specifications.	Podemos modificar nuestro producto/servicio según sus especificaciones.
Here are testimonials from our customers.	Tengo aquí recomendaciones de nuestros clientes.

Handling Acceptance, Skepticism, Indifference

Yes, I agree we have an excellent track record.	Sí, estoy de acuerdo en que tenemos un excelente historial.
Yes, we are proud of our product/service.	Sí, nos sentimos orgullosos de nuestro producto/servicio.
Our company is very satisfied with our product(s)/service(s).	Nuestra compañía se siente muy satisfecha de nuestros productos/servicios.
Thank you for that compliment.	Gracias por su cumplido.

Perhaps you are not aware of the problems in your operations department.

Perhaps you are not aware that our customers find our product/service very effective.

Our product/service has been successful in most companies/organizations.

Let me explain what this product/service can do for your company.

Our prices are extremely competitive.

Do you realize what this product/service can do for your organization?

Do you know how much this product/service could save you each year?

Are you aware of what this could do for your company?

Quizás no conozca los problemas de su departamento de operaciones.

Quizás no sepa usted que nuestros clientes encuentran nuestro producto/servicio muy eficaz.

Nuestro producto/servicio ha tenido éxito en la mayoría de las compañías/organizaciones/empresas.

Permítame explicarle lo que este producto/servicio **puede hacer para su compañía.**

Nuestros precios son muy competitivos.

¿Se da usted cuenta de lo que este producto/servicio puede hacer para su organización?

¿Se da usted cuenta de lo que este producto/servicio le puede ahorrar cada año?

¿Se percata usted de lo que esto puede hacer para su compañía?

The Close

May I order this product/service for you?

How many do you want?

When would you like it installed?

¿Le puedo tomar un pedido para este producto/servicio?

¿Cuántos desea?

¿Cuándo desea que se le instale?

| When would you like it delivered? | ¿**Cuándo desea que se le entregue?** |

THE NEGOTIATING MEETING

Reading people is key. Who is the decision maker? Is she a take-charge type, or is she looking for you to take the lead? Listening is a critical skill, whether you are leading the negotiations or are a member of a negotiating team.

Businessmen and women in Latin cultures are considered to be tough negotiators. Always calculate enough bargaining space into your initial offer to allow for concessions. Be prepared for rather long and vigorous negotiations, and don't accept an offer too quickly. Ask for time to think about the offer in order to reassure the other party that they have made a reasonable move.

Also, look for the bottom line. What are the key issues on each side? Is what you are negotiating perceived as a zero-sum game? Turn it into a win-win game.

"Cómo negociar el contrato"

SR. JONES: *Quisiéramos que el contrato estipulara que "No hay otras garantías implícitas aparte de la aquí declarada."*

SRTA. BUSTAMANTE: *Insistiríamos en que la garantía estipulara que "No se asumen otras garantías aparte de la aquí declarada."*

SR. JONES: *En la mayoría de nuestros contratos se utiliza "implícita."*

SRTA. BUSTAMANTE: *En nuestro país se usa la palabra "asumir."*

SR. JONES: *Bien. Acordemos usar la palabra "asumir."*

"Negotiating the Contract"

MR. JONES: *We would want the warranty to say "No warranty is implied other than what is stated."*

MS. BUSTAMANTE: *We would insist that it says "No warranty is assumed other than what is stated."*

MR. JONES: *Most of our contracts use "implied."*

MS. BUSTAMANTE: *In our country the word "assumed" is used.*

MR. JONES: *Okay. We'll agree to the word "assumed."*

Key Words

Accept (to)	Aceptar
Acceptable	Aceptable
Agree (to)	Estar de acuerdo
Agreement	Acuerdo
Conflict	Conflicto
Contract	Contrato
Disagree (to)	Discrepar/No estar de acuerdo
Guarantee	Garantía
Issue	Asunto
Item	Tema
Key issues	Temas claves
Lawyer	Abogado
Negotiate (to)	Negociar
Offer	Oferta
Point	Punto
Proposal	Propuesta
Propose (to)	Proponer
Reject (to)	Rechazar
Rejection	Rechazo
Unacceptable	Inadmisible
Warranty	Garantía

I want to introduce my partner.	**Deseo presentarle a mi socio.**
I want to introduce our lawyer.	Deseo presentarle a nuestro abogado.
Please introduce yourself.	Por favor, preséntese.
Please introduce the other people (who are) with you.	Por favor, presente a las otras personas que le acompañan.
Has everyone arrived?	**¿Han llegado todos?**
Is everyone here?	**¿Están todos aquí?**
Is everyone comfortable?	¿Están todos cómodos?
Could we begin?	**¿Podríamos comenzar?**
May we begin?	¿Podemos comenzar?
Can we begin?	¿Comenzamos?
Let's begin.	Comencemos.
Are there any questions before we begin?	¿Alguien tiene una pregunta antes de comenzar?

Stating the Issues

Let's each of us state the issues.	**Que cada cual hable de los temas.**
Let's each of us present our positions.	Que cada cual presente nuestras posiciones.
What are the issues we need to cover in this meeting?	**¿Cuáles son los temas a abarcar en esta reunión?**
What is the purpose of this meeting?	**¿Cuál es el propósito de esta reunión?**
What objectives would you like to accomplish in this meeting?	¿Cuáles son los objetivos que les gustaría lograr en esta reunión?
Why is this meeting necessary?	¿Por qué es necesaria esta reunión?
What are the key issues as you see them?	En su opinión, ¿cuáles son los temas claves?

What is missing?	¿Falta algo?
Is anyone confused about our purpose here today?	¿Hay alguien que no entienda bien nuestro propósito de hoy?
What is it you need us to do?	¿Qué hacemos?/¿Qué quiere(n) que hagames?
Which points are not clear?	**¿Cuáles son los puntos que no están claros?**
Let's go over the details again.	Volvamos a repasar los detalles.
Has everything been covered?	¿Se ha abarcado todo?
We have a problem with . . .	**Tenemos un problema con . . .**
credit and payment.	**el crédito y el pago.**
deadlines.	**las fechas límite.**
delivery and terms.	**la entrega y las condiciones.**
guarantees.	**las garantías.**
licensing.	**las licencias.**
warranties.	**las garantías.**

Disagreement, Ambivalence, and Reaching an Agreement

We disagree with these points.	**Discrepamos con estos puntos.**
We don't agree.	**No estamos de acuerdo.**
That's unacceptable.	**Eso no es aceptable.**
Why do you disagree with this provision?	**¿Por qué no está de acuerdo con esta disposición?**
Why do you reject this provision?	**¿Por qué rechaza usted esta disposición?**
There is still too much keeping us apart.	**Todavía hay mucho que nos mantiene apartados.**
We must continue to negotiate.	**Debemos continuar con nuestra negociación.**

We must continue our efforts.	Debemos continuar nuestros esfuerzos.
You certainly don't expect us to accept that.	**Ciertamente, no espera usted que aceptemos eso.**
Unfortunately, you are not offering enough.	Desgraciadamente, no ofrece usted lo suficiente.
We need more.	**Necesitamos más.**
Who will pay for delivery?	**¿Quién pagará la entrega?**
Who will pay for insurance?	**¿Quién pagará el seguro?**
We wish to propose . . .	**Quisiéramos proponer . . .**
We wish to counter propose . . .	Quisiéramos rebatir la propuesta . . .
What is your counter offer?	**¿Cuál es su contraoferta?**
We are prepared to . . .	Estamos preparados para . . .
You should know the following . . .	**Usted debería saber lo siguiente . . .**
Our lawyers have informed us . . .	**Nuestros abogados nos han informado . . .**
We expect payment in 30/60/90 days.	**Esperamos el pago en treinta/sesenta/novente días.**
Is there any discount for early payment?	**¿Hay algún descuento por pronto pago?**
Can you provide us with a letter of credit?	**¿Nos puede proporcionar una carta de crédito?**
What is your guarantee?	**¿Cuál es su garantía?**
We are getting close.	**Nos estamos acercando.**
I'm beginning to see your point.	**Comienzo a ver su punto de vista.**
Now I understand your point.	Ahora entiendo su punto de vista.
Give us some time to think this over.	**Dénnos tiempo para pensarlo.**

Let's plan another meeting.	**Planeemos otra reunión.**
We agree except for . . .	Estamos de acuerdo excepto por . . .
the cost.	el costo.
the delivery date.	la fecha de entrega.
the guarantee.	la garantía.
the legal costs.	el costo legal.
the price.	el precio.
the shipping.	el transporte.
We agree with some of your points.	Estamos de acuerdo con algunos de sus puntos.
We seem to agree in general.	**Parece que en general estamos de acuerdo.**
We agree with your point.	Estamos de acuerdo en eso.
What is left to discuss?	**¿De qué más hay que hablar?**
This is our final offer.	Esta es nuestra oferta definitiva.
Is that your final offer?	**¿Es esa su oferta definitiva?**

Inking the Deal

Once a deal is reached, you'd want to celebrate, of course. But note that people may celebrate and congratulate each other in different ways in different cultures: bowing, shaking hands, offering a drink or toast, and so forth. If you are not sure of the cultural norms, as usual, the rule of thumb is to follow your hosts.

We agree.	Estamos de acuerdo.
We accept your offer.	**Aceptamos su oferta.**
This point/offer is acceptable.	**Este punto/**esta oferta es **aceptable.**
We have an agreement.	**Tenemos un acuerdo.**
We have the deal.	Tenemos un trato.

We worked hard, let's have an agreement.	Hemos trabajado duro, tengamos un acuerdo.
We need a written document by Friday.	**Necesitamos un documento escrito para el viernes.**
The documents must be signed by all parties.	**Todas las partes deben firmar el documento.**
Who will draft the agreement?	**¿Quién redactará el acuerdo?**
We will draft/type it.	Nosotros lo redactaremos/ escribiremos.
We will send you a draft of the agreement.	**Le enviaremos un borrador del acuerdo.**
We will send a draft of the agreement for your comments.	Le enviaremos un borrador del acuerdo para que lo revise.
Thank you for your efforts.	Gracias por sus esfuerzos.
It was very nice working with you.	**Nos agradó mucho trabajar con usted.**
If you have any questions, please let us know.	**En caso de tener alguna pregunta, sírvase comunicárnoslo.**
We will be in touch.	**Nos mantendremos en contacto.**

THE TRAINING SESSION

Are you conducting the session, or are you there to be trained? If you're giving the session, make sure the training is constructed from the participant's point of view. Too often, training is organized more for the expert than the learner.

There may be a cultural aspect to consider when designing training programs. It's important to know how best to provide information to people in other business cultures. Advanced discussions with those in the country or a region of a country eliminates most of the surprises and difficulties.

You may wish to review two of the sections in this chapter for words and phrases to begin and open the training session with "The General Business Meeting" and "The Presentation or Speech."

"Adiestramiento"

SR. SMITH: *Vamos a hablar ahora sobre el "Desarrollo de una visión conjunta." Si se fijan en el cuaderno de trabajo, página viente y siete, verán una lista de las principales ideas que forman este concepto. Srta. Crespo, sabria usted decirnos algo acerca de cómo comienza este proceso?*

SRTA. CRESPO: *Sí. Creo que una visión conjunta comienza con la dirección de una organización, la cual ha de declarar un comunicado de su misión, una lista de sus objetivos, los cuales darán impulso a dicha organización.*

SR. SMITH: *Muy bien dicho. Sr. Ríos, ¿qué haría usted entonces para estimular a los empleados a seguir tales objetivos direccionales?*

SR. RÍOS: *Supongo que mediante un proceso interactivo, como un grupo de trabajo, o una serie de reuniones de comités, en las que participaran los empleados para determinar cómo pueden implementarse tales objetivos en el nivel de trabajo real.*

"Being Trained"

MR. SMITH: *We are now going to talk about "Developing a Shared Vision." If you look in your workbook on page 27, you'll see a list of the principal ideas behind this concept. Ms. Crespo, could you speculate on how this process begins?*

Ms. Crespo: *Yes. I believe a shared vision starts with the management of the organization establishing a mission statement, a list of management objectives, that will drive the organization.*

Mr. Smith: *Very good. Mr. Ríos, how then do you get employees to buy into these organizational objectives?*

Mr. Ríos: *I would guess by having some interactive process, like a task force or a series of committee meetings, where employees can participate in determining how these objectives can be implemented at the actual work level.*

Key Words

Ask/have a question (to)	Preguntar/Tener una pregunta
Be confused (to)	Estar confundido
Classroom	Salón de clase/(Aula de) clase
Course	Curso
Notepad	Bloc de notas
Pencil	Lápiz
Pen	Pluma/Bolígrafo
Seminar	Seminario
Group work	Trabajo en grupo
Train (to)	Adiestrar/Formar
Training session	Sesión de adiestramiento/ Sesión deformación
Understand (to)	Comprender
Workbook	Cuaderno de trabajo
Workshop	Taller de trabajo

Today, I'm conducting training in . . .	**Hoy, voy a impartir una sesión de formación sobre . . .**

| our policies. | **nuestra política.** |
| our procedures. | nuestros procedimientos. |

The training program today covers our new . . .	**El programa de formación de hoy abarca . . .**
financial reports.	**nuestros nuevos informes financieros.**
marketing reports.	nuestros nuevos informes de marketing.
organization.	nuestra nueva organización.
sales reports.	nuestros informes de venta.
system(s).	nuestro/nuestros sistema(s).

I would like to . . .	**Me gustaría . . .**
convince you . . .	convencerles . . .
discuss . . .	hablar sobre . . .
encourage dialogue on . . .	**animarlos a dialogar sobre . . .**
have your feedback regarding . . .	conocer su reacción acerca de . . .
lead a discussion on . . .	dirigir una charla sobre . . .
participate in . . .	participar en . . .
provide information on . . .	proporcionar información acerca de . . .

Is there any question about the agenda?	¿Hay alguna pregunta sobre la agenda?
Does everyone have all the materials?	**¿Tienen todos el material?**
Do you have any questions before we begin?	¿Hay alguna pregunta antes de comenzar?
Could you repeat that question?	**¿Puede repetir esa pregunta?**
Does everyone understand the question?	¿Todos entienden la pregunta?
Does everyone understand the issues?	¿Todos entienden los temas?

Let's begin.	Comencemos.
Can I clarify anything?	**¿Puedo aclarar algo?**
What do you think about this?	**¿Qué piensa usted sobre esto?**
Would anyone like to respond?	**¿Desea responder alguien?**
Are there any other ideas?	¿Hay otras ideas?
Let's break out into teams to solve this problem.	**Separémonos en grupos para resolver este problema.**
Who will report on your solutions?	**¿Quién informará sobre sus soluciones?**
That concludes the training on . . .	**Así concluye la formación sobre . . .**
I'll be happy to answer any questions.	Gustosamente contestaré cualquiera pregunta.
If you have any further questions, I'll be here for a while.	Si alguien tiene más preguntas, permaneceré aquí un rato.
Please contact me if you have further questions.	Por favor, comuníquense conmigo en caso de tener alguna otra pregunta.
Thank you for your attention.	Gracias por su atención.

Types of Room Set-Up or Style*

Classroom	Sala de clase/(Aula de) clase
Conference table	Mesa de conferencias
Dais	Tarima
Podium	Podio
Theater	Teatro
U-shaped	En forma de U

---

*Please refer back to the section "The Presentation or Speech" of this chapter to find the terms for common audiovisual aids.

Types of Charts and Graphs

Bar chart	Gráfico de barras
Display	Exposición
Dotted line	Línea de puntos
Exponential	Exponente
Histogram	Histograma
Horizontal bar chart	Gráfico de barras horizontal
Line graph	Gráfico de líneas
Linear	Lineal
Logarithmic scale	Escala logarítmica
Organization chart	Gráfico de organización
Pie chart	Gráfico circunferencial
Regression	Retroceso
Solid line	Línea continua
Stacked	Apilado
Table	Tabla
XY scatter	Dispersión de XY

Parts of Charts and Graphs

Arc	Arco
Area	Area
Arrow	Flecha
Beginning	Comienzo
Bell shaped	En forma acampanada
Box	Caja
Bullet	Punto
Circle	Círculo
Column	Columna
Curve	Curva
Dash	Guión
Diagram	Diagrama
Dotted line	Línea de puntos
Edge	Borde
Ellipse	Elipse
End	Final
First	Primero
Grid	Malla

Heading	Encabezamiento
Label	Etiqueta
Last	Último
Layout	Trazado
Line	Línea
Logo	Logotipo
Map	Mapa
Maximum	Máximo
Middle	Medio
Minimum	Mínimo
Numbers	Números
Object	Objeto
Origin	Origen
Percentage	Porcentaje
Polygon	Polígono
Right angle	Angulo recto
Row	Fila
Scale	Escala
Shadow	Sombra
Slice	Pedazo
Space	Espacio
Square	Cuadrado
Rectangle	Rectángulo
Shadow	Sombra
Table	Tabla
Text	Texto
Triangle	Triángulo
Title	Título
Values	Valores

Positions

Bottom	Pie (de)/Parte inferior
Center	Centro
Horizontal	Horizontal
Inside	Dentro/Interior
Left	Izquierdo/a
Outside	Fuera/Exterior

Right	Derecho/a
Side	Lado
Top	Superior (parte)
Touching	Que juntan
Vertical	Vertical
X-axis	Eje de abscisas
Y-axis	Eje de ordenadas
Z-axis	Eje de altura

Other Symbols and Formatting Designs

Asterisk	Asterisco
Blank	Blanco
Bold	Negrita
Crosshatched	Entretejido
Dash	Guión
Pound sign	Cuadradillo/Almohadilla
Shaded	Sombreado
Solid	Sólido
Star	Estrella
Underlined	Subrayado

Colors

Aqua	Aguamarina
Black	Negro
Blue	Azul
Brown	Marrón
Green	Verde
Orange	Naranja
Purple	Violeta
Red	Rojo
Yellow	Amarillo

THE TRADE SHOW

The trade show is a cross between a sales call and a mass presentation. If you are part of the team presenting your company's products or services, you

71

usually have only a brief time to talk about them. If you are attending just to learn about what other companies are offering, it helps to be organized. There are many exhibits to see, many people to meet, and many contacts to make.

You might also like to review the section "The Sales Call" in this chapter, and the section "Business Cards" in Chapter 1.

"Cómo dar información"

SRTA. SMITH: *¿Quisiera un folleto?*

ASISTENTE: *Sí. ¿Podría ver una demostración de su servicio?*

SRTA. SMITH: *Usted puede ver el menú en el monitor. Seleccionaremos la opción dos.*

ASISTENTE: *¿Es su sistema compatible con Windows?*

"Giving Information"

MS. SMITH: *Would you like a brochure?*

ATTENDEE: *Yes. Can I see a demonstration of your service?*

MS. SMITH: *You can see the menu on the monitor. We'll just select option 2.*

ATTENDEE: *Is your system compatible with Windows?*

Key Words

Badge	Insignia
Booth	Caseta
Brochure	Folleto
Demonstrate (to)	Demostrar
Demonstration	Demostración
Exhibit	Exposición

Literature	Información
Message center	Central de mensajes
Register (to)	Inscribirse
Registration	Inscripción
Trade show	Exposición comercial

I want to register for the trade show.
Quiero inscribirme para la exposición comercial.

Where do I get my badge?
¿Dónde puedo obtener una insignia?

Where is . . .
¿Dónde se encuentra . . .
  the business center?
    la central de negocios?
  check-in?
    el lugar para inscribirse?
  the information desk?
    información?
  the message center?
    la central de mensajes?
  the shipping center?
    la central de transporte?
  ticket sales office?
    la taquilla de boletos?

I would like to reserve . . .
Quisiera reservar . . .
  a booth.
    una caseta.
  a room at the conference center.
    un salón en el centro de conferencias.

I would like to rent (a) . . .
Quisiera alquilar . . .
  color monitor.
    un monitor de colores.
  computer.
    una computadora.
  computer cable.
    un cable de computadora.
  microphone.
    un micrófono.
  slide projector.
    un proyector de diapositivas.

  sound system.
    un sistema de sonido.
  speaker.
    un altavoz.
  table.
    una mesa.
  television.
    una televisión.

There is a problem with . . .	**Hay un problema con . . .**
the electrical line.	la línea eléctrica.
my booth.	mi caseta.
the location of my booth.	**la posición de mi caseta.**
I need . . .	**Necesito . . .**
chairs.	sillas.
display tables.	mesas de exposición.
electricity.	electricidad.
an easel.	**caballete.**
extension cords.	alargos.
My materials have not arrived.	**Mis materiales no han llegado.**
Please deliver these to booth number 124.	Por favor, entréguelos a la caseto número ciento veinte y cuatro.
Hi, my name is . . .	Hola, me llamo . . .
What's yours?	¿Cómo se llama usted?
My name is . . .	Me llamo . . .
My company/ organization is . . .	Mi empresa/organización es . . .
My position is . . .	Mi cargo es . . .
Are you familiar with our products/services?	**¿Conoce nuestros productos/servicios?**
What can I tell you about them?	¿Qué quiere saber sobre ellos?
Can I explain anything to you?	¿Desea que le explique algo?
Please take a brochure.	**Por favor, tome un folleto.**
Please write your name, address, and phone number.	Por favor, escriba su nombre, dirección y número de teléfono.
Do you have any questions?	¿Tiene usted alguna pregunta?
Can I help you?	¿Puedo ayudarle?

May I have your business card?	¿Me puede dar una de sus tarjetas?
What is your e-mail address?	¿Cuál es su dirección eletrónica?
You can visit our Web site.	**Puede visitar nuestro sitio Web.**
Would you like to see . . .	**¿Quisiera ver . . .**
a brochure?	un folleto?
a demonstration?	**una demostración?**
Do you have a brochure in . . .	¿Tiene un folleto . . .
English?	en inglés?
Spanish?	en español?
What can I tell you about the product/service?	¿Qué puedo decirle acerca del producto/servicio?
My company will be giving a demonstration in the conference room.	**Mi empresa hará una demostración en el salón de conferencias.**
We will be demonstrating the product/service . . .*	Haremos una demostración del producto/servicio . . .
later.	más tarde.
tomorrow.	mañana.
at 10:00 A.M.	a las diez de la mãnana.
at 2:00 P.M.	a las dos de la tarde.
Can you come back tomorrow at . . .	¿Puede regresar mañana a las . . .
11:00 a.m.?	once de le mañana.
3:00 P.M.?	tres de la tarde.
Can I contact you to keep you informed about our products/services?	**¿Me puedo comunicar con usted para mantenerle informado acerca de nuestros productos/** servicios?

---

*See section "Telling Time" in Chapter 6 for more information on how to tell time in Spanish.

Can I have . . .	¿Me puede dar . . .
a list of your products/ services?	una lista de sus productos/servicios?
your business card?	su tarjeta?
your catalog?	su catálogo?

Can you tell me more about . . .	**¿Me puede dar más información sobre . . .**
the delivery options.	**opciones de entrega?**
next year's model.	el modelo del próximo año?
your new system.	su nuevo sistema?

Do you have more information on . . .	¿Tiene usted más informacion acerca . . .
your company's history.	del historial de su compañía?
your other products.	de sus otros productos?
your system that is being developed.	del sistema que están desarrollando?

| Please explain your guarantee/warrantee. | **Por favor, explique sus garantías.** |

| Please speak more slowly. | Por favor, hable más despacio. |

Could you repeat that?	¿Puede repetir eso?
I understand.	Entiendo.
I am not interested.	**No estoy interesado/ interesada.**

| May I give you a call? | ¿Puedo llamarle por teléfono? |

| I'll give you a call. | Le llamaré por teléfono. |
| Please call me. | Por favor, llámeme por teléfono. |

| It was nice meeting you. | Me alegra haberle conocido. |

| Perhaps I'll see you later. | Quizás nos veamos después. |

| Thank you for stopping by. | Gracias por visitarnos. |

| Thank you for showing me your products. | Gracias por mostrarme sus productos. |

76

ATTENDING A CONFERENCE OR SEMINAR

You can accomplish several objectives by attending a conference or seminar. Obviously you can learn new information, points of view, and better ways of doing something. You can also make important contacts within your industry or field. Also, through questions, you can provide the conference or seminar with your own experiences and information, and express your own or your company's opinions.

Conferences can be large auditorium affairs or small seminars. Taking good notes is key. Check with other attendees on information that you aren't sure of. This can also be a way to make interesting and useful contacts.

Remember to write a note to your new contacts as soon as you can after the conference. A personal note, a phone call, or an e-mail goes a long way to continue and solidify a contact.

"Cómo hacer contactos"

SRTA. JOHNSON: *Veo que está usted con la empresa Neumáticos Garcés.*

SR. RÍOS: *Así es. Con mi asistencia espero aprender cómo comercializar en este país. ¿Me puede dar su tarjeta?*

SRTA. JOHNSON: *Sí, y me gustaría tener una de las suyas también. ¿Qué le pareció el conferenciante en el almuerzo?*

SR. RÍOS: *Así así. Me hubiera gustado si hubiese dado más detalles sobre la forma en que resolvió sus problemas técnicos.*

"Making Contacts"

MS. JOHNSON: *I see you're with Neumáticos Garcés?*

MR. RÍOS: *Yes. I'm hoping to learn more about how to market in this country. May I have your business card?*
MS. JOHNSON: *Yes. I would like one of yours as well. How did you like the speaker at lunch?*
MR. RÍOS: *So-so. I would have liked it if she would have been more specific about how she solved the technical problems.*

Key Words

Ballroom	Sala
Business card	Tarjeta de presentación
Cocktail party	Cóctel
Conference room	Salón de conferencias
Introductions	Presentaciones
Luncheon	Almuerzo
Make contacts (to)	Hacer contactos
Message	Mensaje
Presentation/Talk/ Speech	Presentación/Charla/Discurso

Please introduce yourself.	Por favor, preséntese.
Before we begin the meeting, let's introduce ourselves.	Antes de comenzar la reunión, preséntese cada cual.
Beginning on my left/right please state your name, company, and position/ title.	Comenzando por mi izquierda/derecha, por favor dé su nombre, compañía y cargo/título.
My name is . . .	Me llamo . . .
My company/organization is . . .	Mi empresa/organización es . . .
My position is . . .	Mi cargo es . . .

I hope to get . . .	**Espero obtener en** esta/**este** conferencia/**seminario . . .**
information	información.
a better understanding	**un mejor entendimiento.**
useful data	datos útiles.
out of this conference/seminar.	

Questions

Could you please repeat what you just said?	**Por favor, ¿podría repetir lo que acaba de decir?**
I didn't understand your second point.	**No entendí su segundo punto.**
Why/How did you reach that conclusion?	**¿Por qué/cómo llegó a esa conclusión?**

Close

| Could we receive a tape of this conference/ seminar? | ¿Se nos podría dar una cinta de esta conferencia/ seminario? |
| Thank you for the information. | Gracias por su información. |

CONDUCTING AN INTERVIEW

Are you interviewing someone for your own department? Are you in human resources, screening applicants for a job? Getting beyond the details of a resume is the key to a successful interview.

"La entrevista"

SRTA. SMITH: *¿Por qué quiere dejar su trabajo actual?*

SR. RIVERO: *No hay posibilidad de ascenso para mí. No puedo salir de esta posición, y no hay oportunidades para mí.*

SRTA. SMITH: ¿Y qué clase de oportunidades busca usted?

SR. RIVERO: Me gustaría dirigir todo un proyecto de software. Ahora, soy uno de tantos programadores.

"The Interview"

MS. SMITH: *Why do you want to leave your present job?*

MR. RIVERO: *There is no chance for advancement for me. I'm stuck in my position. And there are no challenges for me.*

MS. SMITH: *What kind of challenges are you seeking?*

MR. RIVERO: *I would like to be in charge of an entire software project. Now I'm only one of the many programmers.*

Key Words

Ad	Anuncio
Benefits	Beneficios
Boss	Jefe
Career	Carrera
Experience	Experiencia
Goals	Metas/Objetivos
Job	Empleo
Interview	Entrevista
Objective	Objetivo
Offer	Oferta
Organization	Organización
Reference	Referencia
Resume	Curriculum Vitae/Resumen
Salary	Sueldo
Skills	Habilidades

Jaime Robledo
Calle Desamparados No. 790
Victoria del Campo, Colombia
792–4652

Objetivos

Busca una posición superior en una empresa internacional. Puede viajar a todas partes del mundo.

Experiencia
profesional

Turbinas Montealegre, S.A. Victoria del Campo, Colombia.
Desde 1989 hasta el presente.

Analista Superior Financiero en el departamento de finanzas de la corporación. Estructuró e implementó un programa de reducción de costos para toda la compañía. Le ahorró a la misma $2 millones de dólares en inventario.

Compañía Nacional de Transportes, S.A., Los Naranjos, Colombia. Desde 1985 hasta 1989.

Analista financiero en el departamento de contabilidad de la corporación. Encargado de análisis rutinarios y especiales de informes financieros emitidos por la corporación a los accionistas.

Educación

Licenciatura en contabilidad, Universidad de Cali.

Referencias

Sr. D. Juan Carlos Jiménez, Turbinas Montealegre, S.A. Teléfono 493–1596.

Jaime Robledo
Calle Desamparados No. 790
Victoria del Campo, Colombia
792–4652

Objective   Seeking a senior financial position in
an international organization. Will
travel extensively internationally if
necessary.

Professional
Experience   Turbinas Montealegre, S.A., Victorial
del Campo, Columbia 1989 to present.

Senior Financial Analyst in the Corporate Finance Department. Designed
and implemented a companywide
cost-cutting program. Saved $2
million dollars in inventory.

Compañía Nacional de Transportes,
S.A., Los Naranjos, Columbia. 1989 to
1989.

Financial Analyst in the Corporate
Accounting Department. Handled
routine and special analysis of financial reports issued by the company to
shareholders.

Education   B.S. Degree in Accounting, University
of Cali.

Professional
References   Mr. D. Juan Carlos Jiménez, Turbinas
Montealegre, S.A. Telephone:
493–1596.

Do you have a resume?	¿Tiene usted un curriculum vitae/resumen?
Could you review your work experience/ history for me?	¿Podríamos repasar su historial de trabajo/ experiencia?
Please tell me about your education.	Por favor, hábleme de sus estudios.
Please tell me about your jobs.	Por favor, hábleme de sus empleos.
What do you feel were your biggest accomplishments at each of your jobs?	¿Cuáles piensa usted que fueron sus mayores logros en cada empleo?
What was your salary/ compensation at each of your jobs?	¿Cuál era su sueldo/ compensación en cada empleo?
What is your salary/ compensation now?	¿Cuál es ahora su sueldo/compensación?
Do you receive any . . . bonus? deferred compensation? stock options?	¿Recibe usted algún(a)(s) . . . bonificación? compensaciones diferidas? opciones en acciones?
Do you have a . . . 401(k) type plan? pension?	¿Tiene usted . . . un plan de retiro? una pensión?
Why did you leave Turbinas Montealegre and join Transportes Nacionales?	¿Por qué dejó usted la compañía Turbinas Montealegre y se cambió a Transportes Nacionales?
Why do you want to leave Transportes Nacionales now?	¿Por qué quiere dejar ahora a Transportes Nacionales?
What position are you looking for?	¿Qué posición le interesa?

What are you looking for in a position?	¿Qué le interesa a usted de una posición?
What salary/ compensation are you looking for?	**¿Qué sueldo/ compensación le interesa?**
What were some of the problems you experienced?	**¿Cuáles fueron algunos de los problemas que usted tuvo?**
How did you deal with them?	¿Cómo se enfrentó usted a ellos?
How well did you get along with your boss(es)?	¿Cómo se llevó usted con su/sus jefe/jefes?
How well did you get along with your colleagues?	¿Cómo se llevó usted con sus compañeros de trabajo?
Do you have any references?	**¿Tiene usted referencias?**
Can we check with any of these references?	¿Podemos verificar cualquiera de estas referencias?
Do you have any questions for me?	¿Tiene usted alguna pregunta?
What questions do you have?	**¿Qué pregunta tiene?**
How can we be in touch with you?	**¿Cómo podemos mantenernos en contacto con usted?**
Here is my card.	Aquí tiene mi tarjeta.
If you have any questions, please call me.	Si tiene usted alguna pregunta, por favor, llámeme.
My e-mail address is . . .	Mi dirección electrónica es . . .
You will hear from us within . . .	**Le avisaré dentro de . . .**

two days.	**dos días.**
one week.	una semana.
two weeks.	dos semanas.
three weeks.	tres semanas.
one month.	un mes.

We will be in touch with you within . . .	Nos comunicaremos con usted dentro de un plazo de . . .
Do you have any further questions?	¿Tiene usted más preguntas?
I enjoyed talking to you.	**Me agradó hablar con usted.**
It was a pleasure talking to you.	Fue un placer hablar con usted.
Thank you for seeing us.	Gracias por visitarnos.
Good luck to you.	Buena suerte.

In Latin American countries, men still dominate the business profession. As a result, you might encounter a certain amount of skepticism or reserve on their side if you're a successful businesswoman. The best way to fight this is by being well-prepared, quietly confident, and assertive. This will eventually gain you their respect.

3 GETTING OUT

Dining out, attending a sporting event or going to a movie, or just doing some pleasant sightseeing can be a welcome break from meetings and conferences. It's a chance to relax after an intense business day. It's also an opportunity to see and learn about a country, culture, and people.

However, when you engage in these activities with business associates, you have to be as attentive and businesslike as you are in the office. After all, you are merely extending your selling or negotiating from the office to a more casual setting. Thus, you must be very conscious of the boundary separating business from personal affairs. If you do cross that line, you do it deliberately.

A more casual setting can offer the chance to establish or cement relationships, which can be difficult to do in the office. You can get to know your associates and build trust, the bedrock of successful business relationships.

Getting out can mean different things to different people. We cover a number of situations:

> **Getting a Taxi**
> **At the Restaurant**
> **Social Conversation**
> **Sporting Events, Movies,**
>   **Theater, Clubs**
> **Visiting the Partner's or**
>   **Associate's Home**
> **Sightseeing**
> **Shopping**

For most of these activities, we need a taxi. *¡Taxi!*

GETTING A TAXI

"Cómo tomar un taxi"
CHOFER: *¿Dónde quiere ir?*
SR. JONES: *Me gustaría ir a un buen restaurante francés. ¿Sabe usted de alguno cerca?*
CHOFER: *Sí, hay varios. ¿Quiere ir a uno caro o de precio moderado?*
SR. JONES: *Me imagino que a uno de precio moderado.*

"Taking a Taxi"
DRIVER: *Where do you want to go?*
MR. JONES: *I would like to go to a nice French restaurant. Are there any close by?*
DRIVER: *Yes, there are several. Do you want an expensive one or a moderate one?*
MR. JONES: *A moderate one, I guess.*

Taxi!	¡Taxi!
I need a taxi.	Necesito un taxi.
Please call a taxi.	Por favor, llámeme a un taxi.
Take me to . . .	Lléveme a . . .
this address . . .	esta dirección . . .
the restaurant called . . .	el restaurante que se llama . . .
the hotel . . .	el hotel . . .
Please take me to the . . .	Por favor, lléveme . . .
concert hall.	a sala de conciertos.
conference center.	al centro de conferencias.
dock/pier.	al muelle/embarcadero.

| museum. | al museo. |
| opera house. | al teatro de la ópera. |

Turn here.	Gire aquí.
Stop here.	Pare aquí.
Could you wait ten minutes?	¿Puede esperar diez minutos?
How much do I owe?	¿Cuánto le debo?
Keep the change.	Quédese con el cambio.

AT THE RESTAURANT

Here's a chance to learn about the culture you're visiting—through food. If you're adventuresome, you might try dishes indigenous to the country or region. If you are timid, stay with foods you know and perhaps one or two dishes that your host recommends. But even if you don't try many local dishes, you can ask about them and, in doing so, show your interest in the local culture, which will give your host a good impression of you.

"Cómo encontar un restaurante"

SR. CORTÉS: *¿A qué clase de restaurante desea ir esta noche?*
SR. JONES: *Bien puede ser francés o español.*
SR. CORTÉS: *Hay uno francés magnífico en los muelles.*
SR. JONES: *¿No queda eso muy lejos?*
SR. CORTÉS: *Sí, pero tomaremos un taxi.*
SR. JONES: *Fantástico. Vamos.*

"Finding a Restaurant"

MR. CORTÉS: *So, what kind of restaurant do you want to go to tonight?*
MR. JONES: *Either French or Spanish.*

MR. CORTÉS: *There is a great French restaurant at the wharf.*
MR. JONES: *Isn't that far?*
MR. CORTÉS: *Yes, but we'll take a taxi.*
MR. JONES: *Great. Let's go.*

Key Words

Check/Bill	Cuenta/Cuenta
Coats	Abrigos
Drinks	Bebidas
Menu	Menú
Order (to)	Pedir
Restaurant	Restaurante
Restroom	Baño/Aseo
Smoking/	Fumadores/No fumadores
Non-smoking (area)	(Zona de . . .)
Table	Mesa
Waiter/Waitress	Camarero/Camarera
Wine list	Carta de vinos

Good evening.	Buenas noches.
My name is . . . I have a reservation for two/three/four/five.	**Me llamo . . . Tengo una reserva para dos/tres/cuatro/cinco.**
Can I/we check our coat(s)?	¿Puedo guardar mi/nuestros abrigo(s)?
Could we have a drink at the bar first?	**¿Podemos antes tomar una bebida en el bar?**
Could we be seated promptly?	**¿Nos puede sentar cuanto antes?**
Could we have a smoking/non-smoking table/area?	**¿Nos puede dar una mesa en la zona de fumadores/** no fumadores?

Do you have a table . . .	¿Tiene usted una mesa que esté . . .
at a window?	cerca de una ventana?
in a corner?	en una esquina?
in a smoking/ non-smoking area?	en una zona de fumadores/ no fumadores?
in a quiet area?	en un lugar tranquilo?
in the other room?	en el otro salón?
Could we have that table?	¿Nos podría dar aquella mesa?
We don't have much time, could we order quickly?	**No tenemos mucho tiempo, ¿podríamos pedir ya?**
Could we have a menu?	**¿Nos podría dar el menú?**
Do you have a wine list?	¿Tiene usted una carta de vinos?
Here is the menu.	Aquí está el menú.
Here is the wine list.	Aquí está la carta de vinos.
Do you mind if I have a cocktail/a drink?	¿Le parece bien si me tomo un cóctel/una bebida?

 Drinking and smoking are more widespread in Spain and Latin America than in the United States. If you're not a smoker or drinker, and are offered a cigarette or drink, just say *no* nicely. Say, for example, that you are taking medication or that you have a sensitive stomach, without acting shocked about how much your hosts smoke or drink, or trying to teach them a lesson on personal health. They will probably refrain from offering you a cigarette or drink again.

Ordering Drinks

In some countries, giving a toast is expected. Give some thought ahead of time to what toast you can offer. Even write it out. This will greatly impress your hosts and go a long way to establish you as a world traveler.

I would like to order a/an . . .	**Me gustaría pedir . . .**
apéritif.	**un aperitivo.**
drink.	un trago.
beer.	una cerveza.
cocktail.	un cóctel.
glass of wine.	una copa de vino.
juice.	un jugo zumo.
coke.	una coca-cola.
mineral water with gas.	un agua mineral con gas.
mineral water without gas.	un agua mineral sin gas.

What types of wines do you have?	¿Qué clase de vinos tienen?
Could you recommend a local wine?	**¿Nos podría recomendar un vino del país?**
Do you have Beaujolais Nouveau?	¿Tienen Beaujolais Nouveau?
I would like a glass of white/red wine.	**Me gustaría una copa de vino blanco/tinto.**
I would like to make a toast.	**Quisiera hacer un brindis.**

"Cómo pedir la cena"
CAMARERO: *¿Puedo tomar su orden?*
SR. SMITH: *¿Tiene usted algún plato típico?*
CAMARERO: *Sí, tenemos paella.*
SR. DÍAZ: *Me parece muy bien. Déme ese.*
SR. SMITH: *A mí me trae el bisté, poco cocinado.*
CAMARERO: *Gracias.*

"Ordering Dinner"
WAITER: *May I take your order?*

MR. SMITH: *Do you have any local specialties?*
WAITER: *Yes, we have paella.*
MS. DÍAZ: *That sounds very good. I think I'll have that.*
MR. SMITH: *I'll have the steak, medium rare.*
WAITER: *Thank you.*

Key Words

Appetizer	Aperitivo
Dessert	Postre
Entrée/Main course	Plato principal
Fruit	Fruta
Prix fixe	Precio fijo
Salad	Ensalada
Soup	Sopa
Vegetable	Verduras

Americans traveling abroad often worry about the safety of local foods. This is one of the widely held misconceptions among visitors to Latin America. Any major city or capital of Spain, Mexico, or Argentina (or other Latin American countries) offers a wide array of usually excellent restaurants and eateries. Of course, bad experiences are possible, as they are anywhere in the United States.

If you're not a fan of spicy local foods, you can avoid them at a restaurant. If you are invited to a home, however, and served a local specialty that you're not fond of, you'll have to eat it. The last thing you want to do is hurt the feelings of your host. Eat lightly and with a smile.

Waiter!/Waitress!   **¡Camarero!/**¡Camarera!

Do you have any specialties?	¿Tiene usted alguna **especialidad de la casa?**
What are your specialties of the day?	¿Cuál es la especialidad del día?
I/We are ready to order.	Estoy listo/**Estamos listos para pedir.**
Would you like an appetizer?	¿Quisiera un aperitivo?
Yes, I would like an appetizer.	**Sí, me gustaría un aperitivo.**
No, I would like just a main course.	**No, sólo déme el plato principal.**
I recommend . . .	Le recomiendo . . .
the chicken.	el pollo.
the fish.	el pescado.
the pork.	el puerco cerdo.
the steak.	el bisté.
the vegetarian platter.	el plato vegetariano/la comida vegeteriana.
I would like the prix fixe meal.	**Quisiera la comida de precio fijo.**
What are you going to order?	¿Qué va a pedir usted?
I'm saving room for dessert.	**Voy a dejar lugar para el postre.**
I would like my meat . . .	**Me gustaría la carne . . .**
medium.	**al punto.**
medium rare.	poca cocinada/poco hecha.
medium well.	media cocinada/algo hecha.
rare.	vuelta y vuelta.
well done.	bien cocinada/bien hecha.
Could we have some . . .	¿Nos puede traer . . .
butter?	mantequilla?
bread?	pan?
horseradish?	rábano picante?

ketchup?	ketchup?
lemon?	limón?
mayonnaise?	mayonesa?
mustard?	mostaza?
pepper?	pimienta?
salt?	sal?
sugar?	azúcar?
water?	agua?

Could we have a little more?	¿Nos puede traer un poco más?
Could we have a . . .	¿Nos podría dar . . .
cup?	una taza?
glass?	un vaso?
fork?	un tenedor?
knife?	un cuchillo?
napkin?	una servilleta?
plate?	un plato?
saucer?	un plato pequeño?
spoon?	una cuchara?
teaspoon?	una cucharilla?
toothpick?	un palillo de dientes?

Appetizers

Antipasto	Antipasto
Bisque	Cabra
Broth	Caldo
Clams	Almejas
Coldcuts	Carnes frías
Salad	Ensalada
Snails/Escargots	Caracoles
Soup	Sopa

Main Courses

Capon	Capón
Chicken	Pollo
Duck	Pato
Filet of beef	Filete de carne

Goose	Ganso
Ham	Jamón
Lamb	Cordero
Liver	Hígado
Lobster	Langosta
Pasta	Pasta
Pork	Puerco/Cerdo
Oysters	Ostras
Quail	Codorniz
Rice	Arroz
Roast beef	Rosbif/Terrera asada
Salmon	Salmón
Sausages	Salchichas
Scallops	Escalope
Shrimp	Camarones/gamba
Sole	Lenguado
Steak	Bisté
Tuna	Atún
Turkey	Pavo
Veal	Ternera
Venison	Carne de venado

Food can be done . . .

Baked	Al horno
Braised	Estofado
Broiled	A la parrilla
Fried	Frito
Grilled	Asado a la parrilla
Marinated	Adobado/marinado
Roasted	Asado
Poached	Escalfado
Sautéed	Sofrito/salteado
Steamed	A vapor
Stewed	Guisado

Vegetables

Artichoke	Alcachofa
Asparagus	Espárrago

Beans	Frijoles (in Latin America)/ Judías (in Spain)
Beets	Remolacha
Cabbage	Col
Carrots	Zanahorias
Cauliflower	Coliflor
Celery	Apio
Corn	Maíz
Cucumbers	Pepino
Eggplant	Berenjena
Leek	Puerro
Lettuce	Lechuga
Lentils	Lentejas
Mushrooms	Setas
Onions	Cebollas
Peas	Guisante
Potatoes	Papas (in Latin America)/ Patatas (in Spain)
Spinach	Espinaca
Tomato	Tomate
Turnips	Nabos
Zucchini	Calabacín

Herbs and Spices

Anise	Anís
Basil	Albahaca
Bay leaf	Hoja de laurel
Capers	Alcaparras
Caraway	Alcaravea
Chives	Cebolleta
Cinnamon	Canela
Dill	Eneldo
Garlic	Ajo
Ginger	Jenjibre
Marjoram	Mejorana
Mint	Menta
Nutmeg	Nuez moscada

Oregano	Orégano
Parsley	Perejil
Pepper	Pimienta
Pimiento	Pimiento
Rosemary	Romero
Saffron	Azafrán
Sage	Salvia
Tarragon	Estragón
Thyme	Tomillo
I would like my potatoes . . .	Me gustaría mis papas/ patatas . . .
baked.	asadas.
boiled.	hervidas.
creamed.	en crema.
french fried.	fritas.
mashed.	molidas.
pureed.	en puré.

Fruits

Apple	Manzana
Apricot	Albaricoque
Banana	Plátano
Blueberries	Arándanos
Cherries	Cerezas
Dates	Dátiles
Figs	Higos
Grapes	Uvas
Grapefruit	Toronja/Pomelo
Kiwi	Kiwi
Mango	Mango
Melon	Melón
Nectarine	Nectarina
Orange	Naranja
Peach	Melocotón
Pear	Pera
Pineapple	Piña
Plums	Ciruelas

Prunes	Ciruelas pasas
Raisins	Uvas pasas
Raspberries	Frambuesas
Strawberries	Fresas
Watermelon	Sandía

Nuts

Almonds	Almendras
Cashews	Anacardos
Chestnuts	Castañas
Hazelnuts	Avellanas
Peanuts	Maní
Pistachios	Pistachos

"Cómo pedir el postre"

SR. ALBORNOZ: *Camarero, quisiéramos pedir postre.*

SRTA. JOHNSON: *¿Tiene usted alguna especialidad de la casa?*

CAMARERO: *Sí, las tenemos, torta holandesa de chocolate, y flan de leche con caramelo y cerezas.*

SRTA. JOHNSON: *Tráigame el primero.*

SR. ALBORNOZ: *No suena mal. Tráigame lo mismo a mí.*

"Ordering Dessert"

MR. ALBORNOZ: *Waiter, we would like to order dessert.*

MS. JOHNSON: *Do you have any specialties of the house?*

WAITER: *Yes, we have a Dutch chocolate cake and a flan with caramel and cherries.*

MS. JOHNSON: *I'll have the first.*

MR. ALBORNOZ: *Sounds good. I'll have the same.*

Would you like to order dessert?	¿Quisiera postre?
No, I think I've had enough.	**No, creo que he comido bastante.**
Yes, do you have a dessert menu?	Sí, ¿tiene usted una carta de postres?
Yes, I would like to order . . .	Sí, me gustaría pedir . . .
a piece of cake.	torta.
a pie.	pastel.
ice cream.	helado.
We have . . .	Tenemos . . .
chocolate ice cream.	helado de chocolate.
strawberry ice cream.	helado de fresa.
sorbet.	sorbete.
vanilla ice cream.	helado de vainilla.
Would you like to have some coffee?	**¿Quisiera tomar café?**
No thank you.	No, gracias.
Yes, I would like . . .	**Sí, me gustaría . . .**
coffee.	**café.**
espresso.	espresso.
cappucino.	cappuccino.
tea.	té.
Would you like your coffee . . .	¿Quiere el café . . .
black?	negro?/solo?
with cream?	con crema?/cortado?
with milk?	con leche?
Do you have decaffeinated coffee?	**¿Tiene café descafeinado?**
What kind of tea?	¿Qué clase de té?
Black	Negro
Earl Grey	Conde Grey
English breakfast	Desayuno inglés

Green	Verde
Oolong	De la China
Do you have . . .	¿Tiene usted . . .
cream?	leche?
sweetener?	azúcar de dieta?/
	edulcorante?
sugar?	azúcar?

When going out to a restaurant with a local business associate, who is expected to pick up the tab? It depends on who is making the invitation, but usually the host pays. Often, regardless of who is the host, Spaniards and Latin Americans, especially men, are very generous as long as you are in their country, and they will insist on paying the bill. This is part of their sense of hospitality. So, show an interest in paying the bill, but don't take it too far. You will reciprocate when they come to visit you in your country.

Paying the Bill

The check, please!	¡La cuenta, por favor!
Allow me to pay the bill. Please be my guest.	Permítame pagar la cuenta. Yo le invito.
Is service included?	¿Está incluido el servicio?*
Do you take credit cards? Which credit cards do you take?	¿Aceptan tarjetas de crédito? ¿Qué tarjetas de crédito aceptan?
Can I pay by check/ traveler's check?	¿Puedo pagar con cheque/ cheque de viaje?

---

* In Spain, service (or gratuity) is always included.

Tipping is not as standardized as it is in the United States, and depends more directly on the quality of service. However, keep in mind that wages are generally low for restaurant and hotel personnel, so be as generous as you can. You'll be rewarded with more attention.

Complaints

I didn't order this.	**Yo no pedí eso.**
What is this item on the bill?	¿Qué pone aquí en la cuenta?
This is too cold.	**Esto está muy frío.**
This must be some mistake.	**Tiene que haber una equivocación.**
May I see the headwaiter please?	¿Puedo hablar con el encargado?

The Rest Room

Where is the rest room/lavatory?	**¿Dónde está el baño?**
Where is the men's room?	¿Dónde está el baño de caballeros?
Where is the ladies' room?	¿Dónde está el baño de señoras?

SOCIAL CONVERSATION

Caution here—in some cultures there is little business discussed during the main part of dinner, only during coffee. In others, there is no prohibition on discussing business at any time. Follow the lead of your hosts or ask if it's proper.

"Una charla entre amigas"
SRTA. CARVAJAL: *¿Qué tal el vuelo?*
SRTA. JOHNSON: *Muy bien.*

101

SRTA. CARVAJAL: *¿Pudo dormir en el avión?*
SRTA. JOHNSON: *Sí. Fue un vuelo sin tropiezos.*
Aquí hace un tiempo magnífico.
SRTA. CARVAJAL: *Sí. Nos gusta esta época del año.*
Vamos a comer, ¿no le parece?
SRTA. JOHNSON: *Me estoy muriendo de hambre.*

"A Social Conversation"
MS. CARVAJAL: *So, how was your flight?*
MS. JOHNSON: *It was just fine.*
MS. CARVAJAL: *Were you able to sleep on the plane?*
MS. JOHNSON: *Yes. It was a smooth flight.*
What great weather you have here!
MS. CARVAJAL: *Yes. We enjoy this time of year.*
Let's go eat, shall we?
MS. JOHNSON: *I'm starving.*

Key Words

Children	Niños
Family	Familia
Hobby	Pasatiempo/Hobby
Husband	Esposo
Interests	Intereses
Sports	Deportes
Weather	Tiempo
Wife	Esposa

Please tell me about your . . .	Por favor, hábleme de su(s) . . .
I'd like to hear about your . . .	Me gustaría saber de su(s) . . .
child/children.	niño(s).
daughter(s).	hija(s).

son(s).	hijo(s).
family.	familia.
grandparents.	abuelos.
husband.	esposo.
parents.	padres.
wife.	esposa.

Please give your family my regards. — **Por favor, salude a su familia de mi parte.**

How do you spend your weekends? — ¿Cómo pasa usted los fines de semana?

Do you like to garden? — ¿Le gusta la jardinería?

Do you have pets? — ¿Tiene usted algún animal?

I have a . . . — Tengo . . .
  cat. — un gato.
  dog. — un perro.
  horse. — un caballo.

Do you like sports? — **¿Le gustan los deportes?**

Yes, I like . . . — **Sí, me gusta el . . .**
  basketball. — **baloncesto.**
  football. — fútbol americano.
  karate. — karate.
  Ping-Pong. — ping pong.
  rugby. — rugby.
  skiing. — esquí.
  scuba. — buceo.
  soccer. — fútbol.

Are you interested in . . . — **¿Le interesa(n) . . .**
  art? — **el arte?**
  books? — los libros?
  classical music? — la música clásica?
  film? — las películas?
  history? — la historia?
  hobbies? — los pasatiempos?/los hobbys?

movies?	el cine?
museums?	los museos?
music?	la música?
opera?	la ópera?
philosophy?	la filosofía?
plays?	las obras de teatro?

Saying Good-bye

The food was excellent.	**La comida estaba deliciosa.**
Will it be difficult to find a taxi?	**¿Se puede conseguir un taxi?**
Please excuse me, but I must go.	**Discúlpeme, por favor, pero me tengo que ir.**
Thank you for a wonderful evening.	**Gracias por esta velada maravillosa.**
I enjoyed our conversation very much.	Disfruté mucho de nuestra conversación.
It was nice talking to you.	**Me agradó hablar con usted.**
I look forward to seeing you . . .	**Espero verle . . .**
at the office.	**en la oficina.**
tomorrow.	mañana.
tomorrow morning.	mañana por la mañana.
tomorrow night.	mañana por la noche.
Please be my guest tomorrow night.	Por favor, permítame invitarle mañana por la noche.
It will be my pleasure.	Con mucho gusto.
Good night.	Buenas noches.

SPORTING EVENTS, MOVIES, THEATER, CLUBS

Do you have an evening or weekend free? Then enjoy the country you're visiting. Don't just eat at the hotel restaurant and watch television in your room.

Get out! An important part of doing business in another culture is learning and appreciating what that culture has to offer. What you learn can get you closer to your business contacts. Seeing a movie, going to the theater, or seeing a sporting event can be a welcome break from an arduous day.

"En el teatro"

SR. RESTREPO: *Le va a gustar esta obra musical. Es una historia de amor.*
SRTA. JONES: *¿Es popular?*
SR. RESTREPO: *No, pero la música es muy buena. Es probable que la quiten el mes próximo.*
SRTA. JONES: *Bien, entonces, vamos a verla.*

"At the Theater"

MR. RESTREPO: *You'll like this musical. It's a love story.*
MS. JONES: *Is it a popular one?*
MR. RESTREPO: *No, but it has very nice music. It may close next month.*
MS. JONES: *Well, then, let's go see it.*

Key Words

Program	*Programa*
Teams	*Equipos*
Ticket	*Boleto/Entrada*
What's playing?	*¿Qué ponen?*
Who is playing?	*¿Quiénes son los actores?*

I would like to go to a . . .	Me gustaría ir a un . . .
basketball match.	partido de baloncesto.
boxing match.	combate de boxeo.

soccer match.	partido de fútbol.
tennis match.	partido de tenis.
How much do tickets cost?	¿Cuánto cuestan los boletos?
I would like one/two tickets.	Déme un boleto/dos boletos.
When does the match/ play/movie begin?	¿A qué hora comienza el partido/la obra/la película?
Who's playing?	¿Quiénes son los actores?
What are the teams?	¿Qué equipos juegan?
May I buy a program?	¿Puedo comprar un programa?

I would like to go to the . . .

Me gustaría ir . . .

ballet.	al ballet.
cinema.	al cine.
concert.	al concierto.
museum.	al museo.
movies.	al cine.
opera.	a la ópera.
orchestra.	a la orquesta.
theater.	al teatro.

I would like a seat in the . . .

Me gustaría una butaca en . . .

balcony.	el balcón.
box seats.	el palco.
front row.	la primera fila.
gallery.	la galería.
mezzanine.	el entrepiso.
orchestra.	la platea.

I would like to see a/an . . .

Me gustaría ver . . .

action movie.	una película de acción.
comedy.	una comedia.
drama.	un drama.

love story.	una historia de amor.
musical.	una obra musical.
mystery.	una película de misterio.
romance.	una película romántica.
science fiction.	una película de ciencia ficción.
western.	una película del oeste.

Does the film have English subtitles?	¿Tiene la película subtítulos en inglés?
May I have a program please?	¿Me puede dar un programa, por favor?
What's playing at the opera tonight?	¿Qué hay esta noche en la ópera?
Who is the conductor?	¿Quién es el director?
I would like to go to a . . .	Me gustaría ir a . . .
disco.	una discoteca.
jazz club.	un club de jazz.
jazz concert.	un concierto de jazz.
nightclub.	un club nocturno.
I'd like to go dancing.	Me gustaría ir a bailar.
Would you like to dance?	¿Le gustaría bailar?
Is there a cover charge?	¿Hay consumo mínimo?
Is there a floor show?	¿Hay un espectáculo?
What time does the floor show start?	¿A qué hora comienza el espectáculo?

What is the best compliment you can give a Spaniard or a Latin American? Spanish has a vast repertoire of words commonly used to express compliments, but none is more meaningful or appreciated than *simpático/a*, which implies, in the mind of the speaker, all that can possibly be nice and pleasant about a person.

Participatory Sports

Is there a gym in the hotel?	¿Hay un gimnasio en el hotel?
Where is the closest gym?	¿Dónde está el gimnasio más cercano?
Is there a place to jog?	¿Hay algún lugar para correr?
Where is the pool?	¿Dónde está la piscina?
Is it heated?	¿Está climatizada?
Are there towels?	¿Hay toallas?

I would like to play . . .
Me gustaría jugar . . .
   golf.
   a golf.
   racket ball.
   a frontenis.
   tennis.
   a tenis.
   volley ball.
   a vóleibol.

I would like to go to the . . .
Me gustaría ir . . .
   beach.
   a la playa.
   lake.
   al lago.

Is swimming allowed?	¿Se permite nadar?
Are there lifeguards?	¿Hay salvavidas?

Are there . . .
¿Hay . . .
   beach chairs
   sillas de playa
   rowboats
   botes de remos
   sailboats
   botes de vela
   towels
   toallas
   umbrellas
   sombrillas
for rent?
para alquilar?

Are there changing rooms?	¿Hay casetas?

And don't forget to bring . . .
Y no olvide traer . . .

   sun glasses.
   gatas de sol.
   suntan lotion.
   bronceador.

I would like to go . . .	Me gustaría ir a . . .
ice skating.	patinar sobre hielo.
skiing.	esquiar.
cross-country skiing.	esquiar a campo travieso./
	esquí de fondo.

VISITING THE PARTNER'S OR ASSOCIATE'S HOME

Here's a chance to get closer to a business host or associate. Ask your contacts or the hotel concierge if flowers or gifts are appropriate. In some cultures, flowers for the wife of an associate can be misunderstood. Usually, a gift from home is safe and most welcome. If your host has children, bringing a small present for them is the best move.

"En la casa"

SRA. VÁZQUEZ: *Bienvenida a nuestra casa.*

SRTA. JOHNSON: *Gracias por invitarme.*

SRA. VÁZQUEZ: *Le presento a mi esposo, Rodrigo.*

SRTA. JOHNSON: *Encantada de conocerle.*

SRA. VÁZQUEZ: *Estos son mis dos hijos, Félix y Emilia.*

SRTA. JOHNSON: *Aquí tiene unos regalitos para los niños.*

SRA. VÁZQUEZ: *Es usted muy amable. Pasemos a la sala.*

"At the Home"

MRS. VÁZQUEZ: *Welcome to our home.*

MS. JOHNSON: *Thank you for having me.*

MRS. VÁZQUEZ: *This is my husband, Rodrigo.*

MS. JOHNSON: *Very nice to meet you.*

MRS. VÁZQUEZ: *And, here are our two children, Félix and Emilia.*

MS. JOHNSON: *Here are small gifts for your children.*

MRS. VÁZQUEZ: *That's very thoughtful of you. Let's move into the living room.*

This is my wife/husband.	Esta/este es mi esposa/esposo.
This is our child.	Este es nuestro hijo.
These are our children.	Estos son nuestros hijos.
This is our cat/dog.	Este es nuestro gato/perro.
Here is a small gift (from the United States).	Aquí tiene un pequeño regalo (de los Estados Unidos).
Make yourself at home.	Siéntase como en su propia casa.
Come, let's show you our home.	Venga, le mostraremos nuestra casa.
What a pretty house.	Qué casa tan bonita.
What a beautiful house you have.	Qué casa tan bonita tiene usted.
This is a very nice neighborhood.	Este es un barrio muy bonito.
Please sit here.	Por favor, siéntese aquí.
Please take a seat.	Por favor, tome asiento.
Please come in the dinning room.	Por favor, pase al comedor.
Would you like a drink before dinner?	¿Desea tomar algo antes de comer?
Dinner was great.	La cena estaba deliciosa.
It was a pleasure having you in our home.	Fue un placer tenerle en nuestra casa.
Thank you for inviting me to your home.	Gracias por invitarme a su casa.

 If invited to a business associate's home, it is expected that you bring a present with you. A bottle of good local wine or a bouquet of fresh flowers is appropriate. If no local wine is available, go for a French or Spanish brand name. In places like Chile, Argentina, and Uruguay, a local brand is always preferred. If there are children in the household and you really want to please your host, also bring a toy for their kids.

SIGHTSEEING

"En la recepción del hotel"
SR. JONES: *¿Qué lugares turísticos se pueden ver aquí?*
EMPLEADO DEL HOTEL: *El museo y los templos.*
SR. JONES: *¿Dónde se encuentran?*
EMPLEADO DEL HOTEL: *El museo queda sólo a tres cuadras de aquí, pero los templos están del otro lado de la ciudad. Hay que tomar un taxi para ir allí.*
SR. JONES: *Voy a ver los templos. ¿Me puede llamar a un taxi?*

"At the Hotel Reception"
MR. JONES: *What kinds of sites are worthwhile to see here?*
HOTEL CLERK: *There is the museum and the temples.*
MR. JONES: *Where are they?*
HOTEL CLERK: *The museum is only three blocks from here, but the temples are on the other side of the city. You need a taxi to get to them.*
MR. JONES: *I'll go and see the temples. Can you get me a taxi?*

| What are the main attractions? | ¿Cuáles son los principales lugares turísticos? |

111

Do you have a guide book of the city?	¿Tiene usted una guía de la ciudad?
Do you have a map of the city?	¿Tiene usted un mapa de la ciudad?
Is there a tour of the city?	¿Hay algún recorrido por la ciudad?
Where does it leave from?	¿De dónde sale?
How much is it?	¿Cuánto cuesta?
How long is it?	¿Qué tiempo toma?/¿Cuánto dura?

I would like to see a/an . . .	Me gustaría ver . . .
amusement park.	un parque de atracciones.
aquarium.	un acuario.
art gallery.	una galería de arte.
botanical garden.	un jardín botánico.
castle.	un castillo.
cathedral.	una catedral.
cave.	una cueva.
church.	una iglesia.
flea market.	un mercado de objetos de segunda mano.
library.	una biblioteca.
museum.	un museo.
park.	un parque.
planetarium.	un planetario.
synagogue.	una sinagoga.
zoo.	un zoológico.

When does the museum open?	¿Cuándo abre el museo?
How much is the admission?	¿Cuánto vale la entrada?
Do you have an English guide?	¿Tiene usted una guía en inglés?
Do you have an audio guide?	¿Tiene usted una guía con audio?

May I take photographs?	¿Puedo tomar fotos?
I do not use flashbulbs.	Yo no uso flash.
I would like to visit the lake.	Me gustaría visitar el lago.
Can I take a bus there?	¿Puedo tomar un autobús allí?
Which bus do I take?	¿Quí autobús debo tomar?
How long is the ride?	¿Cuánto dura el viaje?

SHOPPING

I'm looking for a . . .	Busco . . .
book store.	una librería.
camera store.	una tienda de cámaras fotográficas.
clothing store.	una tienda de ropa.
department store.	una grandes almacenes.
flower shop.	una florería.
hardware store.	una ferretería.
health food store.	una tienda de alimentos naturales.
jewelry store.	una joyería.
leather goods store.	una tienda de artículos de cuero.
liquor store.	una tienda de vinos y licores.
newsstand.	un quiosco de periódicos.
record store.	una tienda de discos.
shoe store.	una zapatería.
shopping center.	un centro comercial.
souvenir shop.	una tienda de souvenirs.
stationery shop.	una papelería.
tobacco store.	un estanco.
toy store.	una juguetería.
I would like to find a . . .	Me gustaría encontrar un . . .
jeweler.	joyero.
photographer.	fotógrafo.

shoemaker.	zapatero.
tailor.	sastre.
Can you help me?	¿Me puede ayudar?
Can you show me . . .	¿Me puede mostrar . . . ?
I'm just browsing.	Sólo estoy mirando.
I'd like to buy . . .	Me gustaría comprar . . .
How much does it cost?	¿Cuánto cuesta?
How much is this in dollars?	¿Cuánto es esto en dólares?
Can you write down the price?	¿Puede anotarme el precio?
Do you have a less/more expensive one?	¿Tiene usted uno más barato/ caro?
Where do I pay?	¿Dónde pago?
Can you gift wrap this?	¿Me lo puede envolver para regalo?
I'd like to return this.	Quisiera devolver esto.
Here is my receipt.	Aquí está mi recibo.

4 GETTING AROUND

This can be a trying time, what with negotiating your flight, getting through customs, dealing with taxis or rental cars, getting to your hotel, and having to speak in a foreign tongue. You may also need to find a cash machine or bank, and maybe a post office or a local Federal Express or UPS center. We're here to help.

Don't underestimate jet lag. The seasoned traveler knows how to best handle it. For the first-time business traveler, it can be a surprise. The excitement of new places and new contacts may temporarily mask it, but jet lag is the inevitable response of the body to a change of daily waking and sleeping routine. It manifests itself as tiredness and sometimes disorientation. The best advice is to try to get some sleep on your flight, and don't rush into a meeting just after you land.

In this chapter, we cover:

> **Can You Help Me?**
> **Airplanes, Airports, and**
>   **Customs**
> **At the Hotel**
> **Car Rentals**
> **At the Train Station**
> **Barber Shop and Beauty Parlor**
> **Cash Machines and Banking**
> **Post Office**
> **In an Emergency: Doctors,**
>   **Dentists, Hospitals,**
>   **Opticians, and the Pharmacy**

We hope you won't need them, but, just in case, we list the words you may find useful in an emergency.

CAN YOU HELP ME?

Excuse me.	**Perdone.**
Could you help me?	**¿Me puede ayudar?**
Yes./No.	**Sí./No.**
I'm sorry.	**Lo siento.**
Thank you very much.	Muchas gracias.
Do you speak English?	**¿Habla usted inglés?**
Do you understand English?	**¿Entiende usted inglés?**
Do you know where the American Embassy is?	**¿Sabe usted dónde está la Embajada norteamericana?**
I don't speak much Spanish.	No hablo mucho español.
I don't understand.	**No lo entiendo.**
Repeat please.	**Repita, por favor.**
Please speak more slowly.	**Por favor, hable más despacio.**
Could you write that down, please?	**¿Me lo puede escribir?**
Spell it, please.	Deletréelo, por favor.
Where is the business center?	¿Dónde está el centro comercial de la ciudad?
Where are the telephones?	**¿Dónde están los teléfonos?**
Where are the rest rooms?	**¿Dónde están los baños?**
Where is the men's bathroom/lavatory?	¿Dónde está el baño/lavabo de caballeros?
Where is the women's bathroom/lavatory?	¿Dónde está el baño/lavabo de señoras?

AIRPLANES, AIRPORTS, AND CUSTOMS

"Cómo pasar la aduana"

FUNCIONARIO DE ADUANA: *¿Son estas sus maletas?*
SR. JONES: *Sí, estas dos. ¿Pasa algo?*
FUNCIONARIO DE ADUANA: *Ábralas.*
SR. JONES: *Sólo mis trajes y ropa interior, y mi armónica. Me gusta tocarla en la habitación del hotel cuando viajo.*
FUNCIONARIO DE ADUANA: *Puede marcharse.*

"Getting Through Customs"

CUSTOMS OFFICIAL: *Are these your bags?*
MR. JONES: *Yes, these two. Is there a problem?*
CUSTOMS OFFICIAL: *Open them.*
MR. JONES: *Just suits and underwear. Plus my harmonica. I like to play it in the hotel room when I travel.*
CUSTOMS OFFICIAL: *You may go.*

Key Words

Arrivals	Llegadas
Baggage pick-up area	Consignación de equipajes
Customs	Aduana
Departures	Salidas
Domestic flights	Vuelos nacionales
Gate	Puerta de embarque
International flights	Vuelos internacionales
Make a reservation (to)	Hacer una reserva

Passport	*Pasaporte*
Take a taxi (to)	*Tomar un taxi*
Ticket	*Boleto/Billete*

Here is/are my . . .
documents.
identification card.

passport.
ticket.

I need to buy (a/an) . . .
business class ticket.

economy ticket.

first-class ticket.
round-trip ticket.
single/one-way ticket.

I'd like/need to . . .
cancel
change
confirm

my reservation.

I need to change my seat.
May I have a smoking/
non-smoking seat?

May I have an aisle/
window seat?

Is there a direct flight
to . . . ?
Is there an earlier/later
flight?

Aquí tiene mi/**mis . . .**
documentos.
tarjeta de identidad./carné
de identidad.
pasaporte.
boleto/billete.

Necesito comprar . . .
un boleto de comerciante./
un boleto de clase business.
un boleto de clase
económica.
un boleto de primera clase.
un boleto de ida y vuelta.
un boleto de ida.

Quisiera/Necesito . . .
cancelar
cambiar
confirmar

mi reserva.

Necesito cambiar mi asiento.
¿Puede darme un asiento de
fumador/no fumador?

**¿Me puede dar un asiento
que dé al pasillo/a la
ventana?**

¿Hay un vuelo directo a . . . ?

¿Hay un vuelo que salga más
temprano/tarde?

AT THE HOTEL

"Cómo obtener la habitación debida"

SRTA. JAMES: *Esta llave de mi cuarto no funciona.*

EMPLEADO: *Lo siento, señora. Le dí la llave que no era. En realidad, tengo que darle otra habitación. Esa ya está ocupada.*

SRTA. JAMES: *¿Puede darme entonces una con vistas?*

EMPLEADO: *Sí, creo que le va a gustar esta habitación. Siento lo ocurrido.*

"Getting the Right Room"

MS. JAMES: *This key to my room won't work.*

CLERK: *I'm sorry, madam, I gave you the wrong key. In fact, I have to give you a different room. That one is actually taken.*

MS. JAMES: *Could you then give me a room with a view?*

CLERK: *Yes, I think you will enjoy this room. Sorry for the problem.*

Key Words

Bag(s)/Luggage	Maleta(s)/Equipaje
Bath	Baño
Confirmation	Confirmación
Credit card	Tarjeta de crédito
Hotel	Hotel
Reservation	Reserva
Room	Habitación

119

I have a reservation in the name of . . .	Tengo una reserva a nombre de . . .
Here is my confirmation.	Aquí tiene mi confirmación.
How much are your rooms?	¿Cuál es la tarifa de una habitación?
What is the price for a double room?	¿Cuál es la tarifa de una habitación doble?
Do you take credit cards?	¿Aceptan (ustedes) tarjetas de crédito?
Which credit cards do you take?	¿Qué tarjetas de crédito aceptan (ustedes)?
Do you have any rooms available?	¿Tienen (ustedes) alguna habitación disponible?
Could you recommend any other hotels?	¿Me puede recomendar otro hotel?

I'd like a . . .
room for one/two night(s).
single/double room.

room with a private bath.
room with a queen/king-size bed.
suite.

Quisiera . . .
una habitación para una noche/do noches.
una habitación simple/doble.
una habitación con baño privado.
una habitación con cama/grande.
una suite.

I need a/an . . .
wake-up call.
late check-out.
fax machine.
telephone.
Internet connection.

Necesito . . .
que me despierten.
salir del hotel más tarde.
un fax.
un teléfono.
una conexión a Internet.

Is there a/an . . .
business center?
Internet connection in my room?

¿Hay . . .
un centro comercial?
una conexión a Internet en mi habitación?

exercise room?	un cuarto de ejercicios?
gym?	un gimnasio?
Jacuzzi?	un Jacuzzi?
photocopier?	una fotocopiadora?
printer?	una impresora?
restaurant in the hotel?	un restaurante en el hotel?
swimming pool?	una piscina?

Can a porter take my bags up to the room? **¿Me pueden llevar las maletas a mi habitación?**

May I leave my bags? **¿Puedo dejar mis maletas?**

Are there any messages for me? **¿Tengo algún mensaje?**

May I see the room? ¿Puedo ver la habitación?

We want adjacent rooms. Queremos habitaciones contiguas.

Problems

The room/bathroom needs cleaning. El baño está sucio.

I need more towels/ blankets. Necesito más toallas/mantas.

The room is too small. La habitación es demasiado pequeña.

I did not receive my paper. No recibí el periódico.

The room is too noisy. Hay demasiado ruido en esta habitación.

The door will not open. La puerta no abre.

The door will not lock. La puerta no cierra.

The telephone does not work. El teléfono no funciona.

The heating/air-conditioning is not working. La calefacción/aire acondicionado no funciona.

Can you turn the heat up? ¿Puede poner la calefacción?

How do I make a telephone call?	¿Cómo puedo hacer una llamada telefónica?
How do I make a local/international telephone call?	¿Cómo puedo hacer una llamada telefónica local/internacional?
I need room service.	Necesito servicio de habitación.
I'd like to order dinner to my room.	Quisiera cenar en mi habitación.
I need laundry service.	Necesito lavar la ropa.
I need these shirts/suits cleaned by tomorrow.	Necesito limpiar estas camisas/estos trajes para mañana a primera hora.
Can I have these clothes cleaned/laundered today?	¿Me pueden limpiar/lavar esta ropa para hoy?
Can you have this stain removed?	¿Se puede quitar esta mancha?
How much does it cost to have this cleaned/laundered?	¿Cuánto cuesta limpiar/lavar esto?
Can I extend my stay one/two day(s)?	¿Puedo quedarme un día o dos más?
Can I have a late check-out?	¿Puedo dejar mi habitación más tarde?
Can I leave my bags at the reception desk after check-out?	¿Puedo dejar mis maletas en la recepción después de salir del hotel?
I want to check out.	Quiero dejar mi habitación.
May I have my bill?	¿Me puede dar mi cuenta?
There is a problem with my bill.	Mi cuentano está bien.
What is this charge for?	¿De qué es este cargo?
Is there an airport shuttle?	¿Hay un servicio de transporte directo al aeropuerto?

What time does it leave?	¿A qué hora sale?
What time is the next one?	¿A qué hora sale el próximo?
I would like a taxi.	Por favor, llámeme un taxi.

CAR RENTALS

"Cómo obtener un carro de cambio automático"

SR. SMILEY: *¿Tiene este carro cambio automático?*

EMPLEADO: *No. ¿Lo necesitaba usted?*

SR. SMILEY: *Sí. Como puede ver en mi confirmación, así exactamente lo pedí.*

EMPLEADO: *Ya veo. Ahora bien, hay un pequeño problema. No tendremos otro carro hasta dentro de una hora.*

SR. SMILEY: *Esperaré. No sé cómo conducir con cambio manual.*

"Getting a Car with Automatic Shift"

MR. SMILEY: *Does this car have an automatic shift?*

CLERK: *No. Did you need that?*

MR. SMILEY: *Yes. You can see from my confirmation that I specifically requested it.*

CLERK: *Yes, I see that. However, there is a slight problem. We won't have one for about one hour.*

MR. SMILEY: *I will wait. I don't know how to drive a stick shift.*

I need to rent a car.	Necesito alquilar un carro.
Here is my reservation number.	Aquí tiene el número de mi reserva.
Here is my driver's license.	Aquí tiene mi licencia de conducir.

Key Words

Automatic shift	Cambio automático
Car	Carro/Coche*
Directions	Direcciones
Driver's license	Licencia de conducir
Gas	Gasolina
Gas station	Gasolinera
Insurance	Seguro
Map	Mapa
Stick shift	Cambio manual

I need . . .	Necesito . . .
air conditioning.	**aire acondicionado.**
an automatic shift.	**cambio automático.**
a compact.	un carro compacto.
a convertible	un descapotable.
an intermediate.	un carro intermedio.
a luxury.	un carro de lujo.
a mid-sized car.	un carro de tamaño mediano.
a standard shift.	un carro con cambio manual.
Is insurance included?	**¿Está incluido el seguro?**
How much is the insurance?	¿Cuánto cuesta el seguro?
I want full insurance.	**Quiero seguro a todo riesgo.**
How is the mileage charged?	**¿Cuál es el cargo de kilometraje?**
Is there unlimited mileage?	**¿Hay kilometraje ilimitado?**

*The word for car is *carro* in Latin America and *coche* in Spain. We will use *carro* from now on in this phrasebook.

Is gas included?	¿Incluye la gasolina?
Do I need to fill the tank when I return?	¿Tengo que llenar el tanque al regresar?
Is there a drop-off charge?	**¿Hay algún cargo al devolverlo?**
Which credit cards do you take?	¿Qué tarjetas de crédito aceptan?
May I pay by check?	¿Puedo pagar con cheque?
I need a map.	**Necesito un mapa.**
I need directions.	**Necesito direcciones.**
Can you help me find . . .	Puede ayudarme a encontrar . . .
How do I get to . . .	Cómo voy . . .
the airport.	al aeropuerto.
a bank.	al banco.
a gas station.	a la gasolinera.
the hotel.	al hotel.
a good restaurant.	a un buen restaurante.
Is this the road to . . . ?	**¿Es este el camino a . . . ?**
Turn right/left.	**Gire a la derecha/izquierda.**
Go straight ahead.	**Siga recto.**
Turn around.	**Dé la vuelta.**
Go two traffic lights and turn right/left.	**Pase dos semáforos y gire a la derecha/izquierda.**
Opposite	Delante
U-turn	Vuelta en U
Next to	Al lado de
Fill it up, please.	**Llene el tanque, por favor.**
I need . . .	Necesito . . .
diesel.	diésel.
regular.	regular.
supreme.	superior.
unleaded.	sin plomo.

Could you check the tire pressure?	¿Puede mirar el aire en las gomas?
Could you check the water?	¿Puede mirar el agua?
How much do I owe you?	¿Cuánto le debo?
Where do I park?	¿Dónde puedo parquear?
Is there parking nearby?	¿Hay un parqueo cerca?
I am having a problem with my car.	Tengo problemas con mi carro.
It won't start.	No arranca.
The battery is dead.	Se descargó la baténa.
I'm out of gas.	Me quedé sin gasolina.
I have a flat tire.	Se me pinchó una goma.
The brakes won't work.	Los frenos no funcionan.
The lights don't work.	Las luces no funcionan.
May I use the phone?	¿Puedo usar el teléfono?
Could you help me?	¿Me puede ayudar?
My car has broken down.	Se me ha roto el carro.
Can you tow it?	¿Lo puede remolcar?
Can you repair it?	¿Lo puede arreglar?
Do you have . . .	¿Tiene usted . . .
a flashlight?	una linterna?
a jack?	un gato?
a screwdriver?	un destornillador?
tools?	unas herramientas?
a wrench?	una llave inglesa?
There's been an accident.	Ha habido un accidente.
I have had an accident.	He tenido un accidente.
People are hurt.	Hay heridos.
It is serious.	Es serio.
It is not serious.	No es serio.
Can we exchange driver's license numbers?	¿Nos damos los números de las licencias de conducir?

| Can we exchange insurance cards? | ¿Nos damos las tarjetas del seguro? |

AT THE TRAIN STATION

Getting around in many countries involves trains. This comes as a surprise to the first-time U.S. business traveler unaccustomed to using trains in the United States. Often a quick trip to another city involves hopping on a train, which is usually quite punctual and pleasant.

Key Words

Arrival time	Hora de llegada
Departure time	Hora de salida
Platform	Plataforma/Andén
Reservation	Reservación
Sleeping car	Coche cama
Ticket	Boleto/Billete
Ticket office	Taquilla
Time	Hora
Timetable	Horario

Where is the ticket office?	¿Dónde está la taquilla?
I want to go to . . .	Quiero ir a . . .
How much does a ticket to . . . cost?	¿Cuánto cuesta el boleto a . . . ?
What gate does the train for . . . leave on?	¿De qué puerta sale el tren para . . . ?
Do I need to change trains?	¿Tengo que cambiar de tren?
Is there a dinning/buffet car?	¿Hay un coche comedor/buffet?

Am I on the right train?   ¿Es este el tren?

Is this an open seat?   ¿Está vacío este asiento?

What stop is this?   ¿Qué parada es esta?

BARBER SHOP AND BEAUTY PARLOR

"En el salón de belleza"

SRTA. JOHNSON: *¿Me puede cortar el pelo este tanto?*

PELUQUERA: *Me parece que es mucho.*

SRTA. JOHNSON: *¿Qué le parece así?*

PELUQUERA: *Sí. Me parece que así lucirá mejor.*

"At the Barber Shop/Beauty Shop"

MS. JOHNSON: *Could you cut my hair about this much?*

HAIRDRESSER: *I think that might be too much.*

MS. JOHNSON: *What about this much?*

HAIRDRESSER: *Yes. I think that will look better.*

Is there a barber shop/ beauty parlor nearby?   ¿Hay una barbería/un salón de belleza cerca?

Do I need an appointment?   ¿Necesito una cita?

Key Words

Blow-dry	Secado de pelo
Haircut	Corte de pelo
Manicure	Manicura
Nails	Uñas
Shampoo	Champú
Shave	Afeitado

I need a haircut.	**Necesito cortarme el pelo.**
I'd like to have a . . .	Me gustaría que me hiciera . . .
blow-dry.	un secado de pelo.
cut.	corte de pelo.
facial.	tratamiento facial.
manicure.	una manicura.
shampoo.	un lavado de pelo.
I'd like a shave.	Me gustaría una afeitada.
Could you trim my mustache/beard?	¿Puede recortarme el bigote/la barba?

CASH MACHINES AND BANKING

Where is the nearest cash machine?	**¿Dónde está el cajero automático más cercano?**
Where is the nearest bank?	¿Dónde está el banco más cercano?
Is there a money exchange office near here?	**¿Hay una oficina de cambio cerca?**
Do you change money?	**¿Cambian dinero?**
What is the exchange rate?	**¿Cuál es la tasa de cambio?**
I'd like to change 100 dollars.	Me gustaría cambiar cien dólares.
I need your passport.	Necesito su pasaporte.

POST OFFICE

| Where is the post office/ FedEx office? | ¿Dónde está correos/la oficina de Federal Express? |
| Do you have over-night service? | ¿Tienen servicio de noche? |

I would like postage for this . . .	Me gustaría un sello para . . .
letter.	esta carta.
package.	este paquete.
postcard.	esta tarjeta postal.

When will the letter/
package arrive?

¿Cuándo llegará la carta/el
paquete?

I'd like to send it . . .
insured.
registered.
overnight.

Quisiera mandarlo . . .
asegurado.
certificado.
para que llegará mañana.

IN AN EMERGENCY: DOCTORS, DENTISTS, HOSPITALS, OPTICIANS, AND PHARMACIES

You'll usually pay for these bills with your credit card or by check. Then when you get home you'll submit the expenses to your medical plan for reimbursement.

"En la farmacia"

SR. JONES: *Tengo una tos muy fuerte. ¿Qué me puede recomendar?*

FARMACÉUTICO: *¿Quiere usted un jarabe o pastillas para la garganta?*

SR. JONES: *¿Tiene usted pastillas con sabor a cereza?*

FARMACÉUTICO: *No, pero las tenemos con sabor a miel.*

"At the Pharmacy"

MR. JONES: *I have a bad cough. Could you recommend something for it?*

PHARMACIST: *Do you want a syrup or lozenges?*

MR. JONES: *Do you have cherry flavored lozenges?*

PHARMACIST: *No, but we have these, honey flavor.*

Key Words

Cold	Catarro
Doctor	Médico
Emergency	Emergencia
Eye doctor	Médico de la vista/Oculista/ Oftalmólogo
Flu	Gripe
Glasses	Lentes
Headache	Dolor de cabeza
I don't feel well.	No me siento bien.
I got hurt.	Me di un golpe.
Nurse	Enfermera
Optician	Óptico
Pharmacist	Farmacéutico
Toothache	Dolor de muelas

I want/need to go to a/an . . .	**Quiero**/necesito **ir a . . .**
dentist.	**un dentista.**
doctor.	un médico.
eye doctor.	un médico de la vista./ oftalmólogo.
hospital.	un hospital.
optician.	un óptico.
pharmacy.	una farmacia.
I need to see a/an . . .	Necesito verme con un . . .
allergist.	alergista.
general practitioner.	médico de medicina general.
gynecologist.	ginecólogo.
internist.	médico de medicina interna.
Please call an ambulance.	**Por favor, llame a una ambulancia.**
Please call a doctor.	**Por favor, llame a un médico.**
Please call the police.	**Por favor, llame a la policia.**
There has been an accident.	**Ha habido un accidente.**

Someone is hurt.	**Hay alguien herido.**
Is there anyone here who speaks English?	**¿Hay alguien aquí que hable inglés?**
Can I have an appointment?	**¿Puedo concertar una cita?**
I'm *not* allergic to penicillin.	*No* **soy alérgico a la penicilina.**
I'm allergic to penicillin.	**Soy alérgico a la penicilina.**
I don't feel well.	**No me siento bien.**
I don't know what I have.	**No sé lo que tengo.**
I think I have a fever.	**Creo que tengo fiebre.**
I have asthma.	**Tengo asma.**

I have a/an . . .	Tengo . . .
backache.	un dolor de espalda.
cold.	un catarro.
constipation.	un estreñimiento.
cough.	una tos.
cut.	una corte.
diarrhea.	una diarrea.
earache.	un dolor de oídos.
hayfever.	una alergia al polen.
headache.	un dolor de cabeza.
heart trouble.	una problema en el corazón.
stomachache.	un dolor de estómago.
pain.	un dolor.

I feel dizzy/sick.	Me siento mareado/mal.
I can't sleep.	No puedo dormir.
Can you fill this prescription for me?	¿Me puede llenar esta receta?

Do you have (a/an) . . .	¿Tiene usted . . .
antacid?	un antiácido?
antiseptic?	un antiséptico?
aspirin?	una aspirina?

Band-Aids?	Curitas? (in Latin America)/ Tiritas? (in Spain)
contact lens solution?	una solución para los lentes de contacto?
disinfectant?	un desinfectante?
eye drops?	unas gotas para los ojos?
sanitary napkins?	compresas sanitarias?
sleeping pills?	pastillas para dormir?
tampons?	tampones?
thermometer?	termómetro?
throat lozenges?	pastillas para la garganta?
vitamins?	vitaminas?
I'll wait for it.	Esperaré a que me lo/la/los/las traiga.

5 GETTING BUSINESSIZED

In this chapter we cover important business vocabulary that has not yet found a place in previous chapters, such as names for office objects, job titles, and terminology used in different departments of a company.

The chapter is organized as follows:

Finding Your Way Around the Office
Office Objects
Titles by Level
Organization Chart of a U.S. Company
Functional Areas of a Company

Getting acclimated to the overseas office means being able to better concentrate on your work.

Let's start at the office as you're just settling in . . .

FINDING YOUR WAY AROUND THE OFFICE

"Cómo aclimatarse ala oficina"

Sr. Cervantes: *Puede usar este escritorio mientras permanezca aquí.*
Srta. Clark: *¿Cómo puedo llamar afuera?*
Sr. Cervantes: *Apriete cualquiera de estos botones para que le den línea.*
Srta. Clark: *También necesito mandar un fax.*
Sr. Cervantes: *Por el pasillo, después de la copiadora.*

"Getting Acclimated to the Office"

MR. CERVANTES: *You can use this desk while you're here.*

MS. CLARK: *How do I dial out?*

MR. CERVANTES: *Press any one of these buttons to get an outside line.*

MS. CLARK: *I also need to send a fax.*

MR. CERVANTES: *Just down the hall, past the copier.*

Key Words

Coffee	Café
Coffee machine	Cafetera
Desk	Escritorio
Chair	Silla
Coat	Abrigo
Computer	Computadora/Ordinador
Copier	Copiadora
Cubicle	Cubículo
Fax	Fax
File	Archivo
Women's room	Baño de señoras
Letter	Carta
Mail	Correo
Manual	Manual
Men's room	Baño de caballeros
Office	Oficina
Pen	Pluma/Bolígrafo
Pencil	Lápiz
Phone	Teléfono
Printer	Impresora
Restroom	Baño
Tea	Té

Spaniards and Latin Americans can be formal or informal at work, depending on the situation. With their peers, they generally display a great deal of camaraderie and share with each other their daily experiences, good or bad. This attitude changes sharply when they are dealing with superiors, in which case a "comfortable" distance is often maintained, unless the boss sets the tone for a more open and friendly discourse.

I'm here to see . . .	Quisiera ver a . . .
Is this the office of . . . ?	¿Es esta la oficina de . . . ?
Can you tell me how to get there?	¿Me puede decir cómo llegar allí?
Yes, I can wait.	Sí, puedo esperar.
Where can I hang my coat?	¿Dónde puedo colgar mi abrigo?
Is there a restroom?	¿Hay un baño?
Where is the copier?	¿Dónde está la copiadora?
Where can I get some . . . coffee? tea? water?	¿Dónde puedo obtener . . . café? té? agua?
Where is the . . . cafeteria? lunch room? women's room? men's room?	¿Dónde está . . . la cafetería? el salón de almorzar?/ comedor? el baño de señoras? el baño de caballeros?
Where is the restroom?	¿Dónde está el baño?
How do I get an outside line?	¿Cómo puedo llamar afuera?

How can I make a local call?	¿Cómo puedo hacer una llamada local?
How can I make a long-distance call?	¿Cómo puedo hacer una llamada de larga distancia?
How can I make an overseas call?	¿Cómo puedo hacer una llamada internacional?

Do you have a/an . . .	¿Hay . . .
cafeteria?	una cafetería?
conference room?	un salón de conferencias?
copier?	una copiadora?
extra desk?	un escritorio extra?
office I can use?	una oficina que pueda usar?
phone?	un teléfono?
telephone directory?	una guía de teléfonos?

Could you show me/us the . . .	¿Me/Nos puede mostrar . . .
elevator?	el elevador?
exit?	la salida?
restroom?	el baño?
staircase?	la escalera?
way out?	la salida?

Where is the . . .	¿Dónde se encuentra el . . .
accounting department?	departamento de contabilidad?
mail room?	cuarto de correo?
personnel department?	departamento de personal?
shipping department?	departamento de envíos?
warehouse?	almacén?

Who is responsible for . . .	¿Quién es el encargado de . . .
arranging my flight?	preparar mi vuelo?
fixing the copier?	arreglar la copiadora?
running the copier?	manejar la copiadora?
sending mail?	enviar el correo?

137

"Cómo enviar un paquete"

SR. SMITH: *Quisiera enviar este paquete a los Estados Unidos.*

EMPLEADO: *¿Cuándo quiere que llegue allí?*

SR. SMITH: *En dos o tres días. ¿Puede ser?*

EMPLEADO: *Claro que sí.*

"Shipping a Package"

MR. SMITH: *I would like to ship this package to the United States.*

CLERK: *How soon do you want it to get there?*

MR. SMITH: *In two to three days. Is that possible?*

CLERK: *Of course.*

OFFICE OBJECTS

Here's an alphabetical list of office objects.

Cabinets	Armarios
Bookcase	Estanterías
File cabinet	Archivo
Hanging cabinets	Gabinetes colgantes
Lateral file	Archivo lateral
Letter/Legal size	Tamaño carta/legal
Mobile file	Archivo móvil
Safe	Caja fuerte
Steel cabinet	Armario de metal
Storage cabinet	Armario de almacenaje
Vertical file	Archivo vertical

Carts and Stands	Carritos y bases
Book cart	Carrito para libros
Computer cart	Carrito para computadoras
Mail cart	Carrito postal
Printer/Fax stand	Base de la impresora/fax
Storage cart	Carrito de almacenaje

Chairs	Sillas
Ergonomic chair	Silla ergonómica
Executive chair	Silla de ejecutivo
Folding chair	Silla plegable
Leather chair	Silla de cuero
Manager chair	Silla de gerente
Stacking chair	Silla apilable
Side chair	Silla lateral
Swivel chair	Silla giratoria

Computer Accessories	Accesorios de computadora
Adapter	Adaptador
Cables	Cables
Data cartridge	Cartucho de datos
Diskette or floppy disk	Disquete o disco flexible
Keyboard	Teclado
Monitor	Monitor
Mouse	Ratón
Mouse pad	Almohadilla de ratón
Power cord	Cordón eléctrico
Surge protector	Protector contra subida de voltaje
Wrist rest	Descansador de muñeca
Zip® drive	Unidad de disco Zip®

Desks	Mesas/Escritorios
Computer desk	Mesa de computadora
Steel desk	Escritorio de metal
Wood desk	Escritorio de madera
Work center	Mesa de trabajo

Desktop Material	Material de escritorio
Glass	Cristal
Leather	Cuero
Metal	Metal
Plastic	Plástico
Steel	Acero
Wood	Madera

139

Furnishings	Muebles
Business card file	Tarjetero
Bookshelves	Estantes de libros
Bulletin board	Tablero
Calendar	Calendario
Chalkboard	Pizarra
Clock	Reloj de pared
Coathook/rack	Gancho para abrigos o percha/Perchero
Coffee table	Mesa de café
Corkboard	Tablero de corcho
Cup	Taza
Desk lamp	Lámpara de mesa
Doorstop/jam	Cuña
Easel	Caballete
Floor lamp	Lámpara de suelo
Floormat	Alfombra
Frame	Marco
Paper clips	Sujeta-papeles
Paper cutter	Cortadora de papel
Pictures	Fotos/Cuadros
Projection screen	Pantalla de proyección
Pushpins	Alfileres marcadores
Punch	Perforadora
Rubber bands	Ligas/Ganas elásticas
Ruler	Regla
Scissors	Tijeras
Stamps	Sellos
Stamp pad	Amohadilla de sellos
Stapler	Grapadora
Stapler remover	Sacagrapas
Tacks	Tachuelas
Tape dispenser	Dispensador de cinta adhesiva
Telephone book	Guía de teléfonos
Three-hole punch	Perforadora triple
Wallboard	Pizarrón

Wallplanner	Planificador de pared
Wastebasket	Cesto de basura

Gotta keep organized.

Organizers	Organizadores
Appointment book	Libro de citas
Basket tray	Cesta
Binders	Carpeta
Bookends	Portalibros
Business card holder	Tarjetero comercial
Desk organizer	Organizador de escritorio
In/Out boxes	Cesta de recibo/envío de correspondencia
Hanging wall pockets	Portapapeles de pared
Magazine rack	Estante de revistas
Pencil caddy	Portalápices
Rolodex® card file	Tarjetero Rolodex®
Stacking letter tray	Bandeja apilable de cartas
Trays	Bandejas
Vertical holder	Organizador vertical

Maybe some day we'll eliminate paperwork, but for now we still need to write things down.

Paper and Forms	Papeles y formularios
Bond	Papel bond
Business cards	Tarjetas de presentación
Business stationery	Papelera comercial
Clipboard	Tablilla
Columnar or accounting sheets	Hojas con columnas ó de contabilidad
Continuous computer paper	Papel continuo de computadora
Computer paper	Papel de computadora
Construction paper	Cartulina de colores

Copier paper	Papel de copiadora
Drafting or architecture paper	Paper de dibujo ó de arquitectura
Envelopes	Sobres
File folder	Carpeta de archivo
Folder	Carpeta
Forms	Formularios
Graph paper	Papel cuadriculado
Hanging file holder	Archivo colgante
Labels	Etiquetas
Large business envelope	Sobre comercial grande
Legal-size paper	Papel tamaño legal
Letterhead	Membrete
Letter opener	Abridor de cartas
Message pads	Bloc de mensajes
Notebooks	Cuadernos
Notepads	Bloc de notas
Post-it® notes	Notas Post-it®
Report covers	Cubiertas para informes
Reporter notebook	Cuaderno para informes
Ruled writing pad	Bloc rayado
Scratch pads	Bloc borrador
Steno pads	Bloc estenográfico
Writing pads	Bloc de notas

Pens and Pencils	Bolígrafos y lápices
Ballpoint pen	Bolígrafo
Correction fluid	Borrador líquido
Erasers	Borradores
Highlighter	Resaltador
Ink pen	Pluma estilográfica
Lead	Grafito
Marker	Marcador
Mechanical pencil	Lápiz mecánico
Pen	Pluma
Pencil	Lápiz
Pencil sharpener	Sacapuntas
Refills	Repuestos

Retractable pen — Pluma retractable
Wood pencil — Lápiz de madera
Writing pen — Pluma de escribir

Printers and Faxes — Impresoras y Faxes

Cartridge — Cartucho
Fax paper — Papel para fax
Inkjet — Impresora de chorro de tinta
Laser — Láser
Replacement cartridge — Cartucho de repuesto
Ribbon — Cinta
Toner cartridge — Cartucho de tinta en polvo
Typewriter ribbon — Cinta de máquina de escribir

Tables — Mesas

Computer table — Mesa de computadora
Conference table — Mesa de conferencia
Drafting/Artist's table — Mesa de dibujo/Mesa de dibujantes
Folding table — Mesa plegable
Utility table — Mesa de servicios

Miscellany — Miscelánea

Batteries — Baterías pilas
Broom — Escoba
Cleaning supplies — Productos de limpieza
Cleaning cloth — Paño de limpiar
Duct tape — Cinta de conductos
Duster — Sacudidor
Extension cord — Extensión eléctrica
Fan — Ventilador
Flashlight — Linterna
Floormat — Alfombra
Glue — Goma de pegar
Lightbulb — Bombilla
Locks — Candados
Mailer — Sobre postal

Masking tape	Cinta de enmascarar
Postal meter	Contador postal
Postal scale	Balanza postal
Scotch® tape	Cinta Scotch®
Shipping tape	Cinta de embalaje
Tape	Cinta adhesiva
Trash bags	Bolsas de basura

TITLES BY LEVEL

A standardized system of titles has been developed within most U.S. firms. For instance, the term *vice president* means a significant level of management, usually also an officer. Officer often designates a level that can approve certain significant expenditures. However, sometimes even within the United States, titles differ. For instance, in most companies and organizations, the term *manager* means a person who heads a subarea of responsibility, like recruiting or training. The person in charge of human resources is typically a vice president or director. However, in a few companies the term *manager* is the equivalent of the title *vice president* or *director*.

When you venture to other countries, titles can be quite dissimilar. For instance, in some countries the term *director* is often equivalent to president or vice president.

Chairman	**Presidente del Consejo de Administración**
President	**Presidente**
Vice president	**Vicepresidente**
Director	**Director**
Manager	**Gerente**
Supervisor	**Supervisor**

Senior analyst	**Analista Superior**
Analyst	**Analista**
Junior analyst	**Analista Adjunto**
Coordinator	**Coordinador**
Administrative assistant	**Ayudante/**Asistente de Administración
Secretary	**Secretaria**
Receptionist	**Recepcionista**

"La política de la oficina"

SR. SMITH: *¿Vio usted al Dr. Sabater cómo quiso dominar la presentación cuando entró el Director Gerente?*

SR. RUIZ: *Sí. Hasta ese momento no dijo nada, pero entonces quiso mostrar que él fue el encargado del informe.*

SR. SMITH: *A nadie le gustó que se atribuyese el informe, sobre todo cuando escasamente lo tocó.*

SR. RUIZ: *¿Ocurre lo mismo en los Estados Unidos?*

"Office Politics"

MR. SMITH: *Did you see Dr. Sabater trying to dominate the presentation when the managing director came into the room?*

MR. RUIZ: *Yes. He was quiet up to then, but then he tried to show that he was responsible for the report.*

MR. SMITH: *He made some people angry for taking all the credit for the report when he hardly worked on it.*

MR. RUIZ: *Do you have people in the United States who do that too?*

145

ORGANIZATION CHART OF A U.S. COMPANY*

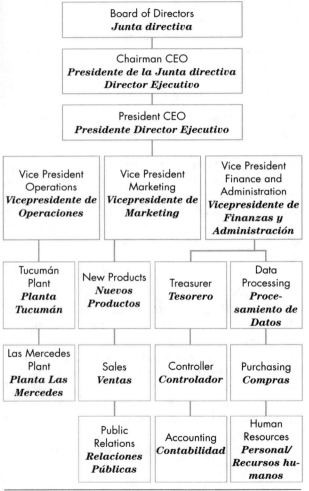

Board of Directors
Junta directiva

Chairman CEO
Presidente de la Junta directiva
Director Ejecutivo

President CEO
Presidente Director Ejecutivo

Vice President Operations
Vicepresidente de Operaciones

Vice President Marketing
Vicepresidente de Marketing

Vice President Finance and Administration
Vicepresidente de Finanzas y Administración

Tucumán Plant
Planta Tucumán

New Products
Nuevos Productos

Treasurer
Tesorero

Data Processing
Proce-samiento de Datos

Las Mercedes Plant
Planta Las Mercedes

Sales
Ventas

Controller
Controlador

Purchasing
Compras

Public Relations
Relaciones Públicas

Accounting
Contabilidad

Human Resources
Personal/ Recursos humanos

* The organization of companies in Spanish-speaking countries corresponds closely to that of companies in the United States.

FUNCTIONAL AREAS OF A COMPANY

Looking for a word in your field of endeavor? You will probably find it below. These are the main areas within a company or organization. Many of these terms, of course, also apply to organizations outside a company. The areas covered are:

Accounting and Finance
Computer Systems (Data Processing)
Human Resources
Legal and International Law
Manufacturing and Operations
Marketing and Sales

Accounting and Finance

(Contabilidad y Finanzas)

What form do I use to submit my expenses?	¿Qué formulario debo usar para someter mis gastos?
Where are your billing records kept?	¿Dónde se guardan los registros de facturación?
Are you on a calendar or fiscal year?	¿Están ustedes en año natural o año fiscal?
When do we close the books?	¿Cuándo cerramos los libros?
Is your organization on the accrual or cash method?	¿Está su organización en un método de acumulación o de efectivo?
Account	Cuenta
Accountant	Contable
Accrual method	Método acumulado
Amortization	Amortización
Assets	Activos
Audit	Auditoría

Balance sheet	Balance general
Bankruptcy	Bancarrota
Billing records	Registros de facturación
Bills	Cuentas
Breakeven	Tener ingresos y gastos iguales
Budget	Presupuesto
Calendar year	Año natural
Capital	Capital
Capital budget	Presupuesto de capital
Capital improvements	Mejoras de capital
Cash	Efectivo
Cash flow	Flujo de efectivo
Cash method	Método de efectivo
Chart of accounts	Diagrama de cuentas
Closing of the books	Cierre de los libros
Command	Orden
Controller	Controlador
Cost	Costo
Cost accounting	Contabilidad de costos
Credit	Crédito
Debit	Débito
Debt	Deuda
Default	Falta de pago
Depreciation	Depreciación
Disbursement	Desembolso
Dividends	Dividendos
Equity	Equidad
Fair market value	Valor de mercado
Financial analyst	Analista financiero
Financial statement	Estado financiero
First In—First Out (FIFO)	Primero en llegar—Primero en salir
Fiscal year	Año fiscal
General ledger	Libro mayor general
Goodwill	Clientela

Gross income	Ingreso bruto
Gross sales	Ventas netas
Income	Ingreso
Income statement	Estado de ingresos
Interest	Interés
Inventory	Inventario
Invoice	Factura
Journal	Diario
Last In—First Out (LIFO)	Último en llegar—Primero en salir
Ledger	Libro mayor
Liabilities	Obligaciónes
Liquid asset	Activo circulante
Margin	Margen
Market value	Valor de mercado
Net earnings	Ganancias netas
Net worth	Activo neto
Operating expenses	Gastos de operación
Overhead	Gastos generales
Payroll	Nómina
Per diem	Por día
Profit	Ganancia
Profit and loss statement	Estado de ganancias y pérdidas
Requisition	Petición
Return on investment	Rendimiento de la inversión
Revenue	Ingreso
Sales	Ventas
Statement of cash flows	Estado de flujo de efectivo
Stock	Acciones
Straight-line depreciation	Depreciación anual uniforme
Trial balance	Balance de comprobación
Voucher	Comprobante

149

Wages	Salarios
Zero-based budgeting	Presupuesto en base de cero

Computer Systems (Data Processing)

Sistemas Computarizados (Procesamiento de Datos)*

What is my password?	¿Cuál es mi contraseña?
How do I get a password?	¿Cómo puedo obtener mi contraseña?
My printer won't work.	Mi impresora no funciona.
Who can help me with my computer?	¿Quién me puede ayudar con mi computadora?
Access (to) the Internet	Acceso al Internet
Access code	Código de acceso
Alt key	Tecla alt
Analog	Analógico
Application	Aplicación
At sign (@)	En la muestra (@)
Attach a file (to)	Adjuntar un archivo
Attachment(s)	Adjuntos
Back slash	Raya vertical posterior/ Contra barra
Backspace key	Tecla de retroceso
Banner ad	Anuncio cartel
BASIC language	Lenguaje BASIC
Baud	Baudio
Beta program	Programa beta
Beta test	Prueba beta
Boot (to)	Arrancar
Broadband	Bancha ancha

---

* See also Telecommunications in the Glossary of Industry Specific Terms.

Browse (to)	Rastrear
Browser	Navegador
Bug	Defecto
Byte	Byte
CD-ROM	CD-ROM
CD-ROM drive	Lector de CD-ROM
Cell	Célula
Central Processing Unit (CPU)	Unidad central de proceso
Chip	Chip
Click (to)	Hacer un clic/pulsar
Clip art	Diseños genéricos
Clock speed	Velocidad de reloj
Close (to)	Cerrar
COBOL language	Lenguaje COBOL
Command	Orden
Communications port	Puerto de comunicaciones
Compatible	Compatible
Compressed file	Archivo comprimido
Control key	Tecla de control
Copy	Copia
Copy (to)	Copiar
Crash	Colisión
Cursor	Cursor
Cut (to)	Cortar
Data	Datos
Database	Base de datos
Debug (to)	Depurar
Delete (to)	Borrar
Delete key	Tecla de borrar
Desktop computer	Computadora de mesa
Desktop publishing	Maquetación
Dialog box	Ventana de diálogo
Digital	Digital
Disk	Disco
Disk drive	Unidad de disco

Diskette	Disquete
Document	Documento
Double-click (to)	Hacer doble clic
Download (to)	Descargar
Drag and drop (to)	Arrastrar y soltar
DRAM—SRAM	DRAM—SRAM
DVD	DVD
E-commerce	E-Commerce/comercio electrónico
E-commerce companies	Compañías de e-Commerce/ comercioelectrónico
Educational software	Software educativo
E-mail	Correo electrónico/e-mail
E-mail (to)	Enviar por correo electrónico
Engine	Motor
Enter (to)	Entrar
Enter key	Tecla de entrada
Entertainment software	Software de espectáculos
Error message	Mensaje erróneo
Escape key	Tecla de salida
Field	Campo
File	Archivo
Flat screen	Pantalla plana
Folder	Carpeta
Font	Tipo de letra
FORTRAN language	Lenguaje FORTRAN
Forward an e-mail (to)	Pasar un correo electrónico
Forward slash	Raya vertical delantera/ barra
Gigabyte	Gigabyte
Graphics	Diagramas
Go online (to)	Conectarse
Hacker	Pirata informático
Hard drive	Mecanismo impulsor duro
Hardware	Hardware

Hertz	Hertzios
Host	Servidor
Host (to)	Servir
Hypertext	Hipertexto
IBM-compatible	Compatible con IBM
Icon	Icono
Insert (to)	Introducir
Install (to)	Instalar
Instructions	Instrucciones
Integrated circuit	Circuito integrado
Internet	Internet
Internet address	Dirección de Internet
Internet advertising	Publicidad de Internet
ISPs (Internet Service Providers)	Proveedor de servicios internet
Key (to)	Entrar
Keyboard	Teclado
Language	Lenguaje
Laptop	Computadora portátil
Laser printer	Impresor Láser
LCD screen	Pantalla LCD
Left click (to)	Pulsar (el botón izquierdo del ratón)
Load (to)	Cargar
Log on/off (to)	Comenzar/terminar la conexión
Mail merge	Fusión postal
Mainframes	Unidades centrales
Maximize (to)	Maximizar
Megahertz	Megaciclo
Memory	Memoria
Menu	Menú
Minimize (to)	Minimizar
Microprocessor (Intel, Motorola)	Microprocesador (Intel, Motorola)
Modem	Módem

Monitor	Monitor
Monitor (to)	Supervisar
Mouse	Ratón
Mouse pad	Almohadilla de ratón
Nanosecond	Nanosegundo
Network	Red
Notebook computer	Computadora portátil
Online	En línea
Open (to)	Abrir
Operating system (Windows, Linux, Unix)	Sistemas operativos (Windows, Linux, Unix)
Palmtop computer	Computadora de bolsillo
Page	Página
Page down/up (to)	Bajar/Subir la página
Parallel port	Puerto paralelo
Password	Contraseña
Paste (to)	Pegar
PC (Personal Computer)	Computadora personal
Plotter	Trazador gráfico
Portal	Portal
Press a button (to)	Apretar un botón
Print (to)	Imprimir
Printer	Impresora
Program	Programa
Program (to)	Programar
Programmable logic devices	Dispositivos de lógica programables
Programmer	Programador
Prompt	Línea de mandatos
Record	Registro
Right-click (to)	Pulsar el butón de la derecha
Save (to)	Guardar
Scan (to)	Buscar

Scanner	Escáner
Screen	Pantalla
Screen (to)	Examinar
Scroll (to)	Enrollar
Search	Búsqueda
Search (to)	Buscar
Search engine	Motor de búsqueda
Serial port	Puerto serie
Server	Servidor
Shift key	Tecla de mayúsculas
Software	Software
Sort (to)	Ordenar
Space bar	Barra de espacio
Speakers	Altavoces
Spell check (to)	Corregir (texto)
Spell-checker	Corrector (de texto)
Surf the Internet (to)	Navegar por Internet
Systems	Sistemas
Tab key	Tabulador
Technical support	Asesoramiento técnico
Telecommuting	Teleconmutar
Teleconferencing	Teleconferenciar
Use (to)	Usar
User	Usuario
User friendly	Convivial
Virus	Virus
Voice recognition	Reconocimiento de voz
Web	Web
Web browser	Navegador de Web
Web page	Página Web
Web site	Sitio Web
Wireless	Inalámbríco
Word processor	Procesador de textos
World Wide Web (WWW)	Red mundial (WWW)
Zip® disk	Disco Zip®
Zip® drive	Unidad de disco Zip®

155

Human Resources   *(Personal)*

Where do you keep the personnel files?	¿Dónde guardan los archivos de personal?
What do you keep in your personnel files?	¿Qué guardan en sus archivos de personal?
What organization regulates the hiring and firing in your country?	¿Qué organización regula el empleo y despido de personal en su país?
How much do you use the Internet for hiring in your country?	¿Utilizan mudro Internet para buscar personal en su país?
How much turnover do you have at this plant?	¿Con quó regularidad se releva al personal en esta planta?
What benefits do you offer?	¿Qué beneficios ofrecen?
How much vacation do you give a new hire?	¿Qué tiempo de vacaciones le dan a un empleado nuevo?
What is your normal retirement age?	¿Cuál es la edad de retiro normal en su empresa?

Absent	Ausente
Advertise a position/job (to)	Anunciar una posición un trabajo
Appraise job performance (to)	Evaluar el desempeño de trabajo
Actuary	Actuario
Background	Antecedentes
Beneficiary	Beneficiario(a)
Bonus	Bonificación
Career	Carrera
Compensation	Compensación
Counsel (to)	Asesorar
Counseling	Asesoramiento

Corporate culture	Cultura corporativa
Cross training	Adiestramiento/formación cruzado integral
Deferred compensation	Compensación diferida
Disability	Incapacidad
Dotted-line responsibility	Responsabilidad de línea de punto
Employee benefits	Beneficios de empleados
Employee turnover	Relevo de empleados
Employment	Empleo
Expatiate	Pérdida de tiempo
Flex-time	Horario flexible
Fringe benefits	Beneficios laborales
Health insurance	Seguro de salud
Human resources	Departamento de personal/ recursos humanos
Human relations	Relaciones personales
Interview	Entrevista
Interview (to)	Entrevistar
Job	Trabajo
Job description	Descripción del trabajo
Job listing/ Advertisement	Relación de trabajos
Job skills	Habilidades del trabajo
Life insurance	Seguro de vida
List a job (to)	Anunciar un trabajo
Manage (to)	Administrar/gestionar
Management	Administración/Gestión
Management training	Adiestramiento de administración/Formación de gestión
Matrix management	Administración de matriz
Merit increase	Aumento por mérito
Micromanage	Microadministrar/ Microgestionar

Morale	Moral
Motivation	Motivación
Nepotism	Nepotismo
On-the-job training	Formación/adiestramiento en el trabajo
Organization	Organización
Organization chart	Diagrama de organización
Paycheck	Cheque de paga
Pension	Pensión
Performance appraisal	Evaluación de desempeño en el trabajo
Personnel	Personal
Personnel file	Archivo de personal
Position	Posición/cargo
Promote (to)	Promover
Promotion	Promoción
Recruiter	Reclutador
Relocation	Traslado
Resume	Curriculum vitae/Resumen
Retire (to)	Retirarse
Retirement plan	Plan de retiro
Restructuring	Reestructurar
Salary	Salario
Salary grade	Grado de salario
Salary survey	Encuesta de salario
Seniority	Antigüedad
Skills	Habilidades
Solid-line responsibility	Responsabilidad de línea entera
Stock options	Opciones sobre acciones
Supervise (to)	Supervisar
Supervisor	Supervisor
Train (to)	Adiestrar/Formar
Training	Adiestramiento/Formación
Turnover	Relevo

Unemployment	Desempleo
Vacation	Vacaciones
Wages	Salarios

Legal and International Law

(Ley Internacional y legal)

What is the procedure to apply for a patent/copyright/trademark in your country?	¿Cuál es el procedimiento para solicitar una patente/un registro de propiedad literaria/marca registrada en su país?
Do you recognize a service mark in your country?	¿Se reconoce una marca de servicio en su país?
What is the procedure to register a prescription drug in your country?	¿Cuál es el procedimiento para registrar un medicamento por prescripción médica en su país?
How much legal work do you do out-of-house?	¿Cuánto trabajo legal hace usted fuera de la empresa?

Affidavit	Declaración jurada
Alibi	Coartada
Appeal	Apelación
Appeal (to)	Apelar
Attorney	Abogado
Bail	Fianza
Bankruptcy	Bancarrota
Bar	Sociedad de abogados
Barrister	Abogado
Bench	Magistratura
Boilerplate	Chapa de caldera
Brief	Relación
Bylaws	Estatutos

Cartel	Cartel
Cease and desist order	Orden de cesar y desistir
Civil law	Derecho civil
Commit a crime (to)	Cometer un crimen
Consideration	Consideración
Contract	Contrato
Copyright	Propiedad literaria
Copyright (to)	Registrar la propiedad literaria
Corpus	Cuerpo de la herencia
Court	Tribunal
Covenant	Convenio
Crime	Crimen
Cross-examination	Contrainterrogatorio
Cross-examine (to)	Contrainterrogar
Damages	Daños
Defense	Defensa
Defraud	Defraude
Defraud (to)	Defraudar
Discovery	Descubrimiento
Evidence	Prueba
Felony	Delito
Fiduciary	Fiduciario
Find (to)	Fallar
Finding	Fallo
Fraud	Fraude
Fraud (to)	Defraudar
Indict (to)	Procesar
Indictment	Procesamiento
In-house	Interno
International law	Ley internacional
Judge	Juez
Judge (to)	Juzgar
Judgment	Juicio
Jury	Jurado

Law	Ley
Law firm	Bufete de abogados
Lawsuit	Pleito
Lawyer	Abogado
Legal	Legal
Litigation	Litigio
Malpractice	Conducta ilegal o inmoral en el ejercicio de una profesión
Motion	Moción
Negligence	Negligencia
Order (to)	Ordenar
Out-of-house	Externo
Patent	Patente
Patent (to)	Patentar
Plaintiff	Demandante
Probate	Validar un testamento
Prosecute (to)	Procesar
Prosecutor	Fiscal
Restrain (to)	Prohibir
Restraining order	Inhibitoria
Service mark	Marca de servicio
Solicitor	Procurador
Sue (to)	Demandar
Suit	Pleito
Tax	Impuesto
Tax (to)	Gravar
Tort	Agravio
Trademark	Marca registrada

Manufacturing and Operations

Where are your main production plants?

(Manufactura y operaciones)

¿Dónde se encuentran sus principales plantas de producción?

How many shifts do you run?	¿Cuántos turnos tienen?
Is your plant unionized?	¿Hay un sindicato en su planta?
What is your through-put at this plant?	¿Cuál es su rendimiento de procesamiento?
How many cars and trucks will you produce at this plant this year?	¿Cuántos carros y camiones producirá usted en esta planta este año?
Where does engineering fit into your organization?	¿Dónde encaja la ingeniería en su organización?
What types of engineers do you employ?	¿Qué clase de ingenieros tienen?
How many engineers do you employ?	¿Cuántos ingenieros tienen?
Accident	Accidente
Assembly line	Línea de ensamblaje
Controls	Controles
Engineer	Ingeniero
Engineer (to)	Tramar/crear
Ear plugs	Tapones de oídos
Fabricate	Fabricar
Factory	Factoría/fábrica
Factory floor	Piso de factoría/Fábrica
Floor	Piso
Foreman	Capataz
Forge (to)	Forjar
Forklift	Elevadora de horquilla
Gasket	Junta
Goggles	Gafas protectores
Inventory	Inventario
Just-in-time inventory	Inventario a tiempo/Just-in-time

Just-in-time manufacture	Manufactura a tiempo/Just-in-time
Machinery	Maquinaria
Manufacture (to)	Manufacturar
Manufacturer	Manufacturero
Model	Modelo
Operate (to)	Operar
Operations	Operaciones
Plant	Planta
Plant manager	Gerente de la planta
Prefabricate	Prefabricar
Procurement	Adquisición
Purchase (to)	Comprar
Purchasing	Compras
Quality	Calidad
Quality control	Control de calidad
Raw materials	Materia prima
Railroad	Ferrocarril
Safety	Seguridad
Safety goggles	Gáfas protectores
Schedule	Horario
Schedule (to)	Programar
Scheduling	Horario
Shift (first, second, third)	Turno (primero, segundo, tercero)
Ship (to)	Enviar
Shipping	Envío
Specifications	Especificaciones
Supervisor	Supervisor
Supplier	Proveedor
Tank	Tanque
Total Quality Management (TQM)	Administración de calidad total
Union	Sindicato
Union contract	Contrato de sindicato

Vat	Tanque
Warehouse	Almacén
Worker(s)	Trabajador(es)

Marketing and Sales — *(Mercadeo y ventas)*

What is your advertising budget for the year?	¿Cuál es su presupuesto publicitario para el año?
Which advertising agency do you use?	¿Cuál es su agencia publicitaria?
Which media do you use, and why?	¿Qué medios usan y por qué?
Who are your product/ service competitors?	¿Quiénes son los competidores de sus productos/servicios?
What is your market share?	¿Cuál es su parte del mercado?

"Quejas de los clientes"

SRTA. JOHNSON: *¿Por qué recibe usted tantas quejas de sus clientes?*
SR. CRUZ: *Esa es la razón por la cual la hemos empleado a usted.*
SRTA. JOHNSON: *Llevemos, pues, un diario de los tipos de quejas que se reciben en una semana.*
SR. CRUZ: *¿Puede encargarse usted de diseñarlo?*
SRTA. JOHNSON: *Sí, lo tendré listo esta tarde.*

"Customer Complaints"

MS. JOHNSON: *Why are you getting so many complaints from your customers?*
MR. CRUZ: *That's why we hired you.*
MS. JOHNSON: *Then let's have the customer representatives keep a log of the various types of complaints for a full week.*

MR. CRUZ: *Could you design the log?*
MS. JOHNSON: *Yes, I'll have it ready this after-noon.*

Account	Cuenta
Account executive	Ejecutivo de cuentas
Ad/Advertisement	Anuncio/Publicidad
Ad campaign	Campaña publicitaria
Advertising	Publicidad
Advertising effectiveness	Efectividad publicitaria
Advertising manager	Gerente publicitario
Advertising objectives	Objetivos publicitarios
Advertising rates	Tarifas publicitarias
Agency	Agencia
Agent	Agente
Art director	Director artístico
Artwork	Material gráfico
Audience	Audiencia
Audience measurement	Medida de la audiencia
Audience profile	Parfil de la audiencia
Bait and switch advertising	Publicidad de gancho
Banner ad	Cartel
Barcode	Código de barras
Barriers to entry	Barreras para entrar
Billboard	Valla publicitaria
Billings	Facturación
Blow-in	Caída
Brochure	Folleto
Brand	Marca
Brand loyalty	Lealtad a una marca
Brand name	Nombre de marca
Broadcast media	Medios de comunicación
Buyers	Compradores
Campaign	Campaña
Captive market	Mercado cautivado
Catalog	Catálogo
Circular	Circular

Circulation	Tirada
Classified advertising	Publicidad por clasificados
Closing date	Hora de cierre
Cold call	Visita sin previo aviso
Commercial	Anuncio
Commodity product	Producto comercial
Competition	Competencia
Competitive advantage	Ventaja competitiva
Consumer	Consumidor
Consumer research	Investigación de consumo
Copy	Copia
Corporate communications	Comunicaciones corporativas
Creative director	Director de creatividad
Creativity	Creatividad
Culture	Cultura
Customer	Cliente
Customer complaints	Quejas de clientes
Customer satisfaction	Satisfación del cliente
Customer service	Servicio al cliente
Database	Base de datos
Demand	Demanda
Demographics	Demográficos
Direct mail	Correo directo
Discount	Descuento
Distribution	Distribución
Economic factors	Factores económicos
Elastic demand	Demanda elástica
Endorsement	Apoyo
Exposure	Exposición
Expressed warranty	Garantía expresada
Focus group	Grupo de enfoque
Forecast	Pronóstico
Frequency	Frecuencia
Fulfillment	Cumplimiento
Galley proofs	Galeras

General sales manager	Gerente general de ventas
Global marketing	Marketing global
Graphic design	Diseño gráfico
Hard sell	Venta forzada
Illustration	Ilustración
Image	Imagen
Implied warranty	Garantía implícita
Impulse buying	Compra por impulso
Incentive	Incentivo
Inelastic demand	Demanda inelástica
Infomercial	Anuncio informativo
Insert	Introducir
Institutional marketing	Mercadeo institucional
Inventory	Inventario
Island display	Escaparate isla
Jobber	Corredor
Junk mail	Propaganda que se recibe por correo
Kiosk	Quiosco
Label	Etiqueta
Layout	Diseño
Lead(s)	Pista
Licensing	Conceder una licencia
Lifestyle	Estilo de vida
List price	Precio de lista
Logo	Logotipo
Magazine	Revista
Mailing list	Lista de distribución
Mail order	Pedido por correo
Margin	Margen
Markdown	Marcar a precio más bajo
Market(s)	Mercado(s)
Market (to)	Comercializar
Marketing	Marketing
Marketing budget	Presupuesto de marketing

Marketing director	Director de marketing
Marketing manager	Gerente de marketing
Marketing plan	Plan de marketing
Market niche	Nicho de marketing
Market penetration	Penetración de marketing
Market research	Investigación de marketing
Market share	Parte del marketing
Mass-marketing	Marketing de masas
Mass media	Medios de comunicación de masas
Media	Medios de comunicación
Media buyer	Comprador de medios de comunicación
Media research	Investigación de medios de comunicación
Merchandise	Mercancía
Merchandising	Comercialización
Message	Mensaje
National account	Cuenta nacional
Needs	Necesidades
New product development	Desarrollo de nuevos productos
News conference	Conferencia de prensa
Newspaper	Periódico
News release	Comunicado de prensa
Niche	Nicho/Segmento de mercado
Niche marketing	Marketing de sectores especializados
Opinion research	Encuesta de opinión
Order form	Formulario de pedidos
Outdoor advertising	Publicidad en exteriores
Outdoor billboards	Vallas publicitarias
Packaging	Embalaje
PMS colors (Pantone Matching System)	Colores PMS (Sistema de Colores Correspondientes al Pantone)
Point-of-sale advertising	Publicidad de punto de venta

Premium	Prima
Price	Precio
Price (to)	Poner precio
Pricing	Fijación de precios
Product(s)	Producto(s)
Product design	Diseño del producto
Product liability	Fiabilidad del producto
Product life cycle	Ciclo de vida del producto
Product launch	Lanzamiento del producto
Product mix	Mezcla del producto
Promotion	Promoción
Prospect	Prospecto
Publicity	Publicidad
Public relations	Relaciones públicas
Publication	Publicación
Qualified lead	Pista autorizada
Radio	Radio
Rate(s)	Tarifa(s)
Rate card	Tarjeta de tarifas
Reach	Alcanzar
Readership	Lectores
Rebate	Descuento
Recall	Retirada
Repetition	Repetición
Research	Investigación
Research report	Informe de investigación
Response(s)	Reacción/Reacciones
Returns and allowances	Devoluciones y concesiones
Rollout	Estiramiento
Sales	Ventas
Sales analysis	Análisis de ventas
Sales contest	Concurso de ventas
Sales force	Personal de ventas
Sales manager	Gerente de ventas
Salesperson	Vendedor
Sales report	Informe de ventas
Sales representative	Representante de ventas

Segmentation	Segmentación
Sell (to)	Vender
Selling	Venta
Services	Servicios
Share of market	Parte del mercado
Shelf life	Conservación de un producto
Slogan	Lema
Specialty product	Producto especializado
Sponsor	Patrocinador
Sponsor (to)	Patronizar
Spot (radio and TV)	Anuncio (radio y TV)
Storyboard	Tablero de guión
Strategy	Estrategia
Subliminal advertising	Publicidad subliminal
Supplier	Proveedor
Supply and demand	Oferta y demanda
Target audience	Público al que se guiere llegar
Target marketing	Marketing dirigido
Television	Televisión
Test group	Grupo de prueba
Test market	Mercado de prueba
Trade magazine	Revista comercial
Trade show	Feria comercial
Trail offer	Oferta de prueba
Unit pricing	Precio unitario
Universal Product Code system (UPC)	Sistema universal del código de producto
Vendor	Vendedor
Wants	Artículos de primera necesidad
Warehouse	Almacén
Warranty	Garantía
Web site	Sitio de Web
Word-of-mouth advertising	Publicidad de boca en boca

6 REFERENCE

Here's a place to find words and phrases for everything we missed in other chapters. For example, this chapter contains some critical information to keep you on schedule, which is so important in any organization, such as expressions used for telling time or words for numbers.

We'll start with words and phrases we hope you'll never have to use, but in an emergency they're critical:

> **Emergency Expressions**
> **Telling Time**
> **Days of the Week**
> **Months of the Year**
> **Seasons of the Year**
> **Ordinal Numbers**
> **Cardinal Numbers**
> **Basic Mathematical Terms**
> **Acronyms and Abbreviations**
> **Countries, Continents, and**
> **Languages**

EMERGENCY EXPRESSIONS

Help!	¡Socorro!/¡Auxilio!
Fire!	¡Fuego!
Hurry!	¡Rápido!
Call an ambulance!	¡Llame a una ambulancia!
Call the police!	¡Llame a la policía!
Call the fire department!	¡Llame a los bomberos!
Stop thief!	¡Detengan al ladrón!
Stop him/her!	¡Párele!
Someone/he/she/they stole my . . .	¡Alguien/él/ella/ellos me han robado mi . . .

bag!	bolso!
briefcase!	maletín!
wallet!	cartera!
watch!	reloj!

Leave me alone!	¡Déjeme en paz!
Can you help me, please!	¡Me puede ayudar, por favor!
Where's the police station?	¿Dónde está la comisaría de policía?
I need a lawyer.	Necesito un abogado.
Can I make a telephone call?	¿Puedo hacer una llamada por teléfono?
Do you speak English?	¿Habla usted inglés?
Can you tell me where the United States Embassy is?	¿Me puede decir dónde se encuentra la Embajada norteamericana?

TELLING TIME

In the United States, most offices use *A.M.* and *P.M.* after the number to distinguish between morning and afternoon hours, for instance, 9 A.M. and 9 P.M. Elsewhere, however, the 24-hour system is often used in offices and for other official purposes. For instance, following 12 noon, the hours are 13, 14 . . . , and so forth, as opposed to 1, 2 . . . , and so forth. An easy way to keep this straight is to subtract or add 12 to the hours you're accustomed to. For instance, if someone says 15:00 hours (spoken as 15 hundred hours), you know that it's really 3 P.M. Or, likewise, if it's 2 P.M. you add 12 to get 14:00 hours. The U.S. army adopted this system to make sure there would be no misunderstanding about what time was meant. But for business there is little confusion: When we say we'll meet at 4, we know that it's *P.M.*, not *A.M.*

Telling time in Spanish is very easy. The two main

words to know are *y* (after the hour) and *menos* (to the hour).

Thus:

las tres y diez (3:10)
las tres menos diez (2:50)

In the last example (2:50), you can also say *las dos y cincuenta.*

Es la . . . is used when referring to one o'clock, and *Son las . . .* is used for any other hour. Both phrases mean "It is. . . ."

What time is it?	**¿Qué hora es?**
It's 10:30 A.M.	**Son las diez y** treinta/**media A.M.**
It's exactly 9:00 A.M.	Son exactamente las nueve de la mañana.
Shortly after 10 a.m.	Unos minutos pasadas las diez de la mañana.
Around noon.	**Alrededor del mediodía.**
It is . . .	**Es la . . .**
one o'clock.	**una en punto.**
one A.M.	**una de la madrugada.**
one P.M.	una de la tarde.
one-fifteen.	una y quince.
one-thirty/half past one.	una y media.
one-thirty-five/quarter to two.	una y treinta y cinco/un cuarto para las dos.
one ten/ten minutes after one.	una y diez/diez minutos pasada la una.
one-fifty/ten to two.	una y cincuenta/diez para las dos.
What year is it?	**¿En qué año estamos?**
It's year 2002.	**Estamos en el año dos mil y dos.**
What date is it?	**¿Cuál es la fecha de hoy?**

Today is Monday,
  August 23, 2002.

**Hoy es lunes, 23 de Agosto
  del 2002.**

What time do we begin?
We begin at 10:30 sharp.

¿Cuándo comenzamos?
**Comenzamos a las diez y
  treinta/media en punto.**

The meeting will start
  at . . .
The meeting will end
  at . . .

La reunión comenzará a
  la/las . . .
La reunión terminará a
  la/las . . .

It's break time.
We will have a coffee
  break at . . .

Hora de hacer un descanso.
**Descansaremos para tomar
  un café a la/las . . .**

Lunch will be served
  at . . .
Lunch will last . . .

Se servirá el almuerzo a
  la/las . . .
El almuerzo durará . . .

I'm early./It's early.

**Llegué temprano./Es
  temprano.**

I'm on time./It's on time.
I'm late./It's late.
I'm too late./It's too late.

Llegué a tiempo./Es a tiempo.
Llegué tarde./Es tarde.
**Llegué demasiado tarde./Es
  demasiado tarde.**

Is this clock right?
It's running slow/fast.
It's five minutes slow/fast.

¿Va bien este reloj?
Está atrasado/adelantado.
Está atrasado/adelantado
  cinco minutos.

When will it start?
In . . .
  about two minutes.
  five minutes.
  one hour.
  a half hour.
  a quarter hour.
  an hour-and-a-half.

¿Cuándo comenzará?
En . . .
  más o menos dos minutos.
  cinco minutos.
  una hora.
  media hora.
  un cuarto de hora.
  hora y media.

Tomorrow/after
  tomorrow/in three days.

Mañana/pasado mañana/en
  tres días.

Next week/month/year.	La semana/el mes/el año próxima/o.
Soon.	**Pronto.**
When did it happen?	**¿Cuándo pasó?**
Five minutes ago.	**Hace cinco minutos.**
A half hour ago.	Hace media hora.
An hour ago.	Hace una hora.
Yesterday/the day before yesterday.	Ayer/anteayer.
Last month/year.	**El mes**/año **pasado.**
Hours/days/months/ years ago.	Hace horas/días/meses/ años.
In the middle of the night/day.	A medianoche/mediodía.
Recently.	**Recientemente.**
Long time ago.	Hace mucho tiempo.
How long did it last?	**¿Cuánto duró?**
(Very) long.	**Mucho tiempo.**
(Very) short.	(Muy) poco tiempo.
A half hour.	**Media hora.**
An hour.	Una hora.
For hours.	Horas.
All day long.	Todo el día.
All night long.	Toda la noche.
All month.	Todo el mes.

"Cómo obtener el huso horario debido."

SR. BELLIDO: *¿Cuál es la diferencia en horas de los Estados Unidos?*

SRTA. CLARK: *Es una hora más tarde.*

SR. BELLIDO: *En otras palabras, cuando son aquí las dos de la tarde . . .*

SRTA. CLARK: *La una de la tarde, en mi país.*

"Getting the time zone right."

MR. BELLIDO: *What is the time difference with the United States?*

MS. CLARK: *It is one hour later.*
MR. BELLIDO: *In other words, when it is 2 in the afternoon here, it is . . .*
MS. CLARK: *One in the afternoon back home.*

What time of day is it?	¿Qué hora del día es?
It's . . .	Es . . .
dawn.	el amanecer.
early morning.	temprano por la mañana.
morning.	**la mañana.**
mid-morning.	media mañana.
late morning.	tarde por la mañana.
noon.	**el mediodía.**
early afternoon.	temprano por la tarde.
mid-afternoon.	**media tarde.**
late afternoon.	tarde por la tarde.
dusk.	el anochecer.
early evening.	temprano por la noche.
evening.	**la noche.**
late evening.	tarde por la noche.
midnight.	**la medianoche.**

DAYS OF THE WEEK

What day of the week is it?	¿Qué día de la semana es?
It's . . .	Es . . .
Monday.	**lunes.**
Tuesday.	**martes.**
Wednesday.	**miércoles.**
Thursday.	**jueves.**
Friday.	**viernes.**
Saturday.	**sábado.**
Sunday.	**domingo.**
Weekday	**Día entre semana**
Weeknight	**Noche entre semana**
Weekend	**Fin de semana**

Yesterday	**Ayer**
The day before yesterday	**Anteayer**
Today	**Hoy**
Tomorrow	**Mañana**
The day after tomorrow	**Pasado mañana**
Last week	**La semana pasada**
This week	**Esta semana**
Next week	**La semana próxima**
On Tuesday	**El martes**
Next Thursday	**El jueves próximo**
When does it take place?	**¿Cuándo tiene lugar?**
Each Tuesday/Tuesdays.	**Cada martes**/los martes.
Once/twice/three times a week/month/year.	Una/dos/tres vece/s por semana/mes/año.

MONTHS OF THE YEAR

What month is it?	**¿En qué mes estamos?**
It's . . .	**Estamos en . . .**
January.	enero.
February.	febrero.
March.	marzo.
April.	abril.
May.	mayo.
June.	junio.
July.	julio.
August.	agosto.
September.	septiembre.
October.	octubre.
November.	noviembre.
December.	diciembre.
Last month.	**El mes pasado.**
This month.	**Este mes.**
Next month.	**El mes próximo.**
Two months ago.	**Hace dos meses.**
In a month.	**En un mes.**

When writing the date in Spanish, the day of the month comes first, followed by the name of the month and then the year. Thus:

5 de mayo del 2000

You can leave out the definite article *el* before the day. If so desired, you can also include the day of the week, which precedes the day of the month. Thus:

jueves, 5 de mayo del 2000 or
jueves, 5 de mayo, 2000 (without *del*)

Days of the week and months of the year are not capitalized in Spanish.

SEASONS OF THE YEAR

What season is it?	**¿En qué estación estamos?**
It's . . .	**Estamos en . . .**
spring.	**primavera.**
summer.	**verano.**
fall.	**otoño.**
winter.	**invierno.**
Last year.	**El año pasado.**
This year.	**Este año.**
Next year.	**El año próximo.**
Two years ago.	**Hace dos años.**
In two years.	**En dos años.**

ORDINAL NUMBERS

What position is it?	**¿Cuál es la posición?**
It's the . . .	**Es la . . .**
first (1st)	**primera (1a.)**
second (2nd)	**segunda (2a.)**
third (3rd)	**tercera (3a.)**
fourth (4th)	**cuarta (4a.)**

fifth (5th)	**quinta (5a.)**
sixth (6th)	**sexta (6a.)**
seventh (7th)	**séptima (7a.)**
eighth (8th)	**octava (8a.)**
ninth (9th)	**novena (9a.)**
tenth (10th)	**décima (10a.)**
position.	posición.

CARDINAL NUMBERS

0 **cero**

1 **uno**	11 **once**
2 **dos**	12 **doce**
3 **tres**	13 **trece**
4 **cuatro**	14 **catorce**
5 **cinco**	15 **quince**
6 **seis**	16 **dieciséis***
7 **siete**	17 **diecisiete**
8 **ocho**	18 **dieciocho**
9 **nueve**	19 **diecinueve**
10 **diez**	20 **veinte**

21 **veinte y uno**	
22 **veinte y dos**	40 **cuarenta**
23 **veinte y tres**	50 **cincuenta**
24 **veinte y cuatro**	60 **sesenta**
25 **veinte y cinco**	70 **setenta**
26 **veinte y seis**	80 **ochenta**
27 **veinte y siete**	90 **noventa**
28 **veinte y ocho**	100 **cien**
29 **veinte y nueve**	101 **ciento uno**
30 **treinta**	110 **ciento diez**

200 **doscientos (-as)**	600 **seiscientos(-as)**
300 **trescientos (-as)**	700 **setecientos (-as)**
400 **cuatrocientos (-as)**	800 **ochocientos (-as)**
500 **quinientos (-as)**	900 **novecientos (-as)**

---

*Counting from 16 to 19, and from 21 to 29 can be done in two ways, both being correct: *diez y seis* or *dieciséis*, or *veinte y uno* or *veintiuno*, etc.

In Spanish, a comma (,) is used instead of a period to mark the decimal point, e.g. 17.5 is written as 17,5. On the other hand, a point (.) is used to separate thousands, e.g. 2,455.12 is written as 2.455,12. The common way, used in the United States, to group the thousands into hundreds, is not used in Spanish. For example the number 1,272 can only be read as *mil doscientos setenta y dos* "one thousand two hundred seventy two."

1,000	mil
10,000	diez mil
100,000	cien mil
1,000,000	un millón
100,000,000	cien millones
1/2	un medio
1/3	un tercio
1/4	un cuarto
1/5	un quinto
1/10	un décimo
1/100	un centésimo
0.1	cero coma uno
0.2	cero coma dos
0.5	cero coma cinco
0.25	cero coma veinte y cinco
0.75	cero coma setenta y cinco

BASIC MATHEMATICAL TERMS

Absolute value	Función absoluta
Acute angle	Angulo agudo
Add (to)	Sumar
Addition	Suma
Algebra	Algebra
Algorithm	Algoritmo
Amortize	Amortizar
Angle	Angulo
Approximation	Aproximación

Area	Area
Asymptote	Asíntota
Average	Promedio
Axis (horizontal/vertical)	Eje (horizontal/vertical)
Bell-shaped curve	Curva acampanada
Binary	Binario
Bimodal distribution	Distribución bimodal
Binomial	Binomio
Boolean algebra	Algebra de Boole
Break-even analysis	Análisis de equilibrio
Calculate (to)	Calcular
Calculator	Calculadora
Calculus	Cálculo
Cardinal number	Número cardinal
Chaos theory	Teoría del caos
Chi-square test	Prueba de Ji-cuadrado
Circumference	Circunferencia
Coefficient	Coeficiente
Compound interest	Interés compuesto
Concave	Cóncavo
Count (to)	Contar
Cone	Cono
Congruent	Congruente
Constant	Constante
Convex	Convexo
Correlation	Correlación
Cube	Cubo
Cubed root	Raíz cúbica
Cylinder	Cilindro
Decimal	Decimal
Delta	Delta
Denominator	Denominador
Dependent variable	Variable dependiente
Depth	Profundidad
Derivative	Derivada
Diameter	Diámetro
Difference	Diferencia

Differentiation	Diferenciación
Digit	Dígito
Dispersion	Dispersión
Divide (to)	Dividir
Division	División
Ellipsis	Elipse
Elliptical	Elíptico
Equation	Ecuación
Exponent	Exponente
F distribution	Distribución en F
Factor	Factor
Factorial	Factorial
Formula	Fórmula
Fraction	Fracción
Future value	Valor futuro
Geometry	Geometría
Geometric figure	Cifra geométrica
Geometric progression	Progresión geométrica
Geometric shape	Forma geométrica
Height	Altura
Histogram	Histograma
Hyperbola	Hipérbola
Hypotenuse	Hipotenusa
Hypothesis	Hipótesis
Imaginary number	Número imaginario
Independent variable	Variable independiente
Inequalities	Desigualdad
Infinity	Infinito
Inflection point	Punto de inflexión
Integer	Entero
Integral	Integral
Integration	Integración
Interest	Interés
Interval	Intervalo
Inverse	Inverso
Irrational number	Número irracional

Length	Longitud
Linear	Lineal
Linear programming	Programación lineal
Logarithm	Logaritmo
Matrix	Matriz
Mean	Media
Median (value)	Valor mediano
Multiple	Múltiple
Multiplication	Multiplicación
Multiply (to)	Multiplicar
Net present value	Valor neto actual
Nominal	Nominal
Null hypothesis	Hipótesis nula
Numerator	Numerador
Obtuse angle	Angulo obtuso
Octagon	Octágono
Optimization	Optimización
Ordinal number	Número ordinal
Origin	Origen
Outline	Cantorno
Parabola	Parábola
Parameter	Parámetro
Parallel	Paralelo
Parallelogram	Paralelogramo
Pascal's triangle	Triángulo de Pascal
Pentagon	Pentágono
Percent	Por ciento
Percentage	Porcentaje
Perpendicular	Perpendicular
Pi	Pi
Plain	Sencillo
Polygon	Polígono
Polynomial	Polinomio
Power	Potencia
Prism	Prisma
Present value	Valor actual

Probability	Probabilidad
Proportion	Proporción
Pyramid	Pirámide
Quadratic equation	Ecuación de segundo grado
Quotient	Cociente
r squared	r cuadrada
Radical sign	Signo radical
Radius	Radio
Random	Aleatorio
Random number	Número aleatorio
Range	Extensión
Rational number	Número racional
Ratio	Proporción
Real	Real
Reciprocal	Recíproco
Rectangular	Rectangular
Regression line	Línea de regresión
Rhomboid	Romboide
Rhombus	Rombo
Right angle	Angulo recto
Sample	Muestra
Scientific notation	Notación científica
Sigma	Sigma
Significance	Importancia
Six sigma	Sigma seis
Skewed distribution	Distribución alabeada
Sphere	Esfera
Square	Cuadrado
Square of a number	Cuadrado de un número
Square root	Raíz cuadrada
Standard deviation	Desviación estándar
Statistics	Estadísticas
Student's t	prueba de diferencia respecto el promedio
Subtract (to)	Restar
Subtraction	Resta
Sum	Suma

T test	Prueba de T
Tri-dimensional	Tridimensional
Variable	Variable
Vector	Vector
Volume	Volumen
Weight	Peso
Weighted average	Promedio ponderado
Width	Anchura
Zero	Cero

ACRONYMS AND ABBREVIATIONS
Acronyms and Abbreviations used in the United States

ABA American Bankers Association	Asociación de banqueros norteamericanos
AD&D Accidental Death and Dismemberment	Muerte accidental y desmembramiento
ADEA Age Discrimination in Employment Act	Discriminación por causa de edad de la ley de empleo
ADP Automated Data Processing	Procesamiento automático de datos
AFL–CIO American Federation of Labor–Congress of Industrial Organizations	Federación norteamericana del congreso laboral de organizaciones industriales
AI Artificial Intelligence	Inteligencia artificial
AICPA American Institute of Certified Public Accountants	Instituto norteamericano de contables públicos certificados
AMA American Management Association	Asociación norteamericana de administración

AMEX American Stock Exchange — Bolsa de valores norteamericana

APB Accounting Principles Board — Junta de principios de contabilidad

APR Annual Percentage Rate — Tasa de porcentaje annual

ARM Adjustable Rate Mortgage — Tasa hipotecaria regulable

ASAP As Soon As Possible — Tan pronto como sea posible

ASTD American Society for Training and Development — Sociedad norteamericana para el adiestramiento y el desarrollo

ATM Automated Teller Machine — Cajero automático

BBB Better Business Bureau — Agencia de buenos negocios

BBS Bulletin Board System — Sistema de tableros

BLS Bureau of Labor Statistics — Departamento de estadísticas laborales

bps bits per second — Dígitos binarios por segundo

BOL or **B/L** Bill of Lading — Conocimiento de embarque

CAD/CAM Computer-Aided Design and Computer-Aided Manufacturing — Diseño asistido por computadora y fabricación asistida por computadora

CAI Computer-Aided Instruction — Instrucción asistida por computadora

CAPM Capital Asset Pricing Model — Modelo de precios de bienes capital

cc copy — copia

CD Compact Disc/ Certificate of Deposit — Disco compacto/ Certificado de depósito

CD-ROM Compact Disc, Read-Only Memory	Disco compacto, sólo lee la memoria
CEO Chief Executive Officer	Director ejecutivo
CERN Conseil Européen pour la Recherche Nucléaire	Consejo europeo de investigación nuclear
CFO Chief Financial Officer	Director financiero
CIF Cost, Insurance, Freight	Costo, seguro, carga
CIS Commonwealth of Independent States	Comunidad de Estados Independientes
CISC Complex Instruction Set Computer	Juego de instrucciones complejas de computadora
c/o care of	Al ciudado de
CO Certificate of Occupancy	Certificado de inquilinato
COBOL Common Business Oriented Language	Lenguaje orientado para comercios comunes
COD Cash on Delivery/ Collect on Delivery	Cóbrese a la entrega
COLA Cost of Living Adjustment	Ajuste del costo de vida
COO Chief Operating Officer	Jefe de operaciones
CPA Certified Public Accountant	Contable público certificado
CPI Consumer Price Index	Indice de precios del consumidor
cpi characters per inch	caracteres por pulgada

CPM Cost Per thousand (M)	Costo por mil
cps characters per second	caracteres por segundo
CPU Central Processing Unit	Unidad central de proceso
CRT Cathode Ray Tube	Tubo de rayos cátodes
CUSIP Committee on Uniform Securities Identification Procedures	Comité de procedimientos de identificaciónde seguridades uniformes
D&B Dun & Bradstreet report (credit report on a company)	Informe de dun & bradstreet (informe económico de una compañía)
DDB Double-Declining-Balance depreciation	Depreciación de balance doble declinante
DJIA Dow Jones Industrial Average	Promedio industrial del dow jones
DOS Disk Operating System	Sistema de operación de discos
DOT Department of Transportation/ Designated Order Turnaround	Departamento de transporte/ cambio de orden designado
DP Data Processing	Procesamiento de datos
DTP Desktop Publishing	Maquetación
EAFE Europe, Australia, Far East	Europa, australia, lejano oriente
EAP Employee Assistance Program	Programa de asistencia a empleados
EC European Community	Comunidad europea (CE)
EEC European Economic Community	Comunidad económica europea (CEE)

EFT Electronic Funds Transfer	Transferencia electrónica de fondos
EIB Export-Import Bank	Banco de exportación e importación
EMU European Economic and Monetary Union	Unión económica y monetaria europea
EOQ Economic Order Quantity	Cantidad de orden económico
EU European Union	Unión europea (UE)
FAA Federal Aviation Administration	Administración federal de aviación
FAQ Frequently Asked Questions	Preguntas frecuentes
FAS Free Alongside Ship	Franco al costado del barco
FASB Financial Accounting Standards Board	Junta de normas financieras contables
FDA Food and Drug Administration	Administración de alimentos y drogas
Fed Federal Reserve System	Sistema de reserva federal
FedEx Federal Express	Federal express
FIFO First In—First Out	Primero en llegar—primero en salir
FMV Fair Market Value	Valor equitativo de mercado
FOB Free On Board	Franco a bordo
FORTRAN Formula Translation	Fórmula de traducción
FTP File Transfer Protocol	Protocolo de transferencia de archivos
FV Future Value	Valor futuro

FYI For Your Information	Para su información
G or GB GigaByte	Gigabyte
G-7 Group of Seven	Grupo de siete naciones nations
G-10 Group of Ten nations	Grupo de diez naciones
GAAP Generally Accepted Accounting Principles	Principios de contabilidad generalmente aceptados
GATT General Agreement on Tariffs and Trade	Convenio general de tarifas y comercio
GDP Gross Domestic Product	Producto bruto nacional
GIM Gross Income Multiplier	Multiplicador de ingresos brutos
GRM Gross Rent Multiplier	Multiplicador de renta bruta
GTC Good Till Canceled	Buena cosecha anulada
GUI Graphical User Interface	Interfaz de usuario gráfico
HDTV High Density Television	Televisión de alta densidad
HMO Health Maintenance Organization	Organización de mantenimiento de la salud
HR Human Resources	Personal/recursos humanos
HTML Hypertext Markup Language	Lenguaje de margen de utilidad hipertexto
HTTP Hypertext Transport Protocol	Protocolo de transporte hipertexto
Hz hertz	Hertzios
IMF International Monetary Fund	Fondo monetario internacional (FMI)

Inc. Incorporated	Constituido
I/O Input-Output	Entrada-salida
IP Internet Protocol	Protocolo internet
IPO Initial Public Offering	Oferta pública inicial
IRC Internet Relay Chat	Charla por transmisión internet
IRR Internal Rate of Return	Tasa de beneficio interna
ISBN International Standard Book Number	Número de libro estándar internacional
ISDN Integrated Services Digital Network	Red digital de servicios integrados (RDSI)
ISSN International Standard Serial Number	Número de serie estándar internacional
ITC International Trade Commission	Comisión internacional de comercio (CIC)
ITO International Trade Organization	Organización internacional de comercio (OIC)
JIT Just-In-Time inventory/ Just-In-Time manufacturing	Inventario a tiempo ó manufactura a tiempo/just-in-time
K or KB Kilobyte	Kilobyte
LAN Local Area Network	Red de área local
LAWN Local Area Wireless Network	Red de área de radio local
LBO Leveraged Buyout	Compra con financiación ajena
L/C Letter of Credit	Carta de crédito
LCD Liquid Crystal Display	Indicador de cristal líquido

LED Light-Emitting Diode — Diodo electroluminoso

LIFO Last In—First Out — Último en llegar—primero en salir

LTC Less Than Carload — Menos que vagón cargado

LTV Loan To Value ratio — Proporción de préstamo a valor

MB or Megs Megabyte — Megabyte

MBO Management By Objectives — Administración por objetivos

MFN Most-Favored Nation — Nación más favorecida

MHz Megahertz — Megaciclo

MICR Magnetic Ink Character Recognition — Reconocimiento de carácter de tinta magnética

MIPS Million Instructions Per Second — Millón de instrucciones por segundo

MIS Management Information Systems — Sistemas informativos de administración

MLM Multi-Level Marketing — Mercado de nivel múltiple

MPT Modern Portfolio Theory — Teoría moderna de cartera de valores

NAFTA North American Free-Trade Agreement — Tratado de libre comercio de américa (TLCAN)

NASA National Aeronautics and Space Administration — Administración nacional de aeronáutica y espacio

NASD National Association of Securities Dealers — Asociación nacional de comerciantes de valores mobiliarios

NASDAQ National Association of Securities Dealers Automated Quotation — Asociación nacional de agentes de obligaciones de presupuestos automáticos

NAV Net Asset Value — Valor de activo neto

NOI Net Operating Income — Ingreso neto de operaciones

NOL Net Operating Loss — Pérdida neta de operaciones

NPV Net Present Value — Valor neto actual

ns nanosecond — nanosegundo

NYSE New York Stock Exchange — Bolsa de valores de nueva york

OBL Ocean Bill of Lading — Conocimiento de embarque oceánico

OCR Optical Character Recognition — Reconocimiento de carácter óptico

OECD Organization for Economic Cooperation and Development — Organización de cooperación económica y desarrollo

OEM Original Equipment Manufacturer — Fabricante de equipo original

OJT On-the-Job Training — Adiestramiento en el trabajo

OPEC Organization of Petroleum Exporting Countries — Organización de países exportadores de petróleo (OPEP)

OPM Other People's Money — El dinero de otros

P&L Profit and Loss statement — Estado de ganancias y pérdidas

PBX Private Branch Exchange — Intercambio privado de sucursal

PC Personal Computer	Computadora personal
PCS Personal Communications Services	Servicio personal de comunicaciones
PDA Personal Digital Assistant	Asistente digital personal
P/E Price/Earnings ratio	Proporción de precios y ganancias
PERT Program Evaluation Review Technique	Técnica de reseñas de evaluación de programas
PGIM Potential Gross Income Multiplier	Multiplicador potencial de ingreso bruto
PIN Personal Identification Number	Número de identificación personal
PMS Pantone Matching System	Sistema igualado pantone
POP Point-of-Purchase display	Exhibición de punto de compra
PPP Purchasing Power Parity	Cambio a la par de fuerza de compra
PV Present Value	Valor actual
R&D Research and Development	Investigación y desarrollo
RAM Random Access Memory	Memoria de acceso aleatorio
RFP Request For Proposal	Solicitud de propuesta
RGB Red, Green, and Blue	Rojo, verde, y azul
RIF Reduction In Force	Reducción vigente
ROI Return On Investment	Rendimiento de la inversión
ROM Read-Only Memory	Memoria inalterable

SDR Special Drawing Rights	Derechos especiales de dibujos
SIG Special Interest Group	Grupo especial de interés
SKU Stock-Keeping Unit	Unidad de mantenimiento de almacenaje
SLIP Serial Line Internet Protocol	Línea de serie de protocol Internet
SMSA Standard Metropolitan Statistical Area	Area de normas de estadísticas metropolitanas
SOP Standard Operating Procedure	Procedimiento estándar de operaciones
SYD Sum-of-the-Year's–Digits depreciation	Depreciación de la suma de los dígitos anuales
T or TB Terabyte	Terabyte
T&E Travel and Entertainment expense	Gasto de viajes y entretenimiento
TIN Taxpayer Identification Number	Número de identificación del contribuyente
TQM Total Quality Management	Administración total de calidad
UPC Universal Product Code	Código universal del producto
URL Uniform Resource Locator	Localizador uniforme de recursos
VAT Value Added Tax	Impuesto sobre el valor añadido (IVA)
VGA Video Graphic Array	Matriz gráfica de vídeo
VP Vice President	vicepresidente
WAIS Wide Area Information Server	Servidor de información de area amplia

WWW World Wide Web	Red mundial
WYSIWYG What You See Is What You Get	Lo que se ve es lo que se obtiene
YTD Year-To-Date	Año hasta la fecha
ZBB Zero Based Budgeting	Presupuesto cero

Acronyms for business-related organizations pertaining to Spanish-speaking countries

AACCLAL Association of American Chambers of Commerce in Latin America

AAPA American Association of Port Authorities (includes Latin America)

Spanish Association of Normalization and Certification

Industrial Latin American Association

Latin American Railroad Association

Latin American Association of Refractory Materials

Latin American Association of Electrical and Electronic Industry

ANCCAL Asociación norteamericana de cámaras de comercio en américa latina

Asociación norteamericana de autoridades de puerto

AENOR Asociación española de normalización y certificación

AILA Asociación industrial de américa latina

ALAF Asociación latinoamericana de ferrocarriles

ALAFAR Asociación latinoamericana de materiales refractorios

ALAINEE Asociación latinoamericana de la industria eléctrica y electrónica

Latin American Association of Railroads and Subways

ALAMyS Asociación latinoamericana de metros y subterráneos

Latin American Association of the Preserves and Food Industry

ALICA Asociación latinoamericana de conservas y de la industia alimenticia

Central American Association of Sustainable Development

ALIDES Alianza para el desarrollo sosteinbile

Latin American Association of the Plastics Industry

ALIPLAST Asociación latinoamericana de la industria plástica

American National Standards Institute

Instituto norteamericano de normas nacionales

Latin American Petrochemical and Chemical Association

APLA Asociación petroguímics y química latiñoamericana

CAISNET Central American Industrial Support Network

Red de apoyo industrial centroamericano

CEDA Caribbean Export Development Agency

Agencia para el desarrollo de la exportación de los estados del caribe

Regional Commission for Electrical Integration

CIER Comisión regional de la integración eléctrica

Confederated Bank of Latin America

COLABANCO Banco confederado de américa latina

Panamanian Commission of Industrial and Technical Standards

COPANIT Comisión panameña de normas industriales y técnicas

Venezuelan Commission of Industrial Standards

COVENIN Comisión venezolana de normas industriales

DANR Dominican American National Roundtable — Conferencia nacional dominicana–norteamericana

DANR Dominican American National Roundtable — Conferencia nacional dominicana–norteamericana

General Administration of Standards and Quality Systems — **DIGENOR** Dirección general de normas y sistemas de calidad

EACC Ecuadorean-American Chamber of Commerce — Cámara de comercio ecuatoriana-norteamericana

ECCLA Exchange and Cooperation Center for Latin America — Centro de intercambio y cooperación para latino américa

ECLAC Economic Commission for Latin America and the Caribbean — **CEPAL** Comisión económica para américa latina y el caribe

FDI Foreign Direct Investment — Inversión directa extranjera

FIBER Foundation for International Business Education and Research — Fundación para la educación de comercio internacional e investigación

FINCA Foundation for International Community Assistance — Fundación para la asistencia de la comunidad internacional

FTAA Free Trade Area of the Americas — Area de comercio libre de las américas

GATS General Agreement on Trade in Services — Pacto general de comercio en servicios

GATT General Agreement on Tariffs and Trade — Pacto general de tarifas y comercio

IAAC Interamerican Accreditation Corporation — Corporación de autorización interamericana

IAI Inter-American Institute for Global Change Research — Instituto interamericano de cambio e investigación mundiales

IBCC International Bureau of Chambers of Commerce — Agencia internacional de cámaras de comercio

Bolivian Institute of Standards and Quality — IBNORCA Instituto boliviano de normas y calidad

IBWC International Boundary and Water Commission — Comisión internacional de límites y agua

Central American Institute of Research and Industrial Technology — ICAITI Instituto centroamericano de Investigación y Technología Industrial

Colombian Institute of Technical Standards and Certification — ICONTEC Instituto colombiano de normas técnicas y certificatión

Latin American Institute of Iron and Steel — ILAFA Instituto latinoamericano del fierro y el acero

National Institute for the Defense of Competition and the Protection of Intellectual Property — INDECOPI Instituto nacional de defensa de la competencia y la protección de la propiedad intelectual

Dominican Institute of Industrial Technology — INDOTEC Instituto dominicano de tecnología industrial

IADB Inter-American Development Bank — IADE Banco de desarrollo interamericano

Central American Institute of Business Administration	**INCAE** Instituto centroamericano de administración de negocios
Ecuadorean Institute of Standards	**INEN** Instituto ecuatoriano de normalización
Costan Rican National Institute of Technical Standards	**INTECO** Instituto nacional costarricense de normas técnicas
National Institute of Technology and Standards	**INTN** Instituto nacional de tecnología y normas
Argentinian Institute of Standards	**IRAM** Instituto argentino de normas
Institute for European American Relations	**IRELA** Instituto de relaciones europes-latinoamericanas
ISO International Standards Organization	Organización de normas internacionales
LAAD Latin American Agribusiness Development Corporation, S.A.	Corporación de desarrollo agri-comercial de latinoamérica, s.a.
LAEA Latin American Economic Association	Asociación económica latinoamericana
LATCO Latin American Trade Council of Oregon	Consejo comercial latinoamericano de oregon
Common Market of the South	**MERCOSUR** Mercado común del sur
NAFTA North American Free Trade Agreement	**TLCAN** Tratado de libre comercio de américa
OAS Organization of American States	**OEA** Organización de estados americanos
Organization of Eastern Caribbean States	**OECS** Organización de estados caribeños orientales

PAU Pan American Union	**UP** Unión panamericana
TIA Telecommunications Industry Association	Asociación de la industria de telecomunicaiones
TRIMs Agreement on Trade–Related Investment Measures	Pacto de medidas de la inversión relacionadas con el comercio
UNCITRAL United National Commission for International Trade Law	**CNUDMI** Comision de las naciones unidas para el deredio mercentil internacional
UUSACC Uruguayan–United States Chamber of Commerce	Cámara de comercio uruguaya–norteamericana
USCIB United States Council for International Business	Consejo de los estados unidos de comercio internacional
USMCOC United States–Mexico Chamber of Commerce	Cámara de comercio mexicana–norteamericana
USTDA United States Trade and Development Agency	Agencia de comercio y desarrollo de los estados unidos
VACCI Venezuelan-American Chamber of Commerce and Industry	Cámara de comercio e industria venezolana-norteamericana

COUNTRIES, CONTINENTS, AND LANGUAGES

Countries

Argentina	Argentina
Australia	Australia
Bolivia	Bolivia
Brazil	Brasil

Canada	Canadá
Chile	Chile
China	China
Colombia	Colombia
Costa Rica	Costa Rica
Cuba	Cuba
Dominican Republic	República Dominicana
Ecuador	Ecuador
Egypt	Egipto
El Salvador	El Salvador
England	Inglaterra
Finland	Finlandia
France	Francia
Germany	Alemania
Great Britain	Gran Bretaña
Greece	Grecia
Guatemala	Guatemala
Haiti	Haití
The Netherlands	Holanda
Honduras	Honduras
Hungary	Hungría
Iceland	Islandia
Iran	Irán
Iraq	Iraq
Ireland	Irlanda
Israel	Israel
Italy	Italia
Japan	Japón
Malaysia	Malaisia
Mexico	México
Morocco	Marruecos
Nicaragua	Nicaragua
Norway	Noruega
Panama	Panamá
Paraguay	Paraguay
Peru	Perú
Poland	Polonia
Portugal	Portugal

Puerto Rico	Puerto Rico
Romania	Rumania
Russia	Rusia
Saudi Arabia	Arabia Saudita
South Africa	África del Sur
Spain	España
Sweden	Suecia
Switzerland	Suiza
Thailand	Tailandia
Taiwan	Taiwán (Formosa)
Turkey	Turquía
United States of America	Estados Unidos de Norteamérica
Uruguay	Uruguay
Venezuela	Venezuela

Continents

Africa	África
North America	América del Norte
South America	América del Sur
Asia	Asia
Australia	Australia
Antarctica	Antártica
Europe	Europa

Languages

Arabic	Árabe
Bengali	Bengalí
Chinese (Cantonese)	Chino (Cantonés)
Chinese (Mandarin)	Chino (Mandarín)
English	Inglés
Finnish	Finlandés
French	Francés
Greek	Griego
German	Alemán
Hebrew	Hebreo
Hungarian	Húngaro

Hindi	Hindi
Italian	Italiano
Japanese	Japonés
Korean	Coreano
Malay	Malayo
Polish	Polaco
Portuguese	Portugués
Russian	Ruso
Spanish	Español
Swedish	Sueco
Thai	Tailandés
Turkish	Turco
Ukranian	Ucraniano

APPENDIX A: Measurements

MILES/KILOMETERS

| 1 kilometer (km) = 0.62 mile | 1 mile = 1.61 km (1,61 km) |

Kilometers	1	5	8	10	15	20	50	75	100	150	200
Miles	0.62	3.1	5	6.2	9.3	12.4	31	46.5	62	93	124

GALLONS/LITERS

| 1 liter (l) = 0.26 gallon | 1 gallon = 3.75 liters (3,75 l) |

Liters	10	15	20	30	40	50	60	70
Gallons	2.6	3.9	5.2	7.8	10.4	13	15.6	18.2

WOMEN'S CLOTHING SIZES

Coats, dresses, suits, skirts, slacks

U.S.	4	6	8	10	12	14	16
Europe & Latin America	36	38	40	42	44	46	48

Blouses, sweaters

U.S.	32/6	34/8	36/10	38/12	40/14	42/16
Europe & Latin America	38/2	40/3	42/4	44/5	46/6	48/7

Shoes

U.S.	4	4½	5	5½	6	6½	7	7½	8	8½	9	9½	10	11
Europe & Latin America	35	35	36	36	37	37	38	38	39	39	40	40	41	42

MEN'S CLOTHING SIZES

Suits, coats

U.S.	34	36	38	40	42	44	46	48
Europe & Latin America	44	46	48	50	52	54	56	58

Slacks

U.S.	30	31	32	33	34	35	36	37	38	39
Europe & Latin America	38	39–40	41	42	43	44–45	46	47	48–49	50

Shirts

U.S.	14	14½	15	15½	16	16½	17	17½	18
Europe & Latin America	36	37	38	39	40	41	42	43	44

Sweaters

U.S.	XS/36	S/38	M/40	L/42	XL/44
Europe & Latin America	42/2	44/3	46–48/4	50/5	52–54/6

Shoes

U.S.	7	7½	8	8½	9	9½	10	10½	11
Europe & Latin America	39	40	41	42	43	43	44	44	45

WEIGHTS AND MEASURES

Weight

Metric U.S.

1 gram (g) = 0.035 ounce	1 ounce = 28.35 grams
100 g = 3.5 ounces	1 pound = 454 grams
1 kilogram (kilo) = 2.2 pounds	100 pounds = 45.4 kilos

Liquid

Metric

1 liter (l) = 4.226 cups
1 l = 2.113 pints
1 l = 1.056 quarts
1 l = 0.264 gallon

U.S.

1 cup = 0.236 l
1 pint = 0.473 l
1 quart = 0.947 l
1 gallon = 3.785 l

TEMPERATURE CONVERSIONS

To Convert Celsius to Fahrenheit

(9/5)C° + 32 = F°
1. Divide by 5
2. Multiply by 9
3. Add 32

To Convert Fahrenheit to Celsius

(F° − 32)5/9 = C°
1. Subtract 32
2. Divide by 9
3. Multiply by 5

Celsius	−17.8	0	10	15.6	23.9	30	37	100
Fahrenheit	0	32	50	60	75	86	98.6	212

APPENDIX B:
Useful Addresses, Telephone Numbers, and Web Sites

Emergency Numbers

	Mexico City	Buenos Aires	Bogotá
Ambulance (*Ambulancia*)	080	100	132 or 428–0111
Fire (*Bomberos*)	080	100	119
Police (*Policía*)	080	100	112 or 156

Embassies/Consulates
In the United States:

MEXICO
Mexican Embassy
1911 Pennsylvania Avenue NW
Washington, DC 20006
Telephone: 202/728–1600

ARGENTINA
Argentinian Embassy
1600 New Hampshire Avenue NW
Washington, DC 20009
Telephone: 202/238–6400

COLOMBIA
Colombian Embassy
2118 Leroy Place NW
Washington, DC 20006
Telephone: 202/387–8338

U.S. embassies in:

MEXICO
Paseo de La Reforma No. 305
Mexico, D.F. 06500
Telephone: 52–5209-9100

ARGENTINA
Avenida Colombia No. 4300
1425 Buenos Aires
Telephone: 54–114-777-4533

COLOMBIA
Calle 22D-B15 No. 47–51
Bogota
Telephone: 571–315-0811

Chambers of Commerce

For the chambers of commerce in Latin America, it is best to contact:

AACCLA
Association of American
Chambers of Commerce in Latin America
1615 H Street NW
Washington, DC 20062
Telephone: 202/463–5485
Fax: 202/463–3126
E-mail: inbox@aaccla.net

Major Airlines

In the United States:

MEXICO
Mexican Airlines (*Mexicana de Aviación*)
Telephone: 800/531–7921

ARGENTINA
Argentinian Airlines (*Aerolíneas Argentinas*)
Telephone: 718/632–1700

COLOMBIA
Colombian Airlines (*AVIANCA*)
Telephone: 800/284–2622

In Latin America:
MEXICO
American Airlines
Telephone: 52–5209–1450

ARGENTINA
American Airlines
Telephone: 54–114–4318–1100

COLOMBIA
American Airlines
Telephone: 571–285–1111

Useful Sites on the Internet

FTAA SECRETARIAT www.ftaa-alca.org
Site maintained by the Inter-American Development
Bank, the Organization of American States, and the
United Nations Economic Commission for Latin America
and the Caribbean.

FUSION INTERAMERICAS www.fusioninteramericas.com
Specializes in delivering hard-to-find goods from the
United States to Latin America.

IWCC INTERNATIONAL www.iwcc.com
Specializing in web design for the entire Latin American
region.

LATINEXPO www.latinexpo.com
Directory of Latin American businesses and products, in
Spanish and English.

LATIN AMERICAN BUSINESS LINK www.labl.com
Offers international trade and e-commerce services to
U.S.–based businesses serving the Hispanic community,
and businesses interested in conducting trade with Latin
America.

LATIN AMERICAN CENTER FOR INTER-AMERICAN
TRADE www.natlaw.com
Online Latin American legal database.

LATIN AMERICAN FAIR AND CONGRESS OF FOOD
INGREDIENTS AND ADDITIVES
www.flaia.com/index_eng.html
A specialized exposition and conference of food
ingredients and additives, drawing buyers from food
processing companies from all over Latin America.

LATIN AMERICAN INVESTMENT SERVICE
www.lafis.com.br
Provides equity information and research on Latin
America.

LATIN AMERICAN MEDIA LINKS www.zonalatina.com
Media resources, Media links, newspapers, magazines,
radio Internet, broadcast television programs, cable television broadcasts, cable television operators, telecommunications media, trade publications, and media trade
advertising.

LATIN AMERICAN NETWORK INFORMATION CENTER
www.lanic.utexas.edu
Provides a wealth of information on Latin American
countries, economy, governments, science, education,
media and communication, and much more.

LATIN BUSINESS EXCHANGE www.lbx.com/leads.html
Trade leads and matchmaking.

LATIN EXCHANGE www.latinexchange.com
Website where businesses can search for and contact
Latino businesses in the U.S. and worldwide.

LATIN EXPORTS www.latinexports.com
Directory of 20,000 companies, including exporters,
suppliers, trading, business opportunities, freight agents,
banks, and chambers of commerce.

LATIN FOCUS www.latin-focus.com
Provides economic and financial analysis for Latin
American markets.

LATIN INTERNET RESOURCES
www.philacol.edu/library/resources/arealatam.html
Areas of the world, links to regions and country
information on the Internet.

LATIN SOURCE www.latinsource.com
Represents specialist economic advisors for Latin
America, with special focus on Mexico, Brazil, Venezuela,
Argentina, and Chile.

NORTH AMERICAN CONGRESS ON LATIN AMERICA
www.nacla.org
Independent non-profit organization that provides
information on major trends in Latin America and its
relations with the United States.

PIERS www.piers.com
Publishes import/export trade information on global
cargo movements transiting in the United States and
Latin American seaports, offering databases and research
reports.

PORVENIR, Inc. www.porvenir.com
Offering a wealth of current Latin American business, economic, and financial information.

WORLD TRADE RESOURCES
www.atnworld.com/Security/wtr.html
International trade directory, worldwide useful resources, import/export links, and international trade show.

APPENDIX C:
Religious and National Holidays in Spanish-Speaking Countries

Principal national holidays (equivalent to Independence Day in the United States) in the following Spanish-speaking countries are:

Country	Holiday
Argentina	July 9
Bolivia	August 6
Chile	September 18
Colombia	July 20
Costa Rica	September 15
Cuba	May 20
Dominican Republic	February 27
Ecuador	August 10
El Salvador	September 15
Guatemala	September 15
Honduras	September 15
Mexico	May 5
Nicaragua	September 15
Panama	November 28
Paraguay	May 14
Peru	July 28
Puerto Rico	July 4 (also July 25)
Spain	October 12
Uruguay	August 25
Venezuela	April 19

The following holidays are commonly observed in Spanish-speaking countries*:

January 1	New Year's Day (*Año Nuevo*)
January 6	Epiphany (*Día de los Reyes Magos*)
April†	Holy Week (*Semana Santa*), in particular, Good Thursday (*Jueves Santo*) and Good Friday (*Viernes Santo*)
May 1	Labor Day (*Día del Trabajo*)
October 12	Columbus Day (*Día de la Raza/Día de la Hispanidad*)
December 24	Christmas Eve (*Nochebuena*)
December 25	Christmas (*Navidad*)
December 31	New Year's Eve (*Víspera de Fin de Año*)

---

*In addition, each Spanish-speaking country observes President's Day, or Day of the Liberator, such as Bolívar (Venezuela), San Martín (Argentina), O'Higgins (Chile), Juárez (Mexico), or Duarte (Dominican Republic).
†This holiday follows the lunar calendar.

APPENDIX D:
Grammar Summary and Verb Charts

A. GRAMMAR SUMMARY

1. EL ARTÍCULO DEFINIDO (THE DEFINITE ARTICLE)

	SINGULAR	PLURAL
masculine	el	los
feminine	la	las

2. EL ARTÍCULO INDEFINIDO (THE INDEFINITE ARTICLE)

	SINGULAR	PLURAL
masculine	un	unos
feminine	una	unas

3. GÉNERO (GENDER)

All Spanish nouns are either masculine or feminine.
Some words can be grouped by gender, but there are
exceptions and it is best to learn the word with its appropriate article.

Masculine words: nouns that end in -o, -r, -n, and -l;
names of items in nature (e.g., mountains); days of the
week and months; words of Greek origin ending in
-ma, -pa, or -ta; verbs, adjectives, etc. used as nouns.

Feminine words: nouns that end in -a, -dad, -tad, -tud,
-ción, -sion, -ez, -umbre, and -ie; names of cities,
towns, and fruits.

4. NÚMERO (NUMBER)

To form the plural for words ending in a vowel, add -s.

For words ending in a consonant or a stressed í or ú,
add -es.

Nouns ending in *z* change to *c* in the plural; e.g., *niños felices*—happy children.

5. ADJETIVOS Y CONCORDANCIA (ADJECTIVES AND AGREEMENT)

All adjectives must agree in number and gender with the nouns they describe.

For agreement with plural nouns, add -*s* or -*es* (if the adjective ends in a consonant) to the adjective.

When an adjective ends in -*o* (in its masculine form), its ending changes into -*a* when it modifies a feminine noun, e.g., *la mujer rica*—the rich woman. For certain adjectives ending in a consonant (or a vowel other than -*o*) in the masculine form, add -*a* for the feminine form; for others, simply use the same form for both genders.

6. PRONOMBRES (PRONOUNS)

SUBJECT PRONOUNS

I	*yo*
you	*tú*
he	*él*
she	*ella*
you (polite)	*usted (Vd.)**
we	*nosotros, nosotras*
you (familiar)	*vosotros, vosotras*
you (polite)	*ustedes (Vds.)*
they	*ellos, ellas*

Note: Subject pronouns are often omitted since the verbal endings show who or what the subject is.

---

* *Usted* and *ustedes* are treated as if they were third person pronouns, though in meaning, they are second person (addressee) pronouns. *Ustedes* is used as both familiar and polite and *vosotros, -as* is not used in Latin America.

Other pronouns, listed according to their corresponding subject pronoun, are:*

	DIRECT OBJECT	INDIRECT OBJECT	POSSESSIVE	PRE-POSITIONAL OBJECT
yo	me	me	mi/mío	mí†
tú	te	te	ti/tuyo	tí†
él/ella/Vd.	lo/la	le	su/suyo	él/ella/Vd.†
nosotros, -as	nos	nos	nuestro	nosotros, -as
vosotros, -as	os	os	vuestro	vosotros, -as
ellos, -as, Vds.	los/las	les	suyo	ellos, -as, Vds.

7. ADJETIVOS Y PRONOMBRES DEMONSTRATIVOS (DEMONSTRATIVE ADJECTIVES AND PRONOUNS)

The demonstrative adjectives are:

	SINGULAR	PLURAL	
this	este, -a	estos, -as	these
that	ese, -a	esos, -as	those
that over there	aquel, -ella	aquellos, -as	those over there

To form demonstrative pronouns, simply add an accent to the first *e* in the word, as in *No me gusta éste*— I don't like this one. There are also neuter pronouns used for general ideas or situations: *esto, eso, aquello*.

8. ADVERBIOS (ADVERBS)

Form adverbs simply by adding *-mente* (which corresponds to -ly in English) to the feminine form of an adjective, as in obviously—*obviamente*.

9. NEGACIÓN (NEGATION)

Form negative sentences by adding *no* before the verb and any pronouns, as in *No lo tengo*—I don't have it.

---

* Reflexive/reciprocal pronouns are *me, te, se, nos, os, se*.
† These pronouns combine with the preposition *con* in the special forms: *conmigo, contigo,* and *consigo*.

Many other negative constructions involve the use of two negative words; e.g., *No tengo nada*—I don't have anything/I have nothing.

10. COMPARACIÓN (COMPARISON)

Form comparative expressions by placing *más*—more or *menos*—less and *que*—than around the quality being compared, e.g., Juan is bigger than Pepe—*Juan es más grande que Pepe;* Juan runs faster than Pepe—*Juan corre más rápidamente que Pepe.* Use *de* instead of *que* before numbers.

To make equal comparisons, use the expressions *tan . . . como* (before adjectives and adverbs) and *tanto . . . como* (before nouns, with which *tanto* must agree). For example, Juan is as big as Pepe—*Juan es tan grande como Pepe;* Juan has as much money as Pepe—*Juan tiene tanto dinero como Pepe.*

Form superlatives by using an article or pronoun (*el* for adjectives, *lo* for adverbs) with the comparative expressions; e.g., Juan is the biggest—*Juan es el más grande;* Pepe is the least big—*Pepe es el menos grande;* Juan runs the fastest—*Juan corre lo más rápidamente.*

Irregular comparative words:

ADJECTIVE	ADVERB	COMPARATIVE
good—*bueno*	well—*bien*	better—*mejor*
bad—*malo*	badly—*mal*	worse—*peor*
much—*mucho*	much—*mucho*	more—*más*
little—*poco*	little—*poco*	less—*menos*
great—*grande*		bigger—*más grande*
		BUT older—*mayor*
		smaller—*más pequeño*
		BUT younger—*menor*

11. Pronombres relativos (Relative pronouns)

que	that, who which
quien	who(m)
el, la, los, las cuales	who, which
el, la, los, las que	who, which, the one(s) that/ who
lo que	what, which (refers to an entire idea)
cuyo, -a, -os, -as	whose (relative adjective)

12. Cambios de ortografía (Spelling changes)

To keep pronunciation consistent and to preserve customary spelling in Spanish, some verbs in certain tenses change their spelling. The rules are:

In verbs ending in -car, c changes to qu before e to keep the sound hard; e.g., busqué—I looked (buscar).

In verbs ending in -quir, qu changes to c before o and a; e.g., delinco—I commit a transgression (from delinquir).

In verbs ending in -zar, z changes to c before e; comencé—I began (from comenzar).

In verbs ending in -gar, g changes to gu before e to keep the g hard; e.g., pagué—I paid (from pagar).

In verbs ending in a consonant + -cer/-cir, c changes to z before o, and a to keep the sound soft; e.g., venzo—I conquered (from vencer).

In verbs ending in -ger/-gir, g changes to j before o and a to keep the sound soft; e.g., cojo—I catch (from coger).

In verbs ending in -guir, gu changes to g before o and a to preserve the sound; e.g., distingo—I distinguish (from distinguir).

In verbs ending in *-guar*, *gu* changes to *güi* before e to keep the "gw" sound; e.g., *averigüé*—I ascertained (from *averiguar*).

In verbs ending in *-eer*, the unstressed *i* between vowels becomes a *y*; e.g., *leyó*—he read (from *leer*).

In stem-changing verbs ending in *-eir*, two consecutive *i*'s become one; e.g., *rio*—he laughed (from *reir*).

In stem-changing verbs beginning with a vowel, an *h* must precede the word-initial diphthong or the initial *i* of the diphthong becomes a *y*; e.g., *huelo*—I smell (sense) (from *oler*).

In verbs with stems ending in *ll* or *ñ*, the *i* of the diphthongs *ie* and *ió* disappears; e.g., *bulló*—it boiled (from *bullir*).

13. CONTRACCIONES (CONTRACTIONS)

de + el = del
a + el = al

B. VERB CHARTS

I. The Forms of Regular Verbs

INDICATIVE

INFINITIVE	PRESENT AND PAST PARTICIPLES	PRESENT INDICATIVE	IMPERFECT	PRETERITE	FUTURE
I. *-ar* ending *hablar* to speak	*hablando* *hablado*	*hablo* *hablas* *habla* *hablamos* *habláis* *hablan*	*hablaba* *hablabas* *hablaba* *hablábamos* *hablabais* *hablaban*	*hablé* *hablaste* *habló* *hablamos* *hablasteis* *hablaron*	*hablaré* *hablarás* *hablará* *hablaremos* *hablaréis* *hablarán*
II. *-er* ending *comer* to eat	*comiendo* *comido*	*como* *comes* *come* *comemos* *coméis* *comen*	*comía* *comías* *comía* *comíamos* *comíais* *comían*	*comí* *comiste* *comió* *comimos* *comisteis* *comieron*	*comeré* *comerás* *comerá* *comeremos* *comeréis* *comerán*
III. *-ir* ending *vivir* to live	*viviendo* *vivido*	*vivo* *vives* *vive* *vivimos* *vivís* *viven*	*vivía* *vivías* *vivía* *vivíamos* *vivíais* *vivían*	*viví* *viviste* *vivió* *vivimos* *vivisteis* *vivieron*	*viviré* *vivirás* *vivirá* *viviremos* *viviréis* *vivirán*

CONDITIONAL	PRESENT PERFECT		PAST PERFECT		PRETERITE PERFECT	
hablaría	he		había		hube	
hablarías	has		habías		hubiste	
hablaría	ha	hablado	había	hablado	hubo	hablado
hablaríamos	hemos		habíamos		hubimos	
hablaríais	habéis		habíais		hubisteis	
hablarían	han		habían		hubieron	
comería	he		había		hube	
comerías	has		habías		hubiste	
comería	ha	comido	había	comido	hubo	comido
comeríamos	hemos		habíamos		hubimos	
comeríais	habéis		habíais		hubisteis	
comerían	han		habían		hubieron	
viviría	he		había		hube	
vivirías	has		habías		hubiste	
viviría	ha	vivido	había	vivido	hubo	vivido
viviríamos	hemos		habíamos		hubimos	
viviríais	habéis		habíais		hubisteis	
vivirían	han		habían		hubieron	

INDICATIVE

	FUTURE PERFECT		CONDITIONAL PERFECT		PRESENT SUBJUNCTIVE
I.	habré habrás habrá habremos habréis habrán	} hablado	habría habrías habría habríamos habríais habrían	} hablado	hable hables hable hablemos habléis hablen
II.	habré habrás habrá habremos habréis habrán	} comido	habría habrías habría habríamos habríais habrían	} comido	coma comas coma comamos comáis coman
III.	habré habrás habrá habremos habréis habrán	} vivido	habría habrías habría habríamos habríais habrían	} vivido	viva vivas viva vivamos viváis vivan

SUBJUNCTIVE

IMPERFECT SUBJUNCTIVE (r)	IMPERFECT SUBJUNCTIVE (s)	FUTURE SUBJUNCTIVE	PRESENT PERFECT SUBJUNCTIVE	
hablara	hablase	hablare	haya	
hablaras	hablases	hablares	hayas	
hablara	hablase	hablare	haya	hablado
habláramos	hablásemos	habláremos	hayamos	
hablarais	hablaseis	hablareis	hayáis	
hablaran	hablasen	hablaren	hayan	
comiera	comiese	comiere	haya	
comieras	comieses	comieres	hayas	
comiera	comiese	comiere	haya	comido
comiéramos	comiésemos	comiéremos	hayamos	
comierais	comieseis	comiereis	hayáis	
comieran	comiesen	comieren	hayan	
viviera	viviese	viviere	haya	
vivieras	vivieses	vivieres	hayas	
viviera	viviese	viviere	haya	vivido
viviéramos	viviésemos	viviéremos	hayamos	
vivierais	vivieseis	viviereis	hayáis	
vivieran	viviesen	vivieren	hayan	

SUBJUNCTIVE

	PAST PERFECT SUBJUNCTIVE (r)		PAST PERFECT SUBJUNCTIVE (s)		FUTURE PERFECT SUBJUNCTIVE	
I.	hubiera hubieras hubiera hubiéramos hubierais hubieran	hablado	hubiese hubieses hubiese hubiésemos hubieseis hubiesen	hablado	hubiere hubieres hubiere hubiéremos hubiereis hubieren	hablado
II.	hubiera hubieras hubiera hubiéramos hubierais hubieran	comido	hubiese hubieses hubiese hubiésemos hubieseis hubiesen	comido	hubiere hubieres hubiere hubiéremos hubiereis hubieren	comido
III.	hubiera hubieras hubiera hubiéramos hubierais hubieran	vivido	hubiese hubieses hubiese hubiésemos hubieseis hubiesen	vivido	hubiere hubieres hubiere hubiéremos hubiereis hubieren	vivido

IMPERATIVE	SIMILARLY CONJUGATED VERBS
¡Habla (tú)! ¡Hable (Vd.)! ¡Hablemos (nosotros)! ¡Hablad (vosotros)! ¡Hablen (Vds.)!	*amar, armar, bailar, callar, cambiar, caminar, colonizar, contabilizar, contar, charlar, dar, emigrar, enviar, exportar, felicitar, firmar, ganar, hurtar, ilustrar, importar, indagar, ingresar, immigrar, juntar, lavar, liquidar, llevar, mandar, nombrar, operar, pelear, quedar, realizar, rentar, robar, saldar, sondear, teclear, tocar, visualizar*
¡Come (tú)! ¡Coma (Vd.)! ¡Comamos (nosotros)! ¡Comed (vosotros)! ¡Coman (Vds.)!	*acceder, beber, ceder, deber, defender, depender, emprender, fenecer, haber, pender, prender*
¡Vive (tú)! ¡Viva (Vd.)! ¡Vivamos (nosotros)! ¡Vivid (vosotros)! ¡Vivan (Vds.)!	*abrir, batir, combatir, cubrir, decidir, empedernir, subir, surtir, plañir, unir*

II. Stem-changing Verbs

1. FIRST-CLASS STEM-CHANGING VERBS

Only the tenses in which changes occur are given the following tables. First-class stem-changing verbs have changes in their stems, but are otherwise conjugated like regular verbs.

a) e>ie

INFINITIVE	PRESENT INDICATIVE	PRESENT SUBJUNCTIVE
pensar to think	*pienso* *piensas* *piensa* *pensamos* *pensáis* *piensan*	*piense* *pienses* *piense* *pensemos* *penséis* *piensen*
perder to lose	*pierdo* *pierdes* *pierde* *perdemos* *perdéis* *pierden*	*pierda* *pierdas* *pierda* *perdamos* *perdáis* *pierdan*

b) o>ue

INFINITIVE	PRESENT INDICATIVE	PRESENT SUBJUNCTIVE
encontrar to find	*encuentro* *encuentras* *encuentra* *encontramos* *encontráis* *encuentran*	*encuentre* *encuentres* *encuentre* *encontremos* *encontréis* *encuentren*
volver to return	*vuelvo* *vuelves* *vuelve* *volvemos* *volvéis* *vuelven*	*vuelva* *vuelvas* *vuelva* *volvamos* *volváis* *vuelvan*

IMPERATIVE	SIMILARLY CONJUGATED VERBS		
piensa *pensad*	acertar apretar asentar calentar cerrar confesar	despertar empezar gobernar negar sentarse temblar	tentar
pierde *perded*	ascender atender defender descender encender entender	extender querer tender	

IMPERATIVE	SIMILARLY CONJUGATED VERBS	
encuentra *encontrad*	acordar almorzar contar costar mostrar probar	recordar
vuelve *volved*	doler llover mover oler poder soler	

2. SECOND-CLASS STEM-CHANGING VERBS

Second-class stem-changing verbs undergo the same changes in their stems as other stem-changing verbs, but undergo additional changes in the preterite tense. They are few in number and all belong to the third conjugation.

a) e>ie/i

INFINITIVE	PRESENT INDICATIVE	PRETERITE
sentir	siento	sentí
to feel	sientes	sentiste
	siente	sintió
	sentimos	sentimos
	sentís	sentisteis
	sienten	sintieron

b) o>ue/u

INFINITIVE	PRESENT INDICATIVE	PRETERITE
dormir	duermo	dormí
to sleep	duermes	durmiste
	duerme	durmió
	dormimos	dormimos
	dormís	dormisteis
	duermen	durmieron

PRESENT SUBJUNCTIVE	IMPERATIVE	SIMILARLY CONJUGATED VERBS	
sienta	*siente*	*arrepentirse*	*referir*
sientas	*sentid*	*diferir*	*sugerir*
sienta		*divertir*	
sintamos		*herir*	
sintáis		*mentir*	
sientan		*preferir*	

PRESENT SUBJUNCTIVE	IMPERATIVE	SIMILARLY CONJUGATED VERBS
duerma	*duerme*	*morir* (past participle: *muerto*)
duermas	*dormid*	
duerma		
durmamos		
durmáis		
duerman		

Verb Charts

3. THIRD-CLASS STEM-CHANGING VERBS

Third-class stem-changing verbs undergo a change
from *e* to *i* in their stems. They are few in number
and all belong to the third conjugation.

a) e>i

INFINITIVE	PRESENT INDICATIVE	PRETERITE
seguir to follow	*sigo* *sigues* *sigue* *seguimos* *seguís* *siguen*	*seguí* *seguiste* *siguió* *seguimos* *seguisteis* *siguieron*

PRESENT SUBJUNCTIVE	IMPERATIVE	SIMILARLY CONJUGATED VERBS	
siga	*sigue*	*competir*	*reír*
sigas	*seguid*	*corregir*	*repetir*
siga		*despedir*	*servir*
sigamos		*elegir*	*vestir*
sigáis		*expedir*	
sigan		*pedir*	

III. Irregular Verb Forms

Spanish verbs can have any or all of four basic types of irregularities in the simple tenses:

a) irregularities in the Present Indicative and Present Subjunctive
b) irregularities in the Preterite and the Imperfect Subjunctive
c) irregularities in the Future and Conditional tenses
d) irregularities in the Imperative

The following chart provides only the forms that are irregular.

INFINITIVE	PRESENT INDICATIVE	PRESENT SUBJUNCTIVE	PRETERITE
adquirir to acquire	adquiero adquieres adquiere adquirimos adquirís adquieren	adquiera adquieras adquiera adquiramos adquiráis adquieran	
andar to go, to roam			anduve anduviste anduvo anduvimos anduvisteis anduvieron
caber to fit into	quepo cabes cabe cabemos cabéis caben	quepa quepas quepa quepamos quepáis quepan	cupe cupiste cupo cupimos cupisteis cupieron
caer to fall	caigo caes cae caemos caéis caen	caiga caigas caiga caigamos caigais caigan	

IMPERFECT SUBJUNCTIVE	FUTURE	CONDITIONAL	IMPERATIVE
anduviera *anduvieras* *anduviera* *anduviéramos* *anduvierais* *anduvieran*			
cupiera *cupieras* *cupiera* *cupiéramos* *cupierais* *cupieran*	*cabré* *cabrás* *cabrá* *cabremos* *cabréis* *cabrán*	*cabría* *cabrías* *cabrías* *cabríamos* *cabríais* *cabrían*	

(continued)

INFINITIVE	PRESENT INDICATIVE	PRESENT SUBJUNCTIVE	PRETERITE
dar to give	*doy* *das* *da* *damos* *dais* *dan*	*dé* *des* *dé* *demos* *deis* *den*	*dí* *diste* *dió* *dimos* *disteis* *dieron*
decir to say	*digo* *dices* *dice* *decimos* *decís* *dicen*	*diga* *digas* *diga* *digamos* *digaís* *digan*	*dije* *dijiste* *dijo* *dijimos* *dijisteis* *dijeron*
hacer to do	*hago* *haces* *hace* *hacemos* *hacéis* *hacen*	*haga* *hagas* *haga* *hagamos* *hagáis* *hagan*	*hice* *hiciste* *hizo* *hicimos* *hicisteis* *hicieron*
oír to hear	*oigo* *oyes* *oye* *oímos* *oís* *oyen*	*oiga* *oigas* *oiga* *oigamos* *oigáis* *oigan*	*oí* *oíste* *oyó* *oímos* *oisteis* *oyeron*
poder to be able to	*puedo* *puedes* *puede* *podemos* *podéis* *pueden*	*pueda* *puedas* *pueda* *podamos* *podáis* *pueden*	*pude* *pudiste* *pudo* *pudimos* *pudisteis* *pudieron*

IMPERFECT SUBJUNCTIVE	FUTURE	CONDITIONAL	IMPERATIVE
diera			
dieras			
diera			
diéramos			
dierais			
dieran			
dijera	diré	diría	
dijeras	dirás	dirías	dí
dijera	dirá	diría	
dijéramos	diremos	diríamos	
dijerais	direis	diríais	
dijeran	dirán	dirían	
hiciera	haré	haría	
hicieras	harás	harías	haz
hiciera	hará	haría	
hiciéramos	haremos	haríamos	
hicierais	haréis	haríais	haced
hicieran	harán	harían	
oyera			
oyeras			
oyera			
oyéramos			
oyerais			
oyeran			
pudiera	podré	podría	
pudieras	podrás	podrías	
pudiera	podrá	podría	
pudiéramos	podremos	podríamos	
pudierais	podréis	podríais	
pudieran	podrán	podrían	

(continued)

INFINITIVE	PRESENT INDICATIVE	PRESENT SUBJUNCTIVE	PRETERITE
poner to put to place	pongo pones pone ponemos ponéis ponen	ponga pongas ponga pongamos pongáis pongan	puse pusiste puso pusimos pusisteis pusieron
querer to like to want to to love (a living being)	quiero quieres quiere queremos queréis quieren	quiera quieras quiera queramos queráis quieran	quise quisiste quiso quisimos quisisteis quisieron
reír to laugh	río ríes ríe reímos reís ríen	ría rías ría riamos riáis rían	rió rieron
saber to know (a fact) to know how to	sé sabes sabe sabemos sabéis saben	sepa sepas sepa sepamos sepáis sepan	supe supiste supo supimos supisteis supieron
salir to go out	salgo sales sale salimos salís salen	salga salgas salga salgamos salgáis salgan	

IMPERFECT SUBJUNCTIVE	FUTURE	CONDITIONAL	IMPERATIVE
pusiera	*pondré*	*pondría*	
pusieras	*pondrás*	*pondrías*	*pon*
pusiera	*pondrá*	*pondría*	
pusiéramos	*pondremos*	*pondríamos*	
pusiérais	*pondréis*	*pondríais*	*poned*
pusieran	*pondrán*	*pondrían*	
quisiera	*querré*	*querría*	
quisieras	*querrás*	*querrías*	
quisiera	*querrá*	*querría*	
quisiéramos	*querremos*	*querríamos*	
quisiérais	*querráis*	*querríais*	
quisieran	*querrán*	*querrían*	
riera			
rieras			
riera			
riéramos			
rierais			
rieran			
supiera	*sabré*	*sabría*	
supieras	*sabrás*	*sabrías*	
supiera	*sabrá*	*sabría*	
supiéramos	*sabremos*	*sabríamos*	
supierais	*sabréis*	*sabríais*	
supieran	*sabrán*	*sabrían*	
	saldré	*saldría*	
	saldrás	*saldrías*	*sal*
	saldrá	*saldría*	
	saldremos	*saldríamos*	
	saldréis	*saldríais*	
	saldrán	*saldría*	

(continued)

INFINITIVE	PRESENT INDICATIVE	PRESENT SUBJUNCTIVE	PRETERITE
tener to have to hold	tengo tienes tiene tenemos tenéis tienen	tenga tengas tenga tengamos tengáis tengan	tuve tuviste tuvo tuvimos tuvisteis tuvieron
traer to bring	traigo traes trae traemos traéis traen	traiga traigas traiga traigamos tragáis traigan	traje trajiste trajo trajimos trajisteis trajeron
valer to be worth	valgo vales vale valemos valéis valen	valga valgas valga valgamos valgáis valgan	
venir to come	vengo vienes viene venimos venís vienen	venga vengas venga vengamos vengáis vengan	vine viniste vino vinimos vinisteis vinieron
ver to see	veo ves ve vemos véis ven	vea veas vea veamos veáis vean	

IMPERFECT SUBJUNCTIVE	FUTURE	CONDITIONAL	IMPERATIVE
tuviera	*tendré*	*tendría*	
tuvieras	*tendrás*	*tendrías*	*ten*
tuviera	*tendrá*	*tendría*	
tuviéramos	*tendremos*	*tendríamos*	
tuvierais	*tendréis*	*tendríais*	
tuvieran	*tendrán*	*tendría*	
trajera			
trajeras			
trajera			
trajéramos			
trajerais			
trajeran			
	valdré	*valdría*	
	valdrás	*valdrías*	
	valdrá	*valdría*	
	valdremos	*valdríamos*	
	valdréis	*valdríais*	
	valdrán	*valdrían*	
viniera	*vendré*	*vendría*	
vinieras	*vendrás*	*vendrías*	*ven*
viniera	*vendrá*	*vendría*	
viniéramos	*vendremos*	*vendríamos*	
viniérais	*vendréis*	*vendríais*	
vinieran	*vendrán*	*vendría*	

IV. Auxiliary Verbs

The following irregular verbs, *ser*, *ir*, and *haber* are used as auxiliary verbs, and their conjugations must be memorized.

SER
To be

PRESENT AND PAST PARTICIPLES	PRESENT INDICATIVE	PRETERITE	IMPERFECT
siendo	*soy*	*fui*	*era*
sido	*eres*	*fuiste*	*eras*
	es	*fue*	*era*
	somos	*fuimos*	*éramos*
	sois	*fuisteis*	*erais*
	son	*fueron*	*eran*

IR
To go

PRESENT AND PAST PARTICIPLES	PRESENT INDICATIVE	PRETERITE	IMPERFECT
yendo	*voy*	*fui*	*iba*
ido	*vas*	*fuiste*	*ibas*
	va	*fue*	*iba*
	vamos	*fuimos*	*íbamos*
	váis	*fuisteis*	*íbais*
	van	*fueron*	*iban*

HABER
To have

PRESENT AND PAST PARTICIPLES	PRESENT INDICATIVE	PRETERITE	FUTURE
habiendo	*he*	*hube*	*habré*
habido	*has*	*hubiste*	*habrás*
	ha	*hubo*	*habrá*
	hemos	*hubimos*	*habremos*
	habéis	*hubisteis*	*habréis*
	han	*hubieron*	*habrán*

PRESENT SUBJUNCTIVE	IMPERFECT SUBJUNCTIVE	IMPERATIVE
sea	*fuera*	*sé*
seas	*fueras*	
sea	*fuera*	
seamos	*fuéramos*	
seais	*fuerais*	
sean	*fueran*	

FUTURE	PRESENT SUBJUNCTIVE	IMPERATIVE
iré	*vaya*	*ve*
irás	*vayas*	*id*
irá	*vaya*	*vayamos/vamos*
iremos	*vayamos*	
iréis	*vayáis*	
irán	*vayan*	

PRESENT SUBJUNCTIVE	IMPERATIVE
haya	*hé*
hayas	*habed*
haya	
hayamos	
hayáis	
hayan	

C. IRREGULAR PAST PARTICIPLES

Past participles are used in the formation of all perfect tenses. The participles in the third column are only used as adjectives, and not with the verb *haber*.

INFINITIVE	PAST PARTICIPLE	ADJECTIVE
abrir	*abierto*	
absorber	*absorbido*	*absorto*
bendecir	*bendecido*	*bendito*
componer	*compuesto*	
cubrir	*cubierto*	
decir	*dicho*	
describir	*descrito*	
disolver	*disuelto*	
escribir	*escrito*	
freir	*freído*	*frito*
hacer	*hecho*	
imprimir	*impreso*	
inscribir	*inscrito*	*inscripto*
morir	*muerto*	
poner	*puesto*	
satisfacer	*satisfecho*	
subscribir	*subscrito*	
ver	*visto*	
volver	*vuelto*	

Note that the derivatives of the above listed verbs contain the same irregularities in their past participles. For example:

INFINITIVE	PAST PARTICIPLE
suponer	*supuesto*
deponer	*depuesto*
entrever	*entrevisto*
prever	*previsto*

deshacer	*deshecho*
disponer	*dispuesto*

D. IRREGULAR GERUNDS

Third conjugation stem-changing verbs undergo stem changes in their gerundive forms.

INFINITIVE	GERUND
dormir	*durmiendo*
erguir	*irguiendo*
sentir	*sintiendo*
pedir	*pidiendo*
podrir	*pudriendo*
venir	*viniendo*

Similar verbs are:

INFINITIVE	GERUND
impedir	*impidiendo*
consentir	*consintiendo*
presentir	*presintiendo*
convenir	*conviniendo*

GLOSSARY OF INDUSTRY-SPECIFIC TERMS

The industries covered in this glossary are*:

Advertising and Public Relations	*Publicidad y Relaciones Públicas*
Agriculture	*Agricultura*
Architecture and Construction	*Arquitectura y Construcción*
Automotive	*Automotriz*
Banking and Finance	*Banca y Comercio*
Engineering	*Ingeniería*
Entertainment, Journalism, and Media	*Entretenimiento, Periodismo y Medios*
Fashion	*Moda*
Government and Government Agencies	*Gobierno y Agencias*
Insurance	*Seguro*
Management Consulting	*Consulta*
Mining and Petroleum	*Minas y Petróleo*
Non-Governmental	*No-Gubernamentales*
Perfume and Fragrance	*Perfume y Fragancia*
Pharmaceutical, Medical, and Dental	*Farmacéutica, Médica, Dental*
Publishing	*Editorial*
Real Estate	*Bienes Raíces*
Shipping and Distribution	*Embarque y Distribución*
Telecommunications	*Telecomunicaciones*
Textiles	*Textiles*
Toys	*Juguetes*
Watches, Scales, and Precision Instruments	*Relojes, Pesas, e Instrumentos de Precisión*
Wine	*Vino*

---

*For the terminology related to computers and computer industry, see Functional Areas of a Company in Chapter 5.

ADVERTISING AND PUBLIC RELATIONS

(See also Marketing and Sales in the section Functional Area of a
Company of Chapter 5)

Account executive	*Ejecutivo contable*
Ad	*Anuncio*
Ad agency	*Agencia de publicidad*
Ad style	*Anuncio de estilo*
Ad time	*Tiempo de anuncio*
Advertise (to)	*Anunciarse*
Advertisement	*Anuncio*
Advertising	*Publicidad*
Agency	*Agencia*
Budget	*Presupuesto*
Campaign	*Campaña*
Message	*Mensaje*
Papers	*Papeles*
Space	*Espacio*
Strategy	*Estrategia*
Vehicle	*Vehículo*
Air (to) / Broadcast (to)	*Emitir/Retransmitir*
Audience	*Público*
Baseline	*Línea de fondo*
Block of commercials	*Bloque de anuncios*
Brand-name promotion	*Promoción de marca*
Broadcast times	*Horario de trans-misión*
Brochure	*Folleto*
Campaign	*Campaña*
Catalog	*Catálogo*
Commercial	*Anuncio*
Commodity	*Mercancía*
Competition	*Competencia*

Consumer research	*Investigación del con sumidor*
Co-operative advertising	*Publicidad cooperativa*
Cost per thousand	*Costo por millar*
Coupon	*Cupón*
Cover	*Cubierta*
Daily press	*Prensa diaria*
Depth of coverage	*Profundidad de cobertura*
Direct marketing	*Marketing directo*
Early adopters	*Circuito de adaptadores*
Effectiveness	*Eficacia*
Endorsement	*Patrocinio*
Focus group	*Grupo de enfoque*
Free shopper's paper	*Periódicos gratuito para el consumidor*
Infomercial	*Infomercial/ Información comercial*
In house	*Interno*
Insert	*Añadidos*
In-store campaign	*Campaña en la tienda*
Introductory campaign	*Campaña de introducción*
Jingle	*Canción publicitaria*
Layout	*Diseño*
Leaflet	*Panfleto*
Listenership	*Oyentes/Audiencia*
Listening rate	*Nivel de oyentes audiencia*
Logo	*Logotipo*

Madison Avenue	*Avenida Madison*
Mail/Letter campaign	*Campaña por correo/por carta*
Market	*Mercado*
Market (to)	*Comercializar*
Marketing	*Marketing*
Market research	*Investigación de marketing*
Mass marketing	*Marketing de masas*
Media	*Medios de comunicación*
Media agent	*Agente de medios de comunicación*
Media plan	*Plan de medios de comunicación*
Merchandise	*Mercancía*
Merchandise (to)	*Comercializar*
Merchandising	*Mercancía*
Misleading advertising	*Publicidad engañosa*
Niche	*Nicho/Segmento de mercado*
Opener	*Abridor*
Packaging	*Embalaje*
Periodical	*Periódico*
Point-of-sale advertising	*Publicidad de punto de venta*
Positioning	*Posición*
Poster advertising	*Publicidad de pancartas*
Premium	*Premium*
Presentation	*Presentación*
Press officer	*Funcionario de prensa*
Press release	*Comunicado de prensa*
Prime time	*Hora de audiencia máxima*

Product	*Producto*
Product information	*Información de producto*
Product life cycle	*Ciclo de vida del producto*
Professional publications	*Publicaciones profesionales*
Promote (to)	*Promover*
Promotion	*Promoción*
Public relations	*Relaciones públicas*
Publicity	*Publicidad*
Radio spot and TV ad	*Anuncio de radio y anuncios de TV*
Readership	*Lectores*
Sales	*Ventas*
Sales promotion	*Promoción de ventas*
Sample	*Muestra*
Sample product	*Producto de muestra*
Selection	*Selección*
Share	*Parte*
Slogan	*Lema*
Space	*Espacio*
Special offer	*Oferta especial*
Sponsor	*Patrocinador*
Sponsor (to)	*Patrocinar*
Sponsorship	*Patrocinio*
Storyboard	*Tablero guión*
Survey	*Encuesta*
Target (to)	*Fijarse un objetivo*
Target group	*Grupo de objetivo*
Target market	*Mercado de objetivo*
Telemarketing	*Telemarketing*
Test market	*Mercado prueba*
Trade show	*Exposición comercial*

Trial	*Prueba*
White space	*Espacio en blanco*
Word-of-mouth advertising	*Publicidad de boca en boca*

AGRICULTURE

Acre	*Acre*
Agronomy	*Agronomía*
Area	*Área*
Arid	*Árido*
Chemical	*Producto químico*
Cotton	*Algodón*
Crop	*Cosecha*
Cropland	*Tierra de cultivo*
Cultivate (to)	*Cultivar*
Cultivation	*Cultivo*
Drought	*Sequía*
Export	*Exportación*
Farm	*Finca/Granja*
Farm (to)	*Cultivar*
Farmers	*Campesinos*
Farm income	*Ingreso de cultivo*
Farming	*Cultivo*
Feedstock	*Almacenamiento de productos alimenticios*
Fertilize (to)	*Fertilizar*
Fertilizer	*Fertilizante*
Grow (to)	*Cultivar*
Harvest	*Cosecha*
Harvest (to)	*Cosechar*

Herbicide	*Herbicida*
Husbandry	*Labranza*
Insecticide	*Insecticida*
Irrigate (to)	*Irrigar*
Irrigation	*Irrigación*
Irrigation system	*Sistema de irrigación*
Land	*Terreno*
Livestock	*Ganado*
Machinery	*Maquinaria*
Pesticide	*Pesticida*
Plant	*Planta*
Plant (to)	*Plantar*
Planting	*Plantar*
Plow (to)	*Surcar*
Potato	*Papa* (in Latin America)/*Patata* (in Spain)
Price	*Precio*
Price supports	*Ayuda a los precios*
Produce (to)	*Producir*
Production	*Producción*
Rice	*Arroz*
Seed (to)	*Sembrar*
Seed	*Semilla*
Seed stock	*Abastecimiento de semillas*
Soil	*Tierra*
Soil conservation	*Conservación de la tierra*
Store	*Tienda*
Subsidy	*Subsidiaria*
Surplus	*Excedente*

Tariff	*Tarifa*
Till (to)	*Labrar*
Tobacco	*Tabaco*
Vegetable	*Verdura*
Wheat	*Trigo*
Yields	*Rendimientos*

ARCHITECTURE AND CONSTRUCTION

Aluminum	*Aluminio*
Architect	*Arquitecto*
Art	*Arte*
Asphalt	*Asfalto*
Blueprint	*Plano*
Brick	*Ladrillo*
Bricklayer	*Albañil*
Build (to)	*Construir*
Builder	*Constructor*
Building	*Construir*
Building materials	*Materiales de construcción*
Carpenter (master/apprentice)	*Carpintero (jefe/aprendiz)*
Cement	*Cemento*
Cement (to)	*Cementar*
Chart (to)	*Diagramar*
Cinder block	*Bloque de ceniza*
Computer design	*Diseño de computación*
Concrete	*Cemento armado*
Construct (to)	*Construir*
Construction	*Construcción*
Cool (to)	*Enfriar*
Demolish (to)	*Demoler*

Design	*Diseño*
Design (to)	*Diseñar*
Designer	*Diseñador*
Destroy (to)	*Destruir*
Develop (to)	*Desarrollar*
Developer	*Promotor*
Dig (to)	*Cavar*
Draft	*Borrador*
Draft (to)	*Esbozar*
Drafting	*Esbozo*
Draw (to)	*Dibujar*
Drawing	*Dibujo*
Elevator	*Asunsor*
Engineer	*Ingeniero*
Excavate (to)	*Excavar*
Excavation	*Excavación*
Fix (to)	*Arreglar*
Fixture	*Instalación fija*
Glass	*Cristal*
Frosted	*Helado*
Insulated	*Aislado*
Plexi	*Plexi*
See-through	*Transparente*
Safety	*de Seguridad*
Gravel	*Grava*
Heat	*Calor*
Heat (to)	*Calentar*
Heating and ventilation	*Calefacción y ventilación*
Implement (to)	*Implementar*
Iron	*Hierro*
Ironworks	*Fundición*

Joiner	*Carpintero*
Joint	*Junta*
Joist	*Viga*
Land	*Tierra*
Lay (to)	*Colocar*
Light	*Luz*
Lighting	*Iluminación*
Material	*Material*
Metal	*Metal*
Measure (to)	*Medir*
Model	*Modelo*
Mortar	*Argamasa*
Office layout	*Diseño de oficina*
Paint	*Pintura*
Paint (to)	*Pintar*
Painter	*Pintor*
Parking	*Parqueo/Aparcamiento*
Plan (to)	*Planificar*
Plans	*Planes*
Plasterer	*Yesero*
Plastic	*Plástico*
Plumber	*Fontanero*
Refurbish (to)	*Restaurar*
Renovate (to)	*Renovar*
Repair (to)	*Reparar*
Replace (to)	*Reemplazar*
Rock	*Piedra*
Steel	*Acero*
Stone(s)	*Piedra*
Structure	*Estructura*
Survey	*Reconocimiento*
Survey (to)	*Reconocer*

Surveyor	*Agrimensor*
Tile (to)	*Azulejar*
Tiles	*Azulejos*
Weather (to)	*Proteger de los elementos*
Welder	*Soldador*
Window	*Ventana*
Wire (to)	*Alambrar*
Wood	*Madera*
Ebony	*Ébano*
Cedar	*Cedro*
Mahogany	*Caoba*
Oak	*Roble*
Pecan	*Nuez*
Pine	*Pino*
Redwood	*Secuoya*

AUTOMOTIVE

ABS brakes	*Frenos ABS*
Airbag	*Airbag*
Aircleaner	*Limpiador de aire*
Air filter	*Filtro de aire*
Air vent	*Conducto de aire*
Antilock brake	*Freno antibloque*
Ashtray	*Cenicero*
Assembly line	*Línea de ensamblaje*
Automatic shift	*Cambio automático*
Automobile	*Automóvil*
Auto show	*Exhibición de automóviles*
Axle	*Eje*
Backlog	*Reserva*
Bearing	*Cojinete*

Belt	*Correa*
Blinker	*Indicador*
Body	*Carrocería*
Body panel	*Panel de carrocería*
Body shop	*Taller de carrocería*
Bonnet	*Capote*
Brake	*Freno*
Brake (to)	*Frenar*
Brake cylinder	*Cilindro de freno*
Bucket seat	*Asiento de compartimiento*
Bumper	*Parachaques*
Bushing	*Buje*
Buy (to)	*Comprar*
Camshaft	*Árbol de levas*
Car	*Carro* (in Latin America)/*Coche* (in Spain)
Carburetor	*Carburador*
Car dealer	*Agente de automóvil*
Car maintenance	*Mantenimiento de carro/coche*
Carpet	*Alfombra*
Catalytic converter	*Convertidor catalítico*
CD player	*Reproductor de CD*
Chassis	*Chasis*
Child seat	*Asiento infantil*
Cigarette lighter	*Encendedor*
Climate control	*Control aclimatador/elimatizador*
Clock	*Reloj*
Cockpit	*Cabina de mando*
Component	*Componente*
Component stage	*Etapa componente*
Computer chip	*Chip de computadora*

Connecting rod	*Varilla de conexión*
Console	*Consola*
Consolidation	*Consolidación*
Convertible	*Descapotable*
Cooling system	*Sistema de refrigeración*
Cooling and heating system	*Sistema de refrigeración y calefacción*
Corporate average fuel economy (CAFE)	*Economía promedio de combustible corporativo*
Chrome	*Cromo*
Competition	*Competencia*
Coolant	*Refrigerante*
Cooling system	*Sistema de refrigeración*
Cost competitiveness	*Competencia de costos*
Crankshaft	*Cigüeñal*
Cream puff	*De paquete*
Cross member	*Miembro cruzado*
Cruise control	*Control de velocidad*
Cup holder	*Sostenedor de tazas*
Customer support	*Asesoramiento de cliente*
Custom-made	*Hecho a la medida*
Cylinder	*Cilindro*
Cylinder lining	*Forro del cilindro*
Cylinder head	*Cabeza del cilindro*
Dashboard	*Consola*
Dealer	*Agente*
Defog (to)	*Desempañar*
Defogger	*Desempañador*
Design	*Diseño*

Designer	*Diseñador*
Diesel	*Diésel*
Differential	*Diferencial*
Dimmer switch	*Botón reductor de luz*
Displacement	*Desplazamiento*
Distributor	*Distribuidor*
Door	*Puerta*
Door handle	*Manilla*
Door lock	*Cerradura*
Door panel	*Panel de la puerta*
Drive (to)	*Conducir*
Driver's seat	*Asiento del chófer*
Drive train	*Eje impulsador*
Electrical harness	*Arreos eléctricos*
Electrical system	*Sistema eléctrico*
Electronic systems	*Sistemas electrónicos*
Emergency flasher	*Destellador de emergencia*
Emission system	*Sistema de emisión*
Engine	*Motor*
Engine block	*Obstrucción de motor*
Engine cradle	*Cuna del motor*
Engineer	*Ingeniero*
Engineering	*Ingeniería*
EPA agency	*Ingeniería*
Exhaust	*Escape*
Exhaust manifold	*Colector de escape*
Exhaust system	*Sistema de escape*
Experimental design	*Diseño experimental*
Exterior	*Exterior*
Fabricate (to)	*Fabricar*
Fabrication	*Fabricación*
Fan	*Ventilador*
Fiberglass	*Fibra de vidrio*

Fill (to)	*Llenar*
Finish	*Terminación*
Four-door	*Cuatro-puertas*
Frame	*Armadura*
Fuel	*Gasolina*
Fuel gage	*Indicator/Calibrador de combustible*
Fuel pump	*Bomba de gasolina*
Fuel tank	*Tanque de gasolina*
Fuse	*Fusible*
Fuse box	*Caja de fusibles*
Garage	*Garaje*
Gasket	*Junta*
Gas	*Gasolina*
Gas cap	*Tapón de la gasolina*
Gas tank	*Tanque de gasolina*
Gauge	*Indicador*
Gear	*Palanca/Marcha*
Gear shift	*Cambio de palanca/ marcha*
Glove compartment	*Compartimiento de guantes*
Headlight	*Farol*
Head rest	*Cabecero*
Heating system	*Sistema de calefacción*
High beam	*Luces altas*
Hood	*Capó*
Hood ornament	*Decoración del capó*
Hubcap	*Tapacubo*
Indicator light	*Luz indicadora*
Interior	*Interior*
Instrument panel	*Panel de instrumentos*
Intake manifold	*Toma de colector*
Inventory	*Inventario*

Jack	*Gato*
Jobber	*Comisionista*
Key	*Llave*
Labor	*Labor*
Leather	*Cuero*
Lemon	*Cacharro*
Light	*Luz*
Light truck	*Camión pequeño*
Light vehicle	*Vehículo pequeño*
Lock	*Cerradura*
Lock (to)	*Cerrar*
Look (to)	*Mirar*
Lot	*Lote*
Machine shop	*Taller de maquinaria*
Machining	*Fabricación*
Maintenance	*Mantenimiento*
Make (to)	*Hacer*
Manual	*Manual*
Miles per hour/ Kilometers per hour	*Millas por hora/ Kilómetros por hora*
Miles per gallon/ Kilometers per gallon	*Millas por galón/ Kilómetros por galón*
Mint condition	*De paquete*
Mirror	*Espejo*
Model	*Modelo*
New model	*Modelo nuevo*
Noise	*Ruido*
Odometer	*Odómetro*
Oil gauge	*Medidor de gasolina*
Oil pressure	*Presión de aceite*
Open (to)	*Abrir*
Overhead cam	*Leva de arriba*

Paint	*Pintura*
Park	*Parqueo/Aparcamiento*
Park (to)	*Parquear/Aparcar*
Parking brake	*Freno de parqueo/de mano*
Part	*Pieza/parte*
Parts distribution	*Distribución de piezas*
Parts manufacturer	*Manufactura de piezas*
Passenger car	*Carro/Coche de pasajeros*
Passenger's seat	*Asiento de pasajeros*
Pedal	*Pedal*
Pickup truck	*Furgoneta*
Piston	*Pistón*
Piston ring	*Anillo de pistón*
Platform	*Plataforma*
Power brake	*Freno eléctrico*
Power window	*Ventana motorizada*
Price	*Precio*
Price tag	*Etiqueta de precio*
Radio	*Radio*
Rear suspension	*Suspensión trasera*
Rearview mirror	*Espejo retrovisor*
Repair shop	*Taller de repazaciones*
Replacement part	*Partes de repuesto*
Reverse (to)	*Dar marcha atrás*
Robot	*Autómata*
Rocker arm	*Brazo del balance*
Run (to)	*Funcionar*
Seal	*Sello*
Seat	*Asiento*
Seat belt	*Cinturón de seguridad*
Sedan	*Sedán*

Service	*Servicio*
Service station	*Estación de servicio*
Shift (to)	*Cambiar*
Shop (to)	*Comprar*
Showroom	*Sala de exposición*
Side mirror	*Espejo lateral*
Signal	*Señal*
Signal (to)	*Señalar*
Sound system	*Sistema de sonido*
Spare tire	*Rueda de repuesto*
Spark plug	*Bujía*
Speedometer	*Indicador de velocidad*
Sports car	*Carro/Coche deportivo*
Stall (to)	*Pararse*
Stamping	*Estampación*
Start (to)	*Arrancar*
Starter	*Arrancador*
Startup	*Arranque*
Station wagon	*Camioneta*
Steer (to)	*Guiar*
Steering wheel	*Volante*
Stick shift	*Palanca de cambio*
Strut	*Amortiguador*
Sunroof	*Techo corredizo*
Supplier	*Proveedor*
Suspension	*Suspensión*
SUV (sports utility vehicle)	*Vehículo de utilidad deportivo/Todoterreno*
Switch	*Interruptor*
System	*Sistema*
Tachometer	*Tacómetro*
Tire	*Llanta/Rueda*
Tool	*Herramienta*
Tool kit	*Caja de herramientas*

Torque	*Fuerza de torsión*
Transmission	*Transmisión*
Truck	*Camión*
Trunk	*Maletero*
Turn (to)	*Doblar/Girar*
Turn over (to)	*Dar la vuelta*
Turn signal	*Señal de doblar/girar*
Twin cap	*Tapadera*
Two-door	*De dos puertas*
Union	*Unión*
Valve	*Válvula*
Van	*Furgoneta*
Vanity mirror	*Espejo de tocador*
Vehicle	*Vehículo*
Vent	*Conducto de ventilación*
Vibration	*Vibración*
Wagon	*Camioneta*
Warning light	*Luces de advertencia*
Wheel	*Rueda*
Window	*Ventana*
Wiper	*Limpiaparabrisa*
Windshield	*Parabrisas*

BANKING AND FINANCE

Account	*Cuenta*
Accrue (to)	*Acumular*
Acquire (to)	*Adquirir*
Acquisition	*Adquisición*
Asset	*Activo*
Assets under management	*Activos bajo gerencia*
Automatic teller machine (ATM)	*Cajero automático*

Back office	*Oficina trasera*
Bail-out	*Saque de apuros*
Bond	*Bono*
Bond market	*Mercado de bonos*
Borrow (to)	*Pedir prestado*
Borrowing	*Préstamo*
Bottom line	*Línea inferior*
Branch	*Sucursal*
Branch manager	*Gerente de sucursal*
Capital	*Capital*
Cash	*Efectivo*
Cash (to)	*Cambiar*
Cashier	*Cajero*
Central bank	*Banco central*
Certificate of deposit (CD)	*Certificado de depósito*
Check	*Cheque*
Checking account	*Cuenta de cheques*
Close (to)	*Cerrar*
Commercial bank	*Banco comercial*
Commercial banking	*Banca comercial*
Commission	*Comisión*
Commodity	*Mercancía*
Corporate bond	*Bono de corporación*
Correspondent banking	*Banca corresponsal*
Cost of funds	*Costo de fondos*
Credit	*Crédito*
Credit card	*Tarjeta de crédito*
Credit limit	*Límite de crédito*
Credit line	*Línea de crédito*
Currency	*Moneda*
Day-trader	*Comerciante diurno*
Debt (short-term, long-term)	*Deuda (a corto plazo, largo plazo)*
Deficit	*Déficit*

Deflation	*Deflación*
Delinquency rate	*Tasa de pago moroso*
Deposit	*Depósito/Ingreso*
Deposit (to)	*Depositar/Ingresar*
Derivatives	*Derivados*
Down payment	*Pago inicial*
Due date	*Fecha de vencimiento*
Earnings	*Ganancias*
Economy	*Economía*
Efficiency ratio	*Proporción de eficiencia*
Exchange rate	*Tasa de cambio*
Fee	*Honorario*
Financial adviser	*Asesor financiero*
Fiscal policy	*Póliza fiscal*
Foreign exchange	*Cambio exterior*
Futures contract	*Contrato*
Go long/short (to)	*Ir lejos/cerca*
Hedge	*Protección con garantía*
Hedge (to)	*Proteger con garantía*
Hedge fund	*Fondo de protección con garantía*
Hedging	*Protección con garantía*
Inflation	*Inflación*
Institutional investor	*Inversionista institucional*
Interest	*Interés*
Interest rate (fixed, floating)	*Tasa de interés (fija, flotante)*
Invest (to)	*Invertir*
Investment	*Inversión*

Investment bank	*Banco inversionista*
Investment banking	*Banca inversionista*
Investment services	*Servicios inversionistas*
Letter of credit (L/C)	*Carta de crédito*
Liability	*Fiabilidad*
Liquid	*Líquido*
Liquidate (to)	*Liquidar*
Lend (to)	*Prestar*
Loan (short-term, long-term, secured)	*Préstamo (a corto plazo, a largo plazo, asegurado)*
Loan (to)	*Prestar*
Loan officer	*Ejecutivo de préstamos*
Loan volume	*Volumen del préstamo*
Loss	*Pérdida*
Merchant bank	*Banco mercantil*
Merchant banking	*Banca mercantil*
Merge (to)	*Unirse/Fusionarse*
Merger	*Unión/Fusión*
Monetary policy	*Póliza monetaria*
Money	*Dinero*
Mortgage	*Hipoteca*
Mortgage (to)	*Hipotecar*
Mutual fund	*Fondo mutuo*
Net	*Neto*
Net interest margin	*Margen de interés neto*
Non-revolving credit	*Crédito no rotativo*
Open (to) an account	*Abrir una cuenta*
Open (to) letter of credit	*Abrir una carta de crédito*
Overdraft	*Sobregiro*
Overdrawn	*Sobregirado*

Pay (to)	*Pagar*
Payment	*Pago*
Percent	*Por ciento*
Portfolio	*Cartera de valores*
Portfolio manager	*Gerente de cartera de valores*
Price	*Precio*
Price (to)	*Poner precio*
Price/Earnings (P/E) ratio	*Proporción de precio/ganancias*
Private banking	*Banca privada*
Profit	*Ganancia*
Profit (to)	*Sacar provecho de/ganar*
Profit margin	*Margen de ganancia/provecho*
Recession	*Recesión*
Repayment	*Reembolso*
Retail banking	*Banca al por menor*
Revolving credit	*Crédito rotativo*
Safe-deposit box	*Caja de seguridad para ingresos*
Save (to)	*Ahorrar*
Savings account	*Cuenta de ahorros*
Security(ies)	*Garantía/Obligaciones*
Securitization	*Garantización*
Share price	*Parte de acción*
Spread	*Propagación*
Stock market	*Mercado de valores*
Stockholder	*Accionista*
Stock	*Acción*
Surplus	*Superávit*
Syndicate	*Sindicato*
Syndicated loan	*Préstamo de sindicato*

Take-over	*Posesionarse*
Tax	*Impuesto*
Tax (to)	*Gravar*
Teller	*Cajero*
Trade (to)	*Comerciar*
Trader	*Comerciante*
Transact (to)	*Negociar*
Transaction	*Transacción*
Transaction cost	*Costo de transacción*
Transfer (to)	*Transferir*
Traveler's check	*Cheque de viajeros*
Treasury bond	*Bono de hacienda*
Trust	*Fideicomiso*
Trust (to)	*Confiar*
Trust officer	*Ejecutivo de fideicomiso*
Underwrite (to)	*Asegurar*
Underwriter	*Asegurador*
Wire	*Cable*
Wire (to)	*Enviar un cable*
Wholesale banking	*Banca al por mayor*
Withdraw (to)	*Retirar*
Withdrawal	*Retiro*

ENGINEERING

Calculus	*Cálculo*
Chemical	*Químico*
Civil	*Civil*
Design	*Diseño*
Develop	*Elaboración*
Engineer	*Ingeniero*
Instrument	*Instrumento*

272

Mathematics	*Matemáticas*
Mechanical	*Mecánico*
Nuclear	*Nuclear*
Science	*Ciencia*
Structural	*Estructural*
Technology	*Tecnología*
Test	*Prueba*

ENTERTAINMENT, JOURNALISM, AND MEDIA
(See also Publishing, Advertising, and Public Relations)

Actor	*Actor*
Artist	*Artista*
Choreographer	*Coreógrafo*
Cinema	*Cine*
Column	*Columna*
Columnist	*Columnista*
Commentary	*Comentario*
Contact	*Contacto*
Correspondent	*Corresponsal*
Dancer	*Bailarín*
Director	*Director*
Edit (to)	*Editar*
Edition	*Edición*
Editor	*Editor*
Editorial	*Editorial*
Editor-in-Chief	*Jede de redacción*
Feature story	*Artículo principal*
Headline	*Titular*
Interpreter	*Intérprete*

Journalism	Periodismo
Journalist	Periodista
Music	Música
Musician	Músico
News (story)	Artículo de noticias
Perform (to)	Actuar
Performance	Actuación
Photographer	Fotógrafo
Post-production	Producción posterior
Producer	Productor
Production	Producción
Radio	Radio
Recording	Grabación
Rehearsal	Ensayo
Report (to)	Informar
Reporter	Periodista
Review	Reseña
Score	Recuento
Script	Libreto
Technician	Técnico
Television	Televisión
Translator	Traductor
Writer	Escritor

FASHION
(See also Textile)

Accessory	Accesorio
Accessorize	Accesorizar
Appearance	Presentación/Presencia
Beauty	Belleza

Bell-bottom	*De campana*
Belt	*Cinturón*
Bias cut	*Corte preferencial*
Blazer	*Chaqueta*
Blouse	*Blusa*
Boot	*Bota*
Boutique	*Tienda de modas/ Boutique*
Bow tie	*Lacito/Pajarita*
Bra	*Ajustador/ Sujetadore*
Buzz	*Zumbido*
Cap	*Gorra*
Collar	*Cuello*
Collection	*Colección*
Corset	*Corsé*
Couturier	*Modisto*
Cover (to)	*Cubrir*
Cravat	*Corbata*
Design	*Diseño*
Design (to)	*Diseñar*
Designer	*Diseñador*
Dinner jacket	*Smoking*
Double-breasted suit	*Traje cruzado*
Dress	*Vestido*
Dressing room	*Cambiador*
Earmuff	*Orejera*
Etiquette	*Etiqueta*
Fabric	*Tela*
Fake fur	*Piel sintética*
Fashion	*Moda*
Fashion show	*Desfile de modas*
Fur	*Piel*

Garment	*Prenda (de ropa)*
Girdle	*Faja*
Glove	*Guante*
Hat	*Sombrero*
Haute Couture	*Alta costura*
Haute couturier	*Modisto de alta costura*
Heel	*Tacón*
Hem	*Dobladillo*
Hem (to)	*Hacer un dobladillo*
Hemline	*Bajo*
Image	*Imagen*
Jacket	*Chaqueta*
Lapel	*Solapa*
Length	*Largo*
Lingerie	*Ropa interior de señoras*
Metallic	*Metálico*
Midiskirt	*Falda midi*
Miniskirt	*Minifalda*
Model	*Modelo*
Model (to)	*Modelar*
Muff	*Manguito*
Necktie	*Corbata*
Nightgown	*Bata de noche*
Non-crease	*Sin raya*
Overcoat	*Abrigo*
Pad	*Almohadilla/Relleno*
Padded	*Rellenado*
Pajamas	*Pijama*
Pants	*Pantalones*

Plastic	*Plástico*
Platform shoes	*Zapatos de plataforma*
Pleat	*Pliegue*
Proportions	*Proporciones*
Raincoat	*Impermeable*
Ready-to-wear	*Listo para ponerse*
Relaxed	*Relajado*
Robe	*Bata de casa*
Runway	*Pasarela*
Sash	*Fajín*
Scarf	*Bufanda*
Seam (finished, unfinished)	*Costura (terminada, sin terminar)*
Season	*Estación/Temporada*
Separates	*Separados*
Shawl	*Chal*
Sheath	*Funda*
Shirt	*Camisa*
Shoe	*Zapato*
Shoulder pad	*Hombrera*
Show	*Espectáculo*
Show (to)	*Mostrar*
Showroom	*Salón de exposición*
Skirt	*Falda*
Sleeve	*Manga*
Sock	*Calcetin*
Stiletto heel	*Tacón de punta*
Stitch (to)	*Coser*
Stitching	*Coser*
Stocking	*Media*
Straight-leg	*Pierna recta*
Style	*Estilo*
Suit	*Traje*
Sweater	*Suéter*

Tailor	Sastre
Tailor (to)	Confeccionar
Tailored	Confeccionado
Tailoring	Confección
Tank top	Media-camiseta
Three-piece suit	Traje de tres piezas
Tie	Corbata
Trousers	Pantalones
T-shirt	Camiseta
Undergarment	Prenda interior
Underwear	Ropa interior
Vest	Chaleco
Waist	Cintura
Wardrobe	Vestuario
Wedge	Calzo

GOVERNMENT AND GOVERNMENT AGENCIES

Administration	Administración
Agency	Agencia
Arts	Artes
Association	Asociacion
Citizen	Ciudadano
Citizenship	Ciudadanía
College	Universidad
Commission	Comisión
Committee	Comité
Community	Comunidad
Cultural	Cultural
Delegation	Delegación
Department	Departamento
Development	Desarrollo

Economic	*Económico*
Education	*Educación*
Environment	*El medio ambiente*
Form	*Formulario*
Government	*Gobierno*
Governmental	*Gubernamental*
Grant	*Subvención*
Highway	*Carretera*
Housing	*Vivienda*
Industrial part	*Parte industrial*
Information	*Información*
Institute	*Instituto*
International	*Internacional*
Legislation	*Legislación*
Long range	*De alto alcance*
Military	*Militar*
Negotiate	*Negociar*
Negotiation	*Negociacion*
Non-government agency	*Agencia no gubernamental*
Non-profit	*Sin lucro*
Office	*Oficina*
Park	*Parque*
Plan	*Plan*
Plan (to)	*Planificar*
Planner	*Planificador*
Policy	*Política*
Political	*Político*
Politics	*Política*
Population	*Población*

Procedure	*Procedimiento*
Proposal	*Propuesta*
Public	*Público*
Public service	*Servicio público*
Recommendation	*Recomendación*
Region	*Región*
Regional	*Regional*
Regional office	*Oficina regional*
Regulation	*Regulación*
Regulatory agency	*Agencia regulatoria*
Report	*Informe*
Representative	*Representante*
Research	*Investigación*
Resources	*Recursos*
Road	*Camino*
Rural	*Rural*
Social	*Social*
Service	*Servicio*
Society	*Sociedad*
Suburb	*Suburbio*
Transportation	*Transporte*
University	*Universidad*
Urban	*Urbano*

INSURANCE

Actuary	*Actuario*
Agent	*Agente*
Annuity	*Anualidad*
Broker	*Comisionista*
Casualty	*Víctima*
Claim	*Reclamo*

Commission	*Comisión*
Coverage	*Cobertura*
Death benefit	*Beneficios de muerte*
Deductible	*Deducible*
Endowment	*Donación*
Face value	*Valor nominal*
Health	*Salud*
Insure (to)	*Asegurar*
Life	*Vida*
Life expectancy	*Esperanza de vida*
Mortality	*Mortalidad*
Peril	*Peligro*
Policy	*Póliza (de seguros)*
Policy owner	*Dueño de póliza*
Premium	*Prima (de seguros)*
Property	*Propiedad*
Reinsurance	*Reaseguro*
Reserve	*Reserva*
Risk	*Riesgo*
Risk management	*Administración de riesgos*
Term	*Plazo*
Underwriter	*Asegurador*
Universal	*Universal*
Variable annuity	*Anualidad variable*
Viatical settlement	*Acuerdo viático*
Whole-life	*Vida*

MANAGEMENT CONSULTING

Account	*Cuenta*
Accounting executive	*Ejecutivo de cuentas*
Bill	*Cuenta*
Bill (to)	*Facturar*
Entrepreneur	*Empresario*
Expert	*Experto*
Fee	*Honorario*
Implement (to)	*Implementar*
Implementation	*Implementación*
Manage (to)	*Administrar*
Management	*Administración*
Organize (to)	*Organizar*
Organization	*Organización*
Organizational development	*Desarrollo de organización*
Presentation	*Presentación*
Project	*Proyecto*
Proposal	*Propuesta*
Recommend (to)	*Recomendar*
Recommendation	*Recomendación*
Report	*Informe*
Report (to)	*Informar*
Specialize (to)	*Especializarse*
Specialist	*Especialista*
Team build (to)	*Edificar a un grupo*
Team building	*Edificación de grupo*
Time sheet	*Hoja de jornales devengados*
Train (to)	*Adiestrar*

Training	*Adiestramiento*
Value	*Valor*
Value-added	*Valor añadido*

MINING AND PETROLEUM

Blasting	*Hacer estallar*
Chemical	*Químico*
Coal	*Carbón*
Conveyor	*Correa*
Cooling	*Refrigeración*
Copper	*Cobre*
Crosscut	*Corte transversal*
Crush (to)	*Triturar*
Crushers	*Trituradores*
Crystal	*Cristal*
Deposit	*Depósito*
Diamond	*Diamante*
Dig (to)	*Cavar*
Digging	*Cavar*
Dredge (to)	*Excavar*
Dredging	*Excavar*
Drilling	*Perforar*
Earth	*Tierra*
Engineer	*Ingeniero*
Engineering	*Ingeniería*
Excavating	*Excavar*
Extraction	*Extracción*
Gas	*Gas*
Gems	*Piedras preciosas*
Geologist	*Geólogo*
Gold	*Oro*

Hydraulic	*Hidráulico*
Iron	*Hierro*
Lead	*Plomo*
Metal	*Metal*
Metallurgist	*Metalúrgico*
Mine	*Mina*
Mine (to)	*Extraer de una mina*
Mineral	*Mineral*
Natural gas	*Gas natural*
Natural resource	*Recurso natural*
Oil	*Petróleo*
Open-pit	*Hoyo abierto*
Ore	*Mineral*
Outcrop	*Afloramiento*
Pit	*Hoyo*
Platform	*Plataforma*
Power	*Energía*
Processing	*Procesamiento*
Pump	*Bomba*
Pump (to)	*Bombear*
Pumping	*Bombear*
Quarry	*Cantera*
Quarry (to)	*Extraer de la cantera*
Refine (to)	*Refinar*
Refinery	*Refinería*
Resource	*Recurso*
Safety	*Seguridad*
Shaft	*Fuste*
Silver	*Plata*
Sluice	*Compuerta*

Sluicing	*Abrir una compuerta*
Smelting	*Fundir*
Strip mining	*Despojamiento de minas*
Surface	*Superficie*
Tin	*Lata*
Ton	*Tonelada*
Truck	*Camión*
Tunnel	*Túnel*
Tunnel (to)	*Hacer un túnel*
Tunneling	*Hacer un túnel*
Vein	*Vena*
Uranium	*Uranio*
Water	*Agua*
Waste	*Desperdicios*
Well	*Pozo*
Zinc	*Zinc*

NON-GOVERNMENTAL

Academic	*Académico*
Analyst	*Analista*
Associate	*Asociado/Socio*
Association	*Asociación*
Center	*Centro*
Charity	*Obra de caridad/ Organización caritativa*
College	*Universidad*
Consult (to)	*Consultar*
Consulting	*Consultar*
Contract	*Contrato*

Contract (to)	*Contratar*
Coordinate	*Coordinar*
Council	*Consejo*
Cultural art	*Arte cultural*
Database	*Base de datos*
Develop (to)	*Desarrollar*
Development	*Desarrollo*
Directory	*Directorio*
Donation	*Donación*
Educate (to)	*Educar*
Education	*Educación*
Educational	*Educacional*
Enterprise	*Empresa*
Fellowship	*Beca*
Foundation	*Fundación*
Fund-raiser	*Recaudador de fondos*
Fund raising	*Recaudación de fondos*
Gift	*Regalo*
Grant	*Subvención*
Information	*Información*
Institute	*Instituto*
Institute (to)	*Instituir*
Institution	*Institución*
Interest group	*Grupo de intereses*
International	*Internacional*
Issue (to)	*Emitir*
Laboratory	*Laboratorio*
Library	*Biblioteca*
Lobbying	*Cabildeo*
Museum	*Museo*

Nonprofit group/ not-for-profit group	*Grupo no lucrativo/* *Grupo con fines no* *lucrativos*
Organization	*Organización*
Philanthropy	*Filantropía*
Professional association	*Asociación profesional*
Program	*Programa*
Publish (to)	*Editar*
Raise funds (to)	*Recaudar fondos*
Report	*Informe*
Report (to)	*Informar*
Research	*Investigación*
Research (to)	*Investigar*
Schools	*Escuelas*
Society	*Sociedad*
Statistic	*Estadística*
Strategy	*Estrategia*
Study	*Estudio*
Survey	*Encuesta*
Survey (to)	*Hacer una encuesta*
University	*Universidad*

PERFUME AND FRAGRANCE

Aerosol	*Atomizador/Aerosol*
Aftershave	*Colonia de* *afeitar/After-shave*
Air freshener	*Refrescador de aire*
Alcohol	*Alcohol*
Aloe	*Áloe*
Aroma	*Aroma*
Base note	*Nota base*
Bath	*Baño*

Bath oil	*Aceite de baño*
Blush	*Colorete*
Citrus	*Cítrico*
Cologne	*Colonia*
Compact	*Compacto*
Cosmetic(s)	*Cosmético(s)*
Cream	*Crema*
Deodorant	*Desodorante*
Essential oil	*Aceite esencial*
Eyeliner	*Delineador de ojos*
Eye shadow	*Sombra de ojos*
Floral	*Floral*
Fragrance	*Fragancia*
Fresh	*Fresco*
Freshner	*Refrescante*
Herbal	*Herbario*
Lemon	*Limón*
Lipstick	*Lápiz de labios*
Mascara	*Máscara para las pestañas*
Middle note	*Nota media*
Nose	*Nariz*
Oil	*Aceite*
Ointment	*Ungüento*
Olfactory	*Olfativo*
Orange	*Naranja*
Oriental	*Oriental*
Perfume	*Perfume*
Powder	*Polvo*
Powdery	*Polvoroso*

Rouge	*Colorete*
Salt	*Sal*
Scent	*Perfume*
Smell	*Oler*
Spicy	*Condimentado*
Soap	*Jabón*
Toiletries	*Artículos de baño*
Top note	*Nota superior*

PHARMACEUTICAL, MEDICAL, AND DENTAL

Anesthesia	*Anestesia*
Antibiotic	*Antibiótico*
Approve (to)	*Aprobar*
Approval	*Aprobación*
Capsule	*Cápsula*
Check-up	*Examen/Revisión*
Clean (to)	*Limpiar*
Cleaning	*Limpieza*
Chemistry	*Química*
Clinical trial	*Prueba clínica*
Disease	*Enfermedad*
Double-blind data	*Datos de obligaciones dobles*
Drug	*Medicina*
Drug trial (Phase I, Phase II, Phase III)	*Prueba de medicina (Fase I, Fase II, Fase III)*
Exam	*Examen*
Examine (to)	*Examinar*
Filling	*Preparación (de una medicina)*

Generic drug	*Medicina genérica*
Hospital	*Hospital*
Laboratory	*Laboratorio*
Manufacture (to)	*Manufacturar*
Magnetic Resonance Imaging (MRI)	*Simulación de resonancia magnética*
Over-the-counter	*Sin receta*
Patent	*Patente*
Patent (to)	*Patentar*
Patented drug	*Medicina patentada*
Patient	*Paciente*
Pharmaceutical company	*Compañía farmacéutica*
Pharmacologist	*Farmacólogo*
Pharmacy	*Farmacia*
Pharmacist	*Farmacéutico*
Pill	*Pastilla*
Placebo	*Placebo*
Poison	*Veneno*
Prescribe (to)	*Recetar*
Prescription	*Receta*
Prescription drug	*Medicina por receta*
Proprietary drug	*Medicina de marca exclusiva*
Rash (skin)	*Salpullido*
Release (to)	*Estrenar*
Research	*Investigación*
Root canal	*Canal de raíz*
Tablet	*Tableta*
Test (to)	*Probar*
Testing	*Probar*

Tests	*Pruebas*
Toxicology	*Toxicología*
Treatment	*Tratamiento*
Veterinary drug	*Medicina veterinaria*
Vitamin	*Vitamina*
X-ray	*Rayos X*

PUBLISHING

Acknowledgments	*Reconocimientos*
Advance	*Adelanto*
Advanced sales	*Ventas adelantadas*
Appendix	*Apéndice*
Art	*Arte*
Asterisk	*Asterisco*
Author	*Autor*
Author's corrections	*Correciones de autor*
Back ad	*Anuncio posterior*
Backlist	*Lista posterior*
Best-seller	*Exito editorial*
Binding	*Encuadernación*
Blockbuster	*Exitazo*
Blurb	*Nota publicitaria*
Body	*Cuerpo*
Bold type	*Negrita*
Book	*Libro*
Book jacket	*Sobrecubierta*
Bookstore	*Librería*
Border	*Borde*
Box	*Caja*
Broadsheet newspaper	*Periódico*
Bullet point	*Puntos*
Byline	*Subtítulo*

Caps (capital letters)	*Mayúsculas*
Caption	*Pie de foto*
Chapter	*Capítulo*
Circulation	*Circulación/Tirada*
Color	*Color*
Color photo	*Foto en colores*
Contents	*Contenido*
Contrast	*Contraste*
Copy editor	*Redactor*
Copyright	*Propiedad literaria*
Cover	*Portada*
Cropping	*Recortar (fotos)*
Dagger	*Cruz*
Deadline	*Fecha tope*
Dots per inch	*Punto por pulgada*
Double-page spread	*Doble página*
Double dagger	*Cruz doble*
Edit (to)	*Corregir/Redactar*
Editing	*Corregir/Redactar*
Editor	*Redactor/Editor*
Electronic publishing	*Publicaciones elec-trónicas*
End papers	*Hojas en blanco (al final de un libro)*
Fact check	*Comprobación de datos*
Flush left/Flush right	*Alinear izquierda/ Alinear derecha*
Font	*Tipo de letra*
Footnote	*Anotación al margen/ Nota alpic*
Front-list	*Lista delantera*
Galley	*Galera*
Galley proof	*Pruebas de galera*

292

Glossary	*Glosario*
Glossy	*Satinado*
Graphics	*Gráficas*
Hardcover	*En pasta*
Illustration	*Ilustración*
Imprint	*Marca*
Index	*Índice*
International paper sizes	*Tamaño internacional de papel*
Introduction	*Introducción*
International Standard Book Number (ISBN)	*Número de Libro Estándard Internacional (ISBN)*
International Standard Serial Number (ISSN)	*Número de Serie Estándard Internacional (ISSN)*
Italics	*Cursivas*
Jacket	*Sobrecubierta*
Justify	*Justificar*
Landscape	*Horizontal*
Layout	*Diseño*
Legend	*Clave*
Logo	*Logotipo*
Loose-leaf	*Hoja de papel suelta*
Lowercase	*Minúscula*
Magazine	*Revista*
Manuscript	*Manuscrito*
Margin	*Margen*
Masthead	*Cabeza de mástil*
Mock-up	*Maqueta*
Newspaper	*Periódico*
Newsstand	*Puesto de periódicos*

INDUSTRY-SPECIFIC TERMS

Page	*Página*
Page number	*Número de página*
Page proofs	*Pruebas de página*
Pagination	*Compaginación*
Paperback	*Libro de bolsillo*
Paragraph	*Párrafo*
Paragraph mark	*Marca de párrafo*
Percentage	*Porcentaje*
Pica	*Cícero*
Point	*Punto*
Portrait	*Vertical*
Printing	*Imprenta*
Prologue	*Prólogo*
Proof	*Prueba*
Proofread (to)	*Corregir*
Proofreader	*Corrector*
Publisher	*Editor*
Publishing	*Editorial*
Pulp	*Pulpa*
Reference	*Referencia*
Reference marks	*Marcas de referencia*
Remaindering	*Saldar*
Reporter	*Reportero*
Resolution	*Resolución*
Royalty(ies)	*Derecho(s) de autor*
Section mark	*Marca de sección*
Sentence	*Oración*
Softcover	*Rústica*
Subscript/Superscript	*Subíndice/Indice superior*
Subscriptions	*Subcripciones*
Tabloid	*Periódico de formato pequeño*
Template	*Plantilla*

Text	*Texto*
Title	*Título*
Trade book	*Libro comercial*
Trim	*Recorte*
Typeface	*Tipo de letra*
Watermark	*Marca de agua*
Word wrap	*Prevención del deslizamiento de filas*
Writer	*Escritor*

REAL ESTATE

Agent	*Agente*
Agreement	*Acuerdo*
Air rights	*Derechos de aire*
Amortization	*Amortización*
Annual percentage rate	*Tasa de porcentaje annual*
Apartment	*Apartamento*
Appraisal	*Evaluación*
Appraise (to)	*Evaluar*
Assessment	*Valoración*
Assign (to)	*Asignar*
Assume	*Asumir*
Assumption	*Suposición*
Attached	*Adjunto*
Attachment	*Adjunto*
Auction	*Subasta*
Balloon mortgage	*Hipoteca balón*
Bankruptcy	*Bancarrota*
Bearing wall	*Pared de soporte*
Bid (to)	*Apostar*
Binder	*Obligado*
Breach of contract	*Incumplimiento de contrato*

Bridge loan	*Préstamo puente*
Broker	*Agente*
Building	*Construcción*
Building codes	*Código de construcción*
Building permit	*Licencia de construcción*
Buy (to)	*Comprar*
Buy-down	*Compra debajo de*
Capitalization	*Capitalización*
Capital gains	*Ganancias de capital*
Cash flow	*Flujo de efectivo*
Caveat emptor	*Riesgo del comprador*
Closing	*Cierre*
Closing costs	*Costos de cierre*
Collateral	*Garantía*
Commitment	*Compromiso*
Condemnation	*Censura*
Condominium	*Condominium*
Contract	*Contrato*
Convey (to)	*Transmitir*
Conveyance	*Cesión*
Cooperative/Co-op	*Cooperativa*
Credit report	*Informe de crédito*
Debt-to-income ratio	*Relación de deuda a ingreso*
Deed	*Escritura*
Default (to)	*Falta de pago*
Depreciation	*Depreciación*
Diversified	*Diversificado*
Down payment	*Pago inicial*
Earnest money	*Dinero de buena fe*
Easement	*Servidumbre*
Eminent domain	*Dominio eminente*

Equity	*Equidad*
Escrow	*Plica*
Foreclosure	*Juicio hipotecario*
First mortgage	*Primera hipoteca*
Flood insurance	*Seguro de inundación*
Free and clear	*Libre de gravamen*
Freehold	*Dominio absoluto*
General contractor	*Contratista general*
Hazard insurance	*Seguro contra riesgos*
Hotel	*Hotel*
Indemnity	*Indemnización*
Industrial	*Industrial*
Industrial park	*Parque industrial*
Insurance	*Seguro*
Interest	*Interés*
Jumbo loan or mortgage	*Préstamo grande o hipoteca*
Land	*Terreno*
Landscaping	*Arquitectura de jardines*
Lease	*Arrendamiento*
Lease (to)	*Arrendar*
Lessee/Lessor	*Arrendatario/ Arrendador*
Let	*Arrendar*
Lien	*Embargo preventivo*
Manufactured housing	*Vivienda manufacturada*
Mortgage	*Hipoteca*
Note	*Nota*

Occupancy	*Inquilinato*
Office	*Oficina*
Option	*Opción*
Outlet center	*Tienda de distribución*
Owner	*Propietario*
Partition	*Tabique*
Points	*Puntos*
Power-of-attorney	*Por poderes*
Prefabricated construction	*Construcción prefabricada*
Prepayment penalty	*Penalidad de prepago*
Principal	*Principal*
Private mortgage insurance	*Seguro de hipoteca privada*
Probate	*Comprobación*
Promissory note	*Nota promisoria*
Property	*Propiedad*
Public sale	*Venta pública*
Real estate	*Bienes raíces (in Latin America)/Propiedad inmobiliaria (in Spain)*
Real estate investment trusts (REITS)	*Inversión de propiedades inmobiliarias de fideicomiso*
Realtor	*Agente de bienes raíces (in Latin America)/ de la propiedad inmobiliaria (in Spain)*
Refinance (to)	*Refinanciar*
Rent	*Alquiler*
Rent (to)	*Alquilar*
Rental	*De alquiler*
Renter	*Casero*

Rescind (to)	Rescindir
Residential	Residencial
Riparian rights	Derechos ribereños
Second mortgage	Segunda hipoteca
Self-storage	Almacenamiento por uno mismo
Sell (to)	Vender
Settle (to)	Acordar
Shopping malls	Centros comerciales
Strip mall	Tira de tiendas
Sublet (to)	Realquilar
Tenant	Inquilino
Tenure	Tenencia
Title	Título
Title insurance	Título de seguro
Title search	Búsqueda de título
Triple-net	Red triple
Trust	Fideicomiso
Utilities	Servicios públicos
Vacant	Vacante
Warranty deed	Escritura de garantía
Zoning	Zonificación

SHIPPING AND DISTRIBUTION

Agent	Agente
Airfreight	Carga aérea
Airport	Aeropuerto
Anchor	Ancla
Barge	Barcaza
Bill	Cuenta
Bill (to)	Facturar

Bill of lading (B/L)	*Conocimiento de embarque*
Boat	*Barco*
Box	*Caja*
Broker	*Agente*
Bulk carrier	*Conductor de carga*
By air	*Por avión*
By land	*Por tierra*
By sea	*Por mar*
Cargo	*Carga*
Carload	*Carga de un vagón*
Carrier	*Conductor*
Certificate	*Certificado*
Charter	*Fletamento*
Charter (to)	*Fletar*
CIF (Costs, Insurance, and Freight)	*Costos, Seguros y Carga*
Combine (to)	*Combinar*
Consign (to)	*Consignar*
Consigner	*Consignador*
Container	*Envase/Contenedor*
Containerization	*Contenedorización*
Container ship	*Carguero portacontenedares*
Corrugated box	*Caja de cartón acanalada*
Cost	*Costo*
Crate	*Cajón de embalaje*
Crew	*Tripulación*
Customs	*Aduana*
Deliver (to)	*Entregar*
Delivery	*Entrega*
Delivery note	*Nota de entrega*
Delivery time	*Tiempo de entrega*

Depot	*Almacén*
Destination	*Destino*
Dispatch	*Despacho*
Dispatch (to)	*Despachar*
Dock	*Muelle*
Dock (to)	*Atracar*
Double hull	*Casco doble*
Duty	*Impuesto*
Estimate	*Estimado*
Estimate (to)	*Estimar*
Ferry	*Transbordador*
Fleet	*Escuadra*
Free on board (FOB)	*Franco a bordo*
Forward	*Transmitir*
Forwarding	*Transmitir*
Forklift	*Carretilla elevadora*
Fragile	*Frágil*
Freight	*Carga*
Freight carrier	*Conductor de carga*
Freight cost	*Costo de carga*
Freighter	*Agente de carga*
Freight weight	*Peso de carga*
Full containerload	*Envase completo de carga*
Goods	*Mercancías*
Guaranteed arrival date	*Fecha de llegada garantizada*
Hazardous materials	*Materiales peligrosos*
Hire (to)	*Emplear*
Hub	*Cubo*
Insurance	*Seguro*
Insure (to)	*Asegurar*

Island	*Isla*
Isothermal container	*Envase isotérmico*
Landing day	*Día de desembarco*
Liner	*Compañía de buques*
Load	*Carga*
Load (to)	*Cargar*
Load capacity	*Capacidad de carga*
Loading	*Cargar*
Loader	*Cargador*
Loan	*Préstamo*
Locks	*Cerraduras*
Lots	*Lotes*
Manager	*Gerente*
Manifest	*Manifiesto*
Merchant ship	*Barco mercantil*
Message center	*Central de mensajes*
Oil tanker	*Petrolero*
Off load (to)	*Descargar*
On load (to)	*Cargar*
Order	*Orden/Pedido*
Order (to)	*Ordenar/Pedir*
Overdraft	*Sobregiro*
Package	*Paquete*
Package (to)	*Empacar*
Packaging	*Empacar*
Packing	*Empacar*
Pallet	*Paleta*
Partial carload	*Carga parcial*
Partial containerload	*Carga de envase parcial*
Pickup (to)	*Recoger*
Port	*Puerto*
Profit	*Ganancia*

Railroad	*Ferrocarril*
Rails	*Ferrocarriles*
Rail yard	*Corral de ferrocarriles*
Refrigerate (to)	*Refrigerar*
Refrigerated tank	*Tanque de refrigeración*
Refrigeration	*Refrigeración*
Reloading	*Recargar*
Rent (to)	*Alquilar*
Route	*Ruta*
Route (to)	*Encaminar*
Scrapping	*Chatarra*
Sea	*Mar*
Sea-lane	*Carril de mar*
Service	*Servicio*
Ship	*Barco*
Ship (to)	*Embarcar*
Shipper	*Fletador*
Station	*Estación*
Storage	*Almacenamiento*
Super tanker	*Supertanque*
Surface	*Superficie*
Tank	*Tanque*
Tanker	*Buque tanque*
Taxes	*Impuestos*
Tie-down (to)	*Amarrar*
Tonnage	*Tonelaje*
Track (to)	*Seguir la pista*
Tracks (railroad)	*Raíles*
Traffic	*Tráfico*
Traffic coordinator	*Coordinador de tráfico*
Train	*Tren*
Transloading	*Carga trasatlántica*
Transport	*Transporte*

Transport (to)	*Transportar*
Transport company	*Compañía de transporte*
Transporting	*Transportar*
Transporter	*Transportador*
Truck	*Camión*
Truck (to)	*Transportar por camión*
Trucking	*Camionaje*
Van	*Furgoneta*
Union	*Sindicato*
Union representative	*Representante de sindicato*
Unload (to)	*Descargar*
Warehouse	*Almacén*
Yard	*Corral*

TELECOMMUNICATIONS

(See also Computer Systems in the section Functional Areas of a Company in Chapter 5.)

Analog	*Analógico*
Bandwidth	*Ancho de banda*
Baud	*Baudio*
Cable	*Cable*
Capacity	*Capacidad*
Cellular	*Celular*
Cellular phone	*Teléfono celular/móvil*
Data	*Datos*
Data transmission	*Transmisión de datos*
Dedicated line	*Línea dedicada*

Digital	*Digital*
Downlink	*Enlace inferior*
DSL line	*Línea del DSL*
E-commerce	*E-commerce/Comercio electrónico*
E-mail	*Correo electrónico/ E-mail*
Fax/Facsimile	*Fax/Facsímil*
Fiber-optical line	*Línea de fibra óptica*
Hertz	*Hertzios*
High speed	*Alta velocidad*
Internet	*Internet*
Intranet	*Intranet*
Identification number (ID number)	*Número de identificación*
Internet Service Providers (ISPs)	*Proveedores de Servicios Internet*
Keyboard	*Teclado*
Keypad	*Almohadilla de teclado*
Local Area Network (LAN)	*Red de Area Local (LAN)*
Line	*Línea*
Link	*Enlace*
Liquid-crystal display	*Indicador de cristal líquido (LCD)*
Local call	*Llamada local*
Long distance	*Larga distancia*
Megahertz	*Megaciclo*
Menu	*Menú*
Mobile phone	*Teléfono móvil*
Modem	*Módem*

Network	*Red*
Palmtop	*Computadora de bolsillo*
Password	*Contraseña*
Personal digital assistant (PDA)	*Ayudante digital personal*
Phone line	*Línea de teléfono*
Resolution	*Resolución*
Satellite	*Satélite*
Security	*Seguridad*
Server	*Servidor*
Telecommunications	*Telecomunicaciones*
Telegram	*Telegrama*
Telephone	*Teléfono*
Transmit (to)	*Transmitir*
Transmission	*Transmisión*
Uplink	*Enlace superior*
Video conferencing	*Video conferencia*
Voice and data transmission	*Transmisión de voz y datos*
Voice mail	*Correo de voz*
Web	*Web*
Web page	*Página web*
Web site	*Sitio web*
Wireless	*Radio*
World Wide Web (WWW)	*Red mundial*

TEXTILE

Acidity	*Acidez*
Acrylic	*Acrílico*
Alkalinity	*Alcanilidad*
Apparel	*Ropa*

Artists	*Artistas*
Bonded types	*Tipos garantizados*
Braid	*Trenza*
Braided	*Trenzado*
Brocade	*Brocado*
Cloth	*Tela/Ropa*
Clothing	*Ropa*
Color	*Color*
Composite fabrics	*Tejidos compuestos*
Conventional methods	*Métodos convencionales*
Converter	*Convertidor*
Cotton	*Algodón*
Crimp	*Rizado*
Cutting	*Corte*
Cutting room	*Cuarto de corte*
Damask	*Damasquinado*
Defect	*Defecto*
Design	*Diseño*
Dry cleaning	*Tintorería*
Dyeing	*Tintura*
Dye	*Tinte*
Dye (to)	*Teñir*
Elasticity	*Elasticidad*
Elongation	*Elongación*
Embroidered	*Bordado*
Engineer	*Ingeniero*
Fabric	*Tela*
Fastness of finishes and colors	*Rapidez de terminados y colores*
Felt	*Fieltro*
Fiber	*Fibra*
Fiber mass	*Masa de fibras*

Fineness	*Excelencia*
Finished cloth	*Tela terminada*
Flame resistance	*Resistente a la llama*
Flax	*Lino*
Flexibility	*Flexibilidad*
Floral	*Floral*
Garment	*Prenda de vestir*
Geometric	*Geométrico*
Hand operations	*Operaciones manuales*
Insulation	*Aislamiento*
Interlacing	*Entrelazar*
Jute	*Yute*
Knit	*Tejer*
Knitted	*Tejido*
Knitting	*Trabajo de punto*
Lace	*Encaje*
Laundering	*Lavar*
Layer	*Capa*
Length	*Largo*
Licensing	*Licenciar*
Linen	*Lino*
Loom	*Telar*
Machinery	*Maquinaria*
Man-made fiber	*Fibra sintética*
Manufacture	*Manufactura*
Manufacturing operations	*Operaciones de manufactura*
Moisture absorption	*Absorción de humedad*
Natural fibers	*Fibras naturales*
Needle	*Aguja*
Needle woven	*Tejido con aguja*

Net	*Red*
Newer construction methods	*Métodos nuevos de construcción*
Nylon	*Nylon*
Ornament	*Ornamento*
Patterns	*Patrón*
Polyester	*Poliéster*
Polyester filament	*Filamento de poliéster*
Porosity	*Porosidad*
Printed	*Impreso*
Printing	*Imprenta*
Processing	*Procesamiento*
Production	*Producción*
Quality control	*Control de la calidad*
Quality label	*Etiqueta de calidad*
Rayon	*Rayón*
Reaction to heat, sunlight, chemicals	*Reacción al calor, luz solar, productos químicos*
Resistance to creases	*Resistencia a arrugas*
Resistance to pesticides, disease	*Resistencia a pesticidas, enfermedad*
Rug	*Alfombra*
Sew (to)	*Coser*
Sewing	*Coser*
Silk	*Seda*
Silk-screen (to)	*Serigrafía*
Spandex	*Fibra elástica (utilizada en la fabricación de tejidos)*
Specialization	*Especialización*

Spinning	Hilado
Stable-fiber	Fibra estable
Strength	Fuerza
Structure	Estructura
Synthetic fabric	Tejido sintético
Synthetic fiber	Fibra sintética

Tapestry	Tapiz
Technicians	Técnicos
Testing	Prueba
Texture	Textura
Thread	Hilo
Trade mark	Marca registrada
Traditional	Tradicional
Treat (to)	Tratar

| Uniform thickness | Grosor uniforme |

| Velvet | Terciopelo |
| Volume of production | Volumen de producción |

Water-repellent	Repelente al agua
Weave	Tejido
Weave (to)	Tejer
Weave and yarn structure	Estructura de tejido y hilado
Weaving	Tejer
Weight per unit area	Peso por unidad de área
Width	Ancho
Wool	Lana
Worsted	De estambre
Woven	Tejido

| Yarn | Hilado |
| Yard | Yarda |

TOYS

Action figure	*Figura de acción*
Activity set	*Juego de actividad*
Age compression	*Compresión de edad*
Airplane	*Aeroplano*
Animal	*Animal*
Articulation	*Articulación*
Art supplies	*Surtidos de arte*
Ball	*Pelota/Bola/Balón*
Battery	*Batería*
Blocks	*Bloques*
Board games	*Juegos de tablero*
Boat	*Bote*
Brand-name toy	*Juguete de marca*
Building blocks	*Bloques para edificar*
Building toys	*Juguetes para edificar*
Car	*Carro* (in Latin America)/*Coche* (in Spain)
Character	*Carácter*
Chemistry set	*Juego de química*
Children	*Niños*
Clay	*Arcilla*
Computer game	*Juego de computadora*
Creator	*Creador*
Dolls	*Muñecas*
Education software	*Software educativo*
Frisbee	*Frisbee*
Fun	*Diversión*
Fun (to have)	*Divertirse*
Game	*Juego*

Glue	*Goma*
Hobby kit	*Juego de pasatiempo*
Hobby horse	*Caballo de pasatiempo*
Hoop	*Aro*
Infant toy	*Juguete infantil*
Kaleidoscope	*Caleidoscopio*
Kit	*Juego*
Kite	*Cometa*
Letter	*Carta*
Marbles	*Canicas*
Microscope	*Microscopio*
Mobile	*Móvil*
Model	*Modelo*
Musical toy	*Juguete musical*
Novelty	*Novedad*
Part	*Pieza*
Picture book	*Libro de dibujos*
Pegboard	*Tablero*
Play	*Juego*
Play (to)	*Jugar*
Playing	*Jugar*
Playing cards	*Barajas*
Plastic	*Plástico*
Plush toy	*Juguete de felpa*
Preschool activity toy	*Juguete de actividad preescolar*
Puppet	*Marioneta*
Puzzle	*Rompecabeza*
Railroad	*Ferrocarril*
Rattle	*Matraca*

Re-issue	*Reemitir*
Riding toy	*Juguete para montar*
Rocket	*Cohete*
Rubber	*Goma*
Science set	*Juego científico*
Soldier	*Soldado*
Sports equipment	*Equipo de deportes*
Stuffed animal	*Animal de peluche*
Stuffed toy	*Juguete de peluche*
Teddy bear	*Osito de peluche*
Top	*Parte superior*
Trading card	*Tarjeta de intercambio*
Train	*Treno*
Vehicles	*Vehículos*
Video game	*Juego de video*
Wagon	*Carrito*
Wood	*Madera*
Woodburning set	*Juego para quemar madera*
Yo-yo	*Yoyo*

WATCHES, SCALES, AND PRECISION INSTRUMENTS

Analog	*Analógico*
Apparatus	*Aparato*
Balances	*Balanza*
Battery	*Batería/Pila*
Brass	*Latón*
Chain	*Cadena*
Chronograph	*Cronógrafo*

Clock	*Reloj*
Coil	*Rollo*
Digital	*Digital*
Display	*Exhibición*
Friction	*Fricción*
Gear	*Engranaje*
Gold	*Oro*
Instrument	*Instrumental*
Integrated circuit	*Circuito integrado*
Jewel	*Joya*
Laboratory	*Laboratorio*
Laser	*Láser*
Mainspring	*Muelle principal*
Measurement	*Medida*
Mechanism	*Mecanismo*
Miniature	*Miniatura*
Miniaturization	*Miniaturización*
Motion	*Movimiento*
Movement	*Movimiento*
Optical	*Óptico*
Oscillate (to)	*Oscilar*
Oscillation	*Oscilación*
Pin	*Alfiler*
Pivot	*Pivote*
Polished	*Pulido*
Precision	*Precisión*
Scale	*Peso*
Self-winding	*De cuerda automática*
Shaft	*Eje*
Silver	*Plata*

Spring	*Muelle*
Spring-driven	*Funcionamiento de muelles*
Steel	*Acero*
Stopwatch	*Cronómetro*
Time	*Tiempo*
Time (to)	*Cronometrar*
Timepiece	*Reloj*
Torque	*Par*
Transistor	*Transitor*
Watch	*Reloj*
Weight	*Peso*
Wheel	*Rueda*
Wristwatch	*Reloj de pulsera*

WINE

Acidity	*Acidez*
Age (to)	*Añejar*
Aging	*Añejamiento*
Alcohol	*Alcohol*
Aroma	*Aroma*
Barrel	*Barril*
Bordeaux	*Bordeaux*
Bottle	*Botella*
Bottle (to)	*Embotellar*
Bottled	*Embotellado*
Bubbles	*Burbujas*
Brandy	*Coñac*
Burgundy	*Burdeos*
Cabernet Sauvigon	*Cabernet Sauvigon*
Cask	*Tonel*
Cellar	*Bodega*
Champagne	*Champaña*
"Character" of the wine	*"Cuerpo" del vino*

Chardonnay	*Chardonnay*
Chianti	*Chianti*
Clarifying	*Aclarar*
Climate	*Clima*
Color	*Color*
Cool	*Fresco*
Cork	*Corcho*
Cork (to)	*Tapar con corcho*
Crush (to)	*Triturar*
Crusher	*Triturador*
Drink (to)	*Beber*
Dry	*Seco*
Estate	*Hacienda*
Ferment (to)	*Fermentar*
Fermentation	*Fermentación*
Flavor	*Sabor*
Flavor (to)	*Saborear*
Flavored wines	*Vinos de sabores*
Fortified wines	*Vinos fortificados*
Grape(s)	*Uva(s)*
Grow (to)	*Cultivar*
Harvest	*Cosechar*
Herb	*Hierba*
Humidity	*Humedad*
Label	*Etiqueta*
Label (to)	*Poner etiquetas*
Merlot	*Merlot*
Must	*Mosto*
Oak	*Roble*
Pinot Noir	*Pinot Noir*

Port	*Oporto*
Precipitate	*Precipitar*
Pulp	*Pulpa*
Red wine	*Vino tinto*
Refine (to)	*Refinar*
Refrigerate (to)	*Refrigerar*
Refrigeration	*Refrigeración*
Region	*Región*
Riesling	*Riesling*
Rosé wine	*Vino rosado*
Seeds	*Semillas*
Sherry	*Jerez*
Soil	*Tierra*
Sparkling wines	*Vinos burbujeantes*
Store (to)	*Almacenar*
Sugar	*Azúcar*
Sweet	*Dulce*
Table wines	*Vinos de mesa*
Tank	*Tanque*
Taste (to)	*Saborear*
Tasting	*Saborear*
Varietals	*Variedades*
Vermouth	*Vermut*
Vine	*Vid/Viña*
Vineyard	*Viñedo*
Vinifera grapes	*Uvas*
Vintage	*Vino añejo*
White wine	*Vino blanco*
Wine	*Vino*
Winery	*Compañía de vinos*
Yeast	*Levadura*

GENERAL GLOSSARY:
English–Spanish

A

Accent	*Acento*
Accept (to)	*Aceptar*
Acceptable	*Aceptable*
Accountability	*Responsabilidad*
Accounting	*Contabilidad*
Accounts receivable	*Cuentas por pagar*
Accounts payable	*Cuentas por cobrar*
Activity	*Actividad*
Ad	*Anuncio*
Address	*Dirección*
Administration	*Administración*
Administrative assistant	*Ayudante/Asistente de administración*
Admission	*Admisión*
Agenda	*Agenda*
Agree (to)	*Acordar/Estar de acuerdo*
Agreement	*Acuerdo*
Airport	*Aeropuerto*
Airport shuttle	*Aeropuerto de enlace*
American	*Norteamericano*
Amusement	*Diversión*
Amusement park	*Parque de diversiones/de alracciones*
Answer	*Respuesta*
Answer (to)	*Contestar*
Answering machine	*Grabadora automática/ Contestador automático*
Apology	*Disculpa*

Appointment	*Cita*
Appraise (to)	*Evaluar*
Aqua	*Aguamarina*
Arc	*Arco*
Area	*Area*
Argue (to)	*Discutir*
Arrow	*Flecha*
Art	*Arte*
Art gallery	*Galería de arte*
Article	*Artículo*
Ask (to)	*Preguntar*
Associate	*Asociado/Socio*
Asterisk	*Asterisco*
Attachment	*Adjunto*
Attention	*Atención*
Audio	*Audio*
Audit	*Intervención/Auditoría*
Audit (to)	*Intervenir/Hacer una auditoría*
Authority	*Autoridad*
Authorize (to)	*Autorizar*
Auto	*Auto*

B

Background	*Antecedentes*
Badge	*Insignia*
Bag	*Maleta*
Balcony	*Balcón*
Ballet	*Ballet*
Bar	*Barra*
Bar chart	*Diagrama de barra*
Bargain (to)	*Negociar*
Basketball	*Baloncesto*
Bathroom	*Baño*

Bed	*Cama*
Begin (to)	*Comenzar*
Beginning	*Comienzo*
Behavior	*Conducta*
Bell-shaped curve	*Curva en forma de campana*
Benefits	*Beneficios*
Bill	*Cuenta*
Bill of sale	*Comprobante de venta*
Bin	*Papelera*
Black	*Negro*
Blackboard	*Pizarra*
Blank	*Blanco*
Blouse	*Blusa*
Blue	*Azul*
Board	*Tablero*
Bold	*Negrita*
Bond	*Fianza*
Bonus	*Bonificación*
Book	*Libro*
Bookmark	*Marcador*
Booth	*Cabina*
Boss	*Jefe*
Bottom	*Pie*
Box	*Palco*
Box seat	*Asiento de palco*
Breakfast	*Desayuno*
Brochure	*Folleto*
Brown	*Carmelita/Marrón*
Buffet	*Buffet*
Building	*Edificio*
Bus	*Autobús*
Business	*Negocio*
Business card	*Tarjeta de presentación*

Business center	*Centro comercial*
Busy	*Ocupado*
Buy (to)	*Comprar*

C

Cabinet	*Gabinete*
Cafe	*Café*
Cake	*Torta*
Calculus	*Cálculo*
Calendar	*Calendario*
Call (to)	*Llamar*
Calling card	*Tarjeta de presentación*
Camera	*Cámara*
Capability	*Capacidad*
Car	*Carro* (in Latin America)/*Coche* (in Spain)
Career	*Carrera*
Car phone	*Teléfono de automóvil*
Cash	*Efectivo*
Cash a check (to)	*Cambiar un cheque*
Cat	*Gato*
Cellular phone	*Teléfono celular/móvil*
Center	*Centro*
Central	*Central*
Central office	*Oficina central*
Central thesis	*Tesis central*
Centralization	*Centralización*
Certified check	*Cheque certificado*
Certified mail	*Correo certificado*
Chair	*Silla*
Chairman	*Presidente del consejo de dirección*

Chairperson	*Presidente/a del consejo de dirección*
Chairwoman	*Presidenta del consejo de dirección*
Chalk	*Tiza*
Change (to)	*Cambiar*
Chart	*Gráfico*
Check	*Cheque*
Check (to)	*Revisar*
Check in (to)	*Registrarse*
Chicken	*Pollo*
Child	*Niño*
Children	*Niños*
Clothing	*Ropa*
Church	*Iglesia*
Cigar	*Puro/Tabaco*
Cigarette	*Cigarrillo*
Circle	*Círculo*
City	*Ciudad*
Classical music	*Música clásica*
Classroom	*Aula/Salón de clase*
Clear (to)	*Despejar*
Clock	*Reloj de pared*
Close (to)	*Cerrar*
Cloudy	*Nublado*
Coach (to)	*Entrenar*
Coaching	*Entrenamiento*
Coat	*Abrigo*
Cocktail	*Cóctel*
Cocktail party	*Cóctel*
Coffee	*Café*
Cold	*Frío*
Cold call	*Llamada sin aviso*
Color	*Color*
Color monitor	*Monitor de colores*

Column	*Columna*
Comedy	*Comedia*
Communicate (to)	*Comunicarse*
Communications	*Comunicaciones*
Compensate (to)	*Compensar*
Compensation	*Compensación*
Compete (to)	*Competir*
Competition	*Competencia*
Competitive price	*Precio competitivo*
Computer	*Computadora* (in Latin America)/ *Ordinador* (in Spain)
Computer cable	*Cable de computadora/ ordenador*
Computer disk	*Disco de computadora/ ordenador*
Computer monitor	*Monitor de computadora/ ordenador*
Concert	*Concierto*
Concert hall	*Salón de conciertos*
Concierge	*Conserje*
Conference	*Conferencia*
Conference call	*Llamada de conferencia*
Conference center	*Centro de conferencias*
Conflict	*Conflicto*
Confirm (to)	*Confirmar*
Confirmation	*Confirmación*
Consult (to)	*Consultar*
Consultant	*Consultante/Asesor*
Convince (to)	*Convencer*
Cool	*Fresco*
Co-owner	*Condueño/ Copropietario*

Co-partner	*Consocio*
Connection	*Conexión*
Contact (to)	*Contactar/Ponerse en contacto con*
Contract	*Contrato*
Contractual obligation	*Obligación contractual*
Converter	*Convertidor*
Convince (to)	*Convencer*
Copier	*Fotocopiadora*
Copy	*Copia*
Copyright	*Derechos literarios*
Corner office	*Oficina de esquina*
Cost	*Costo*
Country	*País*
Course	*Curso*
Cover	*Cubierta*
Cream	*Crema*
Crosshatched	*Entretejido*
Cultural	*Cultural*
Culture	*Cultura*
Curve	*Curva*
Customer	*Cliente*
Customer service	*Servicio al cliente*
Customs	*Aduana*
Cyberspace	*Ciberespacio*

D

Dais	*Tarima*
Dash	*Guión*
Data	*Datos*
Database	*Base de datos*
Date	*Fecha*
Day	*Día*
Daughter	*Hija*

Deadline	*Fecha tope/Límite*
Deal	*Negocio/Trato*
Decentralization	*Descentralización*
Decide (to)	*Decidir*
Decision	*Decisión*
Decision making	*Toma de decisión*
Deferred compensation	*Compesación diferida*
Delivery	*Entrega*
Delivery date	*Fecha de entrega*
Demonstrate (to)	*Demostrar*
Demonstration	*Demostración*
Department	*Departamento*
Desk	*Escritorio*
Design	*Diseño*
Diagram	*Diagrama*
Diagram (to)	*Diagramar*
Dial	*Disco*
Dial (to)	*Discar/Marcar*
Dialogue	*Diálogo*
Dinner	*Cena*
Direct (to)	*Dirigir*
Directions	*Direcciones*
Direct line	*Línea directa*
Director	*Director*
Directory	*Directorio*
Disco	*Discoteca*
Discuss (to)	*Hablar sobre*
Discussion	*Charla*
Display	*Exhibición*
Display (to)	*Exhibir*
Distribute (to)	*Distribuir*
Distribution	*Distribución*
Doctor	*Médico*
Document	*Documento*
Dog	*Perro*

Dollar	*Dólar*
Door	*Puerta*
Download (to)	*Descargar*
Down payment	*Pago inicial*
Downsize (to)	*Reducir*
Dotted line	*Línea de puntos*
Drama	*Drama*
Due	*Vencido*

E

Easel	*Caballete*
Earlier	*Más temprano*
Early	*Temprano*
Edge	*Borde*
Eight	*Ocho*
Electrical line	*Línea eléctrica*
Electricity	*Electricidad*
Ellipse	*Elipse*
E-mail	*Correo electrónico*
Enclosure	*Adjunto*
Encourage (to)	*Animar*
End	*Final*
End (to)	*Finalizar*
Engineer	*Ingeniero*
English	*Inglés*
Enjoy (to)	*Disfrutar*
Enterprise	*Empresa*
Entrance	*Entrada*
Entrepreneur	*Empresario;*
	Hombre/Mujer de
	empresa
Envelope	*Sobre*
Erase (to)	*Borrar*
Eraser	*Borrador*

Espresso	*Espresso*
Evening	*Noche*
Excel software	*Software de Excel*
Exhibit	*Exhibición*
Exhibit (to)	*Exhibir*
Exit	*Salida*
Exit (to)	*Salir*
Expenses	*Gastos*
Experience	*Experiencia*
Exponential	*Exponente*
Export (to)	*Exportar*
Extension	*Extensión*
Extension cord	*Alargo eléctrico*

F

Facilitate (to)	*Facilitar*
Facilitator	*Facilitador*
Fall (season)	*Otoño*
Family	*Familia*
Fax	*Fax*
Fax (to)	*Mandar por fax*
Feedback	*Reacción*
Feedback (to)	*Reaccionar*
Ferry	*Transbordador*
File	*Archivo*
File (to)	*Archivar*
File cabinet	*Archivo*
Film	*Película*
Finance	*Finanza*
Finance (to)	*Financiar*
Financial figures	*Cifras financieras*
Financial report	*Informe financiero*
Find (to)	*Encontrar*
Findings	*Conclusiones*

First	*Primero*
Fish	*Pescado*
Five	*Cinco*
Flat-panel display	*Pantalla plana*
Flight	*Vuelo*
Flower	*Flor*
Folder	*Carpeta*
Follow up (to)	*Dar seguimiento*
Food	*Comida*
Football	*Fútbol americano*
Foreman	*Capataz*
Forward (to)	*Remitir a*
Found	*Encontrado*
Four	*Cuatro*
Front	*Frente*

G

Gain (to)	*Ganar*
Gallery	*Galería*
Gate	*Puerta de embarque*
Geometry	*Geometría*
Give (to)	*Dar*
Glass	*Cristal*
Goal	*Objetivo*
Good	*Bueno(a)*
Good-bye	*Adiós*
Goods	*Mercancías*
Grandparent	*Abuelo(a)*
Grant	*Subsidio*
Graph (to)	*Diagramar*
Graph	*Gráfico*
Green	*Verde*
Grid	*Malla*
Guarantee	*Garantía*

| Guarantee (to) | *Garantizar* |
| Guard | *Guardia* |

H

Handout	*Papel*
Hang up (to)	*Colgar*
Hat	*Sombrero*
Heading	*Encabezamiento*
Health	*Salud*
Hello	*Hola*
Help (to)	*Ayudar*
Helpful	*Servicial*
Histogram	*Histograma*
History	*Historia*
Hobby	*Pasatiempo/Hobby*
Hold (to)	*Aguantar*
Home page	*Página inicial*
Hope (to)	*Esperar*
Horizontal	*Horizontal*
Horizontal bar chart	*Gráfico de barra horizontal*
Horse	*Caballo*
Hot	*Caliente*
Hotel	*Hotel*
Hour	*Hora*
House	*Casa*
Human resources	*Personal/recursos humanos*
Husband	*Esposo*
Hypertext	*Hipertexto*

I

| Ice cream | *Helado* |
| Idea | *Idea* |

330

Illustrate (to)	*Ilustrar*
Illustration	*Ilustración*
Import (to)	*Importar*
Individual	*Individual/Individuo*
Inform (to)	*Informar*
Information	*Información*
Information desk	*Información*
Inside	*Dentro*
Insight	*Perspicacia*
Install (to)	*Instalar*
Installation	*Instalación*
Insurance	*Seguro*
Intelligence	*Inteligencia*
Intelligent	*Inteligente*
International	*Internacional*
International law	*Ley internacional*
Internet	*Internet*
Interview	*Entrevista*
Interview (to)	*Entrevistar*
Introduce (to)	*Presentar*
Introduction	*Introducción*
Inventory	*Inventario*
Invest (to)	*Invertir*
Investment	*Inversión*
Invoice	*Factura*
Invoice (to)	*Facturar*
Issue (to)	*Emitir*
Item	*Artículo*

J

Jazz	*Jazz*
Jazz club	*Club de jazz*
Jewelry	*Joyas*
Job	*Trabajo*

Joke	*Broma*
Joke (to)	*Bromear*

K

Karate	*Karate*
Key issues	*Temas principales*
Know (to)	*Saber*
Knowledge	*Conocimiento*

L

Label	*Etiqueta*
Label (to)	*Poner una etiqueta*
Language	*Lenguaje*
Laptop computer	*Computadora/ Ordenador portátil*
Last	*Ultimo*
Late	*Tarde*
Later	*Más tarde*
Law	*Ley*
Lawsuit	*Pleito*
Lawyer	*Abogado*
Layout	*Diseño*
Lead (to)	*Dirigir*
Leader	*Líder*
Leadership	*Liderazgo*
Leading	*Destacado*
Learn (to)	*Aprender*
Left	*Izquierda*
Legal	*Legal*
Legal cost	*Costo legal*
Letter	*Carta*
Liability	*Fiabilidad*
Library	*Biblioteca*

Light	*Luz*
Light bulb	*Bombilla*
Like (to)	*Gustar*
Limousine	*Limusina*
Line	*Línea*
Linear	*Lineal*
Line graph	*Gráfico de línea*
Link	*Enlace*
List (to)	*Enumerar*
Listen (to)	*Escuchar*
Literature	*Información escrita*
Local	*Local*
Local call	*Llamada local*
Location	*Posición*
Logarithmic scale	*Escala logarítmica*
Logo	*Logotipo*
Log off (to)	*Terminar la conexión*
Log on (to)	*Comenzar la conexión*
Long distance	*Larga distancia*
Long distance call	*Llamada de larga distancia*
Look (to)	*Mirar*
Lotus 1-2-3 software	*Software de Lotus 1-2-3*
Luggage	*Equipaje*
Lunch	*Almuerzo*
Luncheon	*Almuerzo*

M

Magazine	*Revista*
Mail	*Correo*
Mail (to)	*Enviar por correo*
Mailing list	*Lista de distribución*
Mail order	*Pedido por correo*

Mainframe computer	*Computadora/ Ordenador central*
Make (to)	*Hacer*
Management	*Administración/ Gestión*
Manage (to)	*Administrar/Gestionar*
Manager	*Gerente*
Map	*Mapa*
Marker	*Marcador*
Market	*Mercado*
Market (to)	*Comercializar*
Marketing	*Marketing*
Marketing report	*Informe de mercadeo*
Market value	*Valor de mercado*
Material	*Material*
Mathematics	*Matemáticas*
Maximum	*Máximo*
Maybe	*Quizás*
Meat	*Carne*
Media	*Medios de comunicación*
Mediate (to)	*Mediar*
Meet (to)	*Reunirse*
Meeting	*Reunión*
Memo	*Memoranda*
Men's room	*Baño de caballeros*
Mentor	*Mentor*
Mentoring	*Ser mentor*
Menu	*Menú*
Message	*Mensaje*
Message center	*Central de mensajes*
Mezzanine	*Entresuelo*
Microphone	*Micrófono*
Middle	*Medio*

Milk	*Leche*
Mineral water	*Agua mineral*
Minimum	*Mínimo*
Minute	*Minuto*
Mission	*Misión*
Model	*Modelo*
Modem	*Módem*
Money	*Dinero*
Monitor	*Monitor*
Month	*Mes*
Morning	*Mañana*
Mosque	*Mezquita*
Move (to)	*Mover*
Movie	*Película*
Multimedia	*Multimedia*
Museum	*Museo*
Music	*Música*
Musical	*Obra musical*

N

Name	*Nombre*
Name (to)	*Nombrar*
Need (to)	*Necesitar*
Negotiate (to)	*Negociar*
Negotiating	*Negociando*
Network	*Red*
New	*Nuevo*
News	*Noticias*
Newsstand	*Quiosco/Puesto de periódicos*
Night	*Noche*
Nine	*Nueve*
No	*No*

Note	*Nota*
Note (to)	*Anotar*
Note pads	*Bloc de notas*
Number	*Número*
Nurse	*Enfermera(o)*

O

Object	*Objeto*
Objective	*Objetivo*
Offer (to)	*Ofrecer*
Office	*Oficina*
Officer	*Funcionario*
Okay (to)	*Aprobar*
One	*Uno*
Online	*En línea*
Online service	*Servicio en línea*
On/off	*Encendido/apagado*
Open (to)	*Abrir*
Opera	*Ópera*
Operate (to)	*Operar*
Operating system	*Sistema operativo*
Operations	*Operaciones*
Operator	*Operador*
Option	*Opción*
Orange	*Naranja*
Orchestra	*Orquesta*
Organization	*Organización*
Organization chart	*Gráfico de organización*
Organize (to)	*Organizar*
Orientation	*Orientación*
Origin	*Origen*
Outside	*Fuera*
Overhead projector	*Retroproyector*

Package	*Paquete*
Package (to)	*Empacar*
Paper	*Papel*
Page	*Página*
Page (to)	*Enviar un mensaje al beeper*
Pager	*Beeper*
Parent	*Padre*
Park	*Parque*
Part	*Parte/Pieza*
Participant	*Participante*
Participate	*Participar*
Partner	*Socio*
Passport	*Pasaporte*
Password	*Contraseña*
Past due	*Vencido*
Patent	*Patente*
Pause (to)	*Pausar*
Payment	*Pago*
Peer	*Igual*
Pencil	*Lápiz*
Pension	*Pensión*
Percentage	*Porcentaje*
Personnel	*Personal*
Pet	*Animal*
Philosophy	*Filosofía*
Phone	*Teléfono*
Phone (to)	*Telefonear*
Phone call	*Llamada telefónica*
Photocopy (to)	*Fotocopiaz*
Photograph	*Fotografía*
Picture	*Fotografía/Cuadro*
Pie	*Pastel*

Pie chart	*Gráfico circunferencial*
Ping pong	*Ping pong*
Place (to)	*Colocar*
Plan (to)	*Planificar*
Play	*Partido*
Play (to)	*Jugar*
Please	*Por favor*
Podium	*Podio*
Point	*Punto*
Point (to)	*Indicar*
Pointer	*Pista/Indicador*
Police man	*Policía*
Policy	*Política*
Polygon	*Polígono*
Pork	*Puerco*
Portable	*Portátil*
Portable phone	*Teléfono portátil*
Portal	*Portal*
Porter	*Portero*
Position	*Posición*
Post office	*Correos*
Postpone (to)	*Posponer*
Pound key/sign	*Cuadradito/ Almohadilla*
PowerPoint presentation	*Presentación PowerPoint*
Present (to)	*Presentar*
Presentation	*Presentación*
Presenting	*Presentar*
President	*Presidente*
Price	*Precio*
Print (to)	*Imprimir*
Printer	*Impresora*
Problem	*Problema*
Problem solving	*Solución de problema*

Procedure	*Procedimiento*
Process	*Proceso*
Procure (to)	*Procurar*
Produce (to)	*Producir*
Product	*Producto*
Production	*Producción*
Program	*Programa*
Promotion	*Promoción*
Property	*Propiedad*
Propose (to)	*Proponer*
Proposal	*Propuesta*
Provide (to)	*Proveer*
Purchasing agent	*Agente comprador*
Purple	*Morado*
Purpose	*Propósito*

Q

Quality	*Calidad*
Quality control	*Control de calidad*
Query	*Pregunta*
Question	*Pregunta*
Question (to)	*Preguntar*
Q&A	*Pregunta y Respuesta*
Quiet	*Silencio*

R

Rain/rainy	*Lluvia/lluvioso*
Rare	*Raro*
Reboot	*Reiniciar*
Receive (to)	*Recibir*
Receiver	*Auricular*
Reception	*Recepción*
Receptionist	*Recepcionista*

Recommend (to)	*Recomendar*
Recommendation	*Recomendación*
Reconsider (to)	*Reconsiderar*
Record	*Registro*
Record (to)	*Registrar/Grabar*
Recording	*Registro/Grabación*
Rectangle	*Rectángulo*
Red	*Rojo*
Redial (to)	*Volver a marcar*
Referral	*Remisión*
Reference	*Referencia*
Reference (to)	*Referenciar*
Refreshments	*Refrescos*
Refund	*Devolución*
Register (to)	*Registrar*
Regression	*Regresión*
Regression line	*Línea de regresión*
Rehearse	*Ensayar*
Reject (to)	*Rechazar*
Rent	*Alquiler*
Rent (to)	*Alquilar*
Reorganize (to)	*Reorganizar*
Reply	*Contestación*
Reply (to)	*Contestar*
Report	*Informe*
Request (to)	*Solicitar*
Reservation	*Reserva*
Reserve (to)	*Reservar*
Reserved	*Reservado*
Restaurant	*Restaurante*
Restroom	*Baño*
Result	*Resultado*
Resume (to)	*Reanudar*
Return (to)	*Regresar*
Reveal (to)	*Revelar*

Right	*Derecho*
Right angle	*Angulo recto*
Risk	*Riesgo*
Risk (to)	*Arriesgar*
Room	*Habitación*
Row	*Fila*
Rugby	*Rugby*

S

Salary	*Salario*
Sale	*Venta*
Sales call	*Venta*
Sales reports	*Informes de venta*
Sales tax	*Impuesto de venta*
Say (to)	*Decir*
Scale	*Escala*
Scatter diagram	*Diagrama disperso*
Schedule	*Horario*
Science	*Ciencia*
Science fiction	*Ciencia ficción*
Screen	*Pantalla*
Scuba	*Buceo*
Search engine	*Motor de búsqueda*
Season	*Estación*
Second	*Segundo*
Secretary	*Secretaria*
See (to)	*Ver*
Sell (to)	*Vender*
Seminar	*Seminario*
Send (to)	*Enviar*
Service	*Servicio*
Set up (to)	*Montar/Contigurar (in computers)*
Seven	*Siete*

Server	*Servidor*
Service	*Servicio*
Shaded	*Sombreado*
Shadow	*Sombra*
Ship (to)	*Embarcar/Enviar*
Shipment	*Embarque/Envío*
Shipping center	*Central de envíos*
Shoe	*Zapato*
Show (to)	*Mostrar*
Sightseeing	*Visita turística*
Sign (to)	*Firmar*
Six	*Seis*
Skiing	*Esquiar*
Skill	*Habilidad*
Skirt	*Falda*
Slice	*Pedazo*
Slide projector	*Proyector de diapositivas*
Slide	*Diapositiva*
Snack	*Merienda*
Snow	*Nieve*
Snowy	*Nevoso*
Soccer	*Fútbol*
Sock	*Calcetin*
Software	*Software*
Solid	*Entero*
Solid line	*Línea continua*
Solve (a problem) (to)	*Resolver (un problema)*
Son	*Hijo*
Sound system	*Sistema de sonido*
Souvenir	*Souvenir*
Space	*Espacio*
Speak (to)	*Hablar*
Speaker	*Orador/Altavoz*

Special delivery	*Entrega inmediata*
Specialty	*Especialidad*
Specification(s)	*Especificación/ Especificaciones*
Speech	*Discurso*
Spring	*Primavera*
Sports	*Deportes*
Square	*Cuadrado*
Stack	*Pila*
Star	*Estrella*
Start	*Comienzo*
Steak	*Bisté*
Stock	*Acción*
Stockholder	*Accionista*
Stocking	*Media*
Stock options	*Opción sobre acciones*
Stop	*Parada*
Street	*Calle*
Stress	*Tensión*
Style	*Estilo*
Subject	*Tema*
Submit	*Someter*
Suit	*Traje*
Summer	*Verano*
Supervisor	*Supervisor*
Supply	*Suministro*
Supply (to)	*Suministrar*
Support (to)	*Apoyar*
Surf (to)	*Navegar*
Surf the Web	*Navegar por la red*
Switch	*Interruptor*
Switch (to)	*Cambiar*
Switchboard	*Central telefónica*
Synagogue	*Sinagoga*
System	*Sistema*

Table	*Tabla*
Tailor	*Sastre*
Talk (to)	*Hablar*
Tape recorder	*Grabadora*
Tax	*Impuesto*
Tax-exempt	*Exento de impuesto*
Taxi	*Taxi*
Tea	*Té*
Team	*Equipo*
Team building	*Edificación de grupo*
Technical support	*Asesoramiento técnico*
Telephone	*Teléfono*
Telephone directory	*Guía de teléfono*
Telephone number	*Número de teléfono*
Telephone operator	*Operadora de teléfono*
Television	*Televisión*
Temperature	*Temperatura*
Ten	*Diez*
Terminology	*Terminología*
Text	*Texto*
Thank you	*Gracias*
Theater	*Teatro*
Theory	*Teoría*
Thesis	*Tesis*
Three	*Tres*
3-D chart	*Gráfico tridimensional*
Ticket	*Boleto/Billete*
Tie	*Corbata*
Time	*Hora*
Time (to)	*Cronometrar*
Title	*Título*
Tobacco	*Tabaco*

Today	*Hoy*
Tomorrow	*Mañana*
Top	*Superior*
Tour	*Gira*
Tour bus	*Autobús turístico*
Town	*Pueblo*
Trade	*Comercio*
Trade (to)	*Comerciar*
Trademark	*Marca registrada*
Trade show	*Feria comercial*
Trade union	*Sindicato*
Train (to)	*Adiestrar*
Training	*Adiestramiento/ Formación*
Transact (to)	*Negociar*
Transaction	*Transacción*
Transfer (to)	*Transferir*
Transparency	*Transparencia*
Transportation	*Transporte*
Transportation charges	*Cargos de transporte*
Travel	*Viaje*
Travel (to)	*Viajar*
Treasurer	*Tesorero*
Triangle	*Triángulo*
Turn (to)	*Girar*
Two	*Dos*
Type	*Tipo (de imprenta)*
Type (to)	*Escribir a máquina*
Typewriter	*Máquina de escribir*

U

| Umbrella | *Sombrilla/Paraguas* |
| Unacceptable | *Inaceptable* |

Underline	*Subrayar*
Understand (to)	*Entender*
Understanding	*Entendimiento*
Underwear	*Ropa interior*
Union	*Sindicato*
United States of America	*Estados Unidos de Norteamérica*
U-shaped	*En forma de U*
U-turn	*Giro de 180°*

V

Value	*Valor*
Value (to)	*Valorar*
Value added tax	*Impuesto sobre el valor añadido*
Vegetable	*Vegetal/Verdura*
Vegetarian	*Vegetariano*
Vertical	*Vertical*
Via	*Vía*
Vice president	*Vicepresidente*
Video	*Vídeo*
Video (to)	*Grabar en vídeo*
Video conferencing	*Videoconferencia*
Video recorder	*Grabador de vídeo*
Virtual reality	*Realidad virtual*
Vision	*Visión*
Voice mail	*Correo de voz*
Voice recognition	*Reconocimiento de voz*

W

Wait (to)	*Esperar*
Waiting room	*Sala de espera*

Want (to)	*Querer*
Warm	*Templado*
Warranty	*Garantía*
Watch (to)	*Vigilar*
Water	*Agua*
Weather	*Tiempo*
Web access	*Acceso a Internet*
Week	*Semana*
Well	*Bien*
Well done	*Bien hecho*
Wife	*Esposa*
Window	*Ventana*
Wine	*Vino*
Wine list	*Lista de vinos*
Winter	*Invierno*
Women's Room	*Baño de señoras*
Word software	*Word*
WordPerfect software	*WordPerfect*
Work (to)	*Trabajar*
Workbook	*Cuaderno de trabajo*
Workshop	*Taller de trabajo*
Work station	*Puesto de trabajo*
World Wide Web	*Red mundial*
Write (to)	*Escribir*

X

X-axis	*Eje de abscisas*
XY scatter	*Dispersión XY*

Y

Y-axis	*Eje de ordenadas*
Yellow	*Amarillo*

Yes	*Sí*
Yield	*Rendimiento*
You're welcome	*Bienvenido*

Z

| Z-axis | *Eje de altura* |
| Zoo | *Zoológico* |

GENERAL GLOSSARY:
Spanish–English

A

Abogado	*Lawyer*
Abrigo	*Coat*
Abrir	*Open (to)*
Abuelo/a	*Grandfather/ Grandmother*
Acceso a Web	*Web access*
Acceso a Internet	*Web access*
Acción	*Stock*
Accionista	*Stockholder*
Acento	*Accent*
Aceptable	*Acceptable*
Aceptar	*Accept (to)*
Acordar	*Agree (to)*
Actividad	*Activity*
Acuerdo	*Agreement*
Adiestramiento	*Training*
Adiestrar	*Train (to)*
Adiós	*Good-bye*
Adjunto	*Attachment*
Adjunto	*Enclosure*
Administración	*Administration*
Administración	*Management*
Administrar	*Manage (to)*
Admisión	*Admission*
Aduana	*Customs*
Aeropuerto	*Airport*
Aeropuerto de enlace	*Airport shuttle*
Agenda	*Agenda*
Agente comprador	*Purchasing agent*
Agua	*Water*

Agua mineral	*Mineral water*
Aguamarina	*Aqua*
Aguantar	*Hold (to)*
Almohadilla	*Pound key*
Almuerzo	*Lunch*
Almuerzo	*Luncheon*
Alquilar	*Rent (to)*
Alquiler	*Rent*
Altavoz	*Speaker*
Amarillo	*Yellow*
Ángulo recto	*Right angle*
Animal	*Pet*
Animar	*Encourage (to)*
Anotar	*Note (to)*
Antecedentes	*Background*
Anuncio	*Ad*
Apoyar	*Support (to)*
Aprender	*Learn (to)*
Aprobar	*Okay (to)*
Arco	*Arc*
Archivar	*File (to)*
Archivo	*File*
Archivo	*File cabinet*
Area	*Area*
Arriesgar	*Risk (to)*
Arte	*Art*
Artículo	*Article*
Artículo	*Item*
Asesor	*Consultant*
Asesoramiento técnico	*Technical support*
Asiento de palco	*Box seat*
Asistente de administración	*Administrative assistant*
Asociado	*Associate*
Asterisco	*Asterisk*

Atención	*Attention*
Audio	*Audio*
Auditoría	*Audit*
Auricular	*Receiver*
Auto	*Auto*
Autobús	*Bus*
Autobús turístico	*Tour bus*
Autoridad	*Authority*
Autorizar	*Authorize (to)*
Ayudar	*Help (to)*
Ayudante	*Assistant*
Azul	*Blue*

B

Balcón	*Balcony*
Baloncesto	*Basketball*
Ballet	*Ballet*
Baño	*Bathroom*
Baño	*Restroom*
Baño de caballeros	*Men's room*
Baño de señoras	*Women's Room*
Barra	*Bar*
Base de datos	*Database*
Beeper	*Pager*
Beneficios	*Benefits*
Biblioteca	*Library*
Bien	*Well*
Bien hecho	*Well done*
Bienvenido	*You're welcome*
Billete	*Ticket*
Bisté	*Steak*
Blanco	*Blank*
Bloc de notas	*Notepad*
Blusa	*Blouse*

Boleto	*Ticket*
Bombilla	*Lightbulb*
Bonificación	*Bonus*
Borde	*Edge*
Borrador	*Eraser*
Borrar	*Erase (to)*
Broma	*Joke*
Bromear	*Joke (to)*
Buceo	*Scuba*
Bueno(a)	*Good*
Buffet	*Buffet*

C

Caballete	*Easel*
Caballo	*Horse*
Cabina	*Booth*
Cable de computadora	*Computer cable* (in Latin America)
Cable de ordenodor	*Computer cable* (in Spain)
Café	*Cafe*
Café	*Coffee*
Calcetin	*Sock*
Cálculo	*Calculus*
Calendario	*Calendar*
Calidad	*Quality*
Caliente	*Hot*
Calle	*Street*
Cama	*Bed*
Cámara	*Camera*
Cambiar	*Change (to)*
Cambiar	*Switch (to)*
Cambiar un cheque	*Cash a check (to)*
Capacidad	*Capability*

Capataz	*Foreman*
Cargos de transporte	*Transportation charges*
Carmelita	*Brown*
Carne	*Meat*
Carpeta	*Folder*
Carrera	*Career*
Carro	*Car* (in Latin America)
Carta	*Letter*
Casa	*House*
Cena	*Dinner*
Central	*Central*
Central de embarques	*Shipping center*
Central de mensajes	*Message center*
Central telefónica	*Switchboard*
Centralización	*Centralization*
Centro	*Center*
Centro comercial	*Business center*
Centro de conferencias	*Conference center*
Cerrar	*Close (to)*
Ciberespacio	*Cyberspace*
Ciencia	*Science*
Ciencia Ficción	*Science fiction*
Cifras financieras	*Financial figures*
Cigarrillo	*Cigarette*
Cinco	*Five*
Círculo	*Circle*
Cita	*Appointment*
Ciudad	*City*
Cliente	*Customer*
Club de jazz	*Jazz club*
Coche	*Car* (in Spain)
Cóctel	*Cocktail*
Cóctel	*Cocktail party*
Colgar	*Hang up (to)*

Colocar	*Place (to)*
Color	*Color*
Columna	*Column*
Comedia	*Comedy*
Comenzar	*Begin (to)*
Comenzar la conexión	*Log on (to)*
Comercializar	*Market (to)*
Comerciar	*Trade (to)*
Comercio	*Trade*
Comida	*Food*
Comienzo	*Beginning*
Comienzo	*Start*
Compensación	*Compensation*
Compensar	*Compensate (to)*
Compesación diferida	*Deferred compensation*
Competencia	*Competition*
Competir	*Compete (to)*
Comprar	*Buy (to)*
Comprobante de venta	*Bill of sale*
Computadora	*Computer* (in Latin America)
Computadora central	*Mainframe computer* (in Latin America)
Computadora portátil	*Laptop computer* (in Latin America)
Comunicaciones	*Communications*
Comunicarse	*Communicate (to)*
Concierto	*Concert*
Conclusiones	*Findings*
Conducta	*Behavior*
Condueño	*Co-owner*
Conexión	*Connection*
Conferencia	*Conference*
Confirmación	*Confirmation*
Confirmar	*Confirm (to)*

354

Conflicto	*Conflict*
Conocimiento	*Knowledge*
Conserje	*Concierge*
Consocio	*Co-partner*
Consultante	*Consultant*
Consultar	*Consult (to)*
Contabilidad	*Accounting*
Contactar	*Contact (to)*
Contestación	*Reply*
Contestador automático	*Answering machine*
Contestar	*Answer (to)*
Contestar	*Reply (to)*
Contraseña	*Password*
Contrato	*Contract*
Control de calidad	*Quality control*
Convencer	*Convince (to)*
Convertidor	*Converter*
Copia	*Copy*
Corbata	*Tie*
Correo	*Mail*
Correo certificado	*Certified mail*
Correo de voz	*Voice mail*
Correo electrónico	*E-mail*
Correos	*Post office*
Costo	*Cost*
Costos legales	*Legal costs*
Crema	*Cream*
Cristal	*Glass*
Cronometrar	*Time (to)*
Cuaderno de trabajo	*Workbook*
Cuadradito	*Pound sign*
Cuadrado	*Square*
Cuatro	*Four*
Cubierta	*Cover*
Cuenta	*Bill*

Cuentas por cobrar	*Accounts payable*
Cuentas por pagar	*Accounts receivable*
Cultura	*Culture*
Cultural	*Cultural*
Curso	*Course*
Curva	*Curve*
Curva en forma de campana	*Bell-shaped curve*
Charla	*Discussion*
Cheque	*Check*
Cheque certificado	*Certified check*

D

Dar	*Give (to)*
Dar seguimiento	*Follow up (to)*
Datos	*Data*
Decidir	*Decide (to)*
Decir	*Say (to)*
Decisión	*Decision*
Demostración	*Demonstration*
Demostrar	*Demonstrate (to)*
Dentro	*Inside*
Departamento	*Department*
Deportes	*Sports*
Derecho	*Right*
Derechos literarios	*Copyright*
Desayuno	*Breakfast*
Descargar	*Download (to)*
Descentralización	*Decentralization*
Despejar	*Clear (to)*
Destacado	*Leading*
Devolución	*Refund*
Día	*Day*

Diagrama	*Diagram*
Diagrama de barra	*Bar chart*
Diagrama disperso	*Scatter diagram*
Diagramar	*Diagram (to)*
Diagramar	*Graph (to)*
Diálogo	*Dialogue*
Diapositiva	*Slide*
Diez	*Ten*
Dinero	*Money*
Dirección	*Address*
Direcciones	*Directions*
Director	*Director*
Directorio	*Directory*
Dirigir	*Direct (to)*
Dirigir	*Lead (to)*
Discar	*Dial (to)*
Disco	*Dial*
Disco de computadora	*Computer disk* (in Latin America)
Disco de ordenador	*Computer disk* (in Spain)
Discoteca	*Disco*
Disculpa	*Apology*
Discurso	*Speech*
Discutir	*Argue (to)*
Discutir	*Discuss (to)*
Diseño	*Design*
Diseño	*Layout*
Disfrutar	*Enjoy (to)*
Dispersión XY	*XY scatter*
Distribución	*Distribution*
Distribuir	*Distribute (to)*
Diversión	*Amusement*
Doblar	*Turn (to)*
Documento	*Document*

Dólar	*Dollar*
Dos	*Two*
Drama	*Drama*

E

Edificación de grupo	*Team building*
Edificio	*Building*
Efectivo	*Cash*
Eje de abscisas	*X-axis*
Eje de altura	*Z-axis*
Eje de ordenadas	*Y-axis*
Electricidad	*Electricity*
Elipse	*Ellipse*
Emitir	*Issue (to)*
Empaquetar	*Package (to)*
Empresa	*Company/enterprise/ firm*
Empresario	*Entrepreneur*
En forma de U	*U-shaped*
En línea	*Online*
Encabezamiento	*Heading*
Encendido/apagado	*(To be) on/off*
Encontrado	*Found*
Encontrar	*Find (to)*
Enfermera(o)	*Nurse*
Enlace	*Link*
Ensayar	*Rehearse*
Entender	*Understand (to)*
Entendimiento	*Understanding*
Entero	*Solid*
Entrada	*Entrance*
Entrega	*Delivery*
Entrega inmediata	*Special delivery*
Entrenamiento	*Coaching*

Entrenar	*Coach (to)*
Entresuelo	*Mezzanine*
Entretejido	*Crosshatched*
Entrevista	*Interview*
Entrevistar	*Interview (to)*
Enumerar	*List (to)*
Enviar	*Send (to)/ship (to)*
Enviar por correo	*Mail (to)*
Enviar un mensaje al beeper	*Page (to)*
Envió	*Shipment*
Equipaje	*Luggage*
Equipo	*Team*
Escala	*Scale*
Escala logarítmica	*Logarithmic scale*
Escribir	*Write (to)*
Escribir a máquina	*Type (to)*
Escritorio	*Desk*
Escuchar	*Listen (to)*
Especialidad	*Specialty*
Especificación	*Specification*
Esperar	*Hope (to)*
Esperar	*Wait (to)*
Esposa	*Wife*
Esposo	*Husband*
Espresso	*Espresso*
Esquiar	*Skiing*
Estación	*Season*
Estados Unidos de Norteamérica	*United States of America*
Estar de acuerdo	*Agree (to)*
Estilo	*Style*
Estrella	*Star*
Etiqueta	*Label*
Evaluar	*Appraise (to)*

Excel	*Excel software*
Exento de impuesto	*Tax-exempt*
Exhibición	*Display*
Exhibición	*Exhibit*
Exhibir	*Display (to)*
Exhibir	*Exhibit (to)*
Experiencia	*Experience*
Explicación	*Point*
Exponente	*Exponential*
Exportar	*Export (to)*
Extensión	*Extension*
Extensión eléctrica	*Extension cord*

F

Facilitador	*Facilitator*
Facilitar	*Facilitate (to)*
Factura	*Invoice*
Facturar	*Invoice (to)*
Falda	*Skirt*
Familia	*Family*
Fax	*Fax*
Fecha	*Date*
Fecha de entrega	*Delivery date*
Fecha tope	*Deadline*
Feria comercial	*Trade show*
Fiabilidad	*Liability*
Fianza	*Bond*
Fila	*Row*
Filosofía	*Philosophy*
Final	*End*
Finalizar	*End (to)*
Financiar	*Finance (to)*
Finanza	*Finance*
Firmar	*Sign (to)*

Flecha	*Arrow*
Flor	*Flower*
Folleto	*Brochure*
Formación	*Training*
Formar	*Train (to)*
Fotocopia	*Photocopy (to)*
Fotocopiadora	*Copier*
Fotografía	*Photograph*
Fotografía	*Picture*
Frente	*Front*
Fresco	*Cool*
Frío	*Cold*
Fuera	*Outside*
Funcionario	*Officer*
Fútbol americano	*Football*
Fútbol	*Soccer*

G

Gabinete	*Cabinet*
Galería	*Gallery*
Galería de arte	*Art gallery*
Ganar	*Gain (to)*
Garantía	*Guarantee*
Garantía	*Warranty*
Garantizar	*Guarantee (to)*
Gastos	*Expenses*
Gato	*Cat*
Geometría	*Geometry*
Gerente	*Manager*
Gestión	*Management*
Gestionar	*Manage (to)*
Gira	*Tour*
Giro de 180°	*U-turn*
Grabación	*Recording*

Grabador de vídeo	*Video recorder*
Grabadora	*Tape recorder*
Grabadora automática	*Answering machine*
Grabar	*Record (to)*
Grabar en vídeo	*Video (to)*
Gracias	*Thank you*
Gráfico	*Chart*
Gráfico circunferencial	*Pie chart*
Gráfico de barra horizontal	*Horizontal bar chart*
Gráfico de línea	*Line graph*
Gráfico de organización	*Organization chart*
Gráfico tridimensional	*3-D chart*
Gráfico	*Graph*
Guardia	*Guard*
Guía de teléfono	*Telephone directory*
Guión	*Dash*
Gustar	*Like (to)*

H

Habilidad(es)	*Skill(s)*
Habitación	*Room*
Hablar	*Speak (to)*
Hablar	*Talk (to)*
Hacer	*Make (to)*
Hacer una auditoría	*Audit (to)*
Helado	*Ice cream*
Hija	*Daughter*
Hijo	*Son*
Hipertexto	*Hypertext*
Histograma	*Histogram*
Historia	*History*
Hola	*Hello*
Hombre (Mujer) de empresa	*Entrepreneurship*

Hora	*Hour*
Hora	*Time*
Horario	*Schedule*
Horizontal	*Horizontal*
Hotel	*Hotel*
Hoy	*Today*

I

Idea	*Idea*
Iglesia	*Church*
Igual	*Peer*
Ilustración	*Illustration*
Ilustrar	*Illustrate (to)*
Importar	*Import (to)*
Impresora	*Printer*
Imprimir	*Print (to)*
Impuesto	*Tax*
Impuesto de venta	*Sales tax*
Impuesto sobre el valor añadido	*Value added tax*
Inaceptable	*Unacceptable*
Indicar	*Point (to)*
Indicador	*Pointer*
Individual	*Individual*
Información	*Information*
Información	*Information desk*
Información escrita	*Literature*
Informar	*Inform (to)*
Informe	*Report*
Informe de mercado	*Marketing report*
Informe financiero	*Financial report*
Informe de venta	*Sales report*
Ingeniero	*Engineer*

Inglés	*English*
Insignia	*Badge*
Instalación	*Installation*
Instalar	*Install (to)*
Instroducción	*Introduction*
Inteligencia	*Intelligence*
Inteligente	*Intelligent*
Internacional	*International*
Internet	*Internet*
Interruptor	*Switch*
Intervención	*Audit*
Intervenir	*Audit (to)*
Introducir	*Introduce (to)*
Inventario	*Inventory*
Inversión	*Investment*
Invertir	*Invest (to)*
Invierno	*Winter*
Izquierda	*Left*

J

Jazz	*Jazz*
Jefe	*Boss*
Joyas	*Jewelry*
Jugar	*Play (to)*

K

Karate	*Karate*

L

Lápiz	*Pencil*
Larga distancia	*Long distance*
Leche	*Milk*

Legal	*Legal*
Lenguaje	*Language*
Ley	*Law*
Ley internacional	*International law*
Libro	*Book*
Líder	*Leader*
Liderazgo	*Leadership*
Limusina	*Limousine*
Línea	*Line*
Línea de puntos	*Dotted line*
Línea de regresión	*Regression line*
Línea continua	*Solid line*
Línea directa	*Direct line*
Línea eléctrica	*Electrical line*
Lineal	*Linear*
Lista de distribución	*Mailing list*
Lista de vinos	*Wine list*
Local	*Local*
Logotipo	*Logo*
Lotus 1-2-3	*Lotus 1-2-3 software*
Luz	*Light*
Llamada de conferencia	*Conference call*
Llamada de larga distancia	*Long distance call*
Llamada local	*Local call*
Llamada sin aviso	*Cold call*
Llamada telefónica	*Phone call*
Llamar	*Call (to)*
Lluvia/lluvioso	*Rain/rainy*

M

Maleta	*Bag*
Malla	*Grid*
Mandar por fax	*Fax (to)*

Manejo	*Management*
Mañana	*Morning*
Mañana	*Tomorrow*
Mapa	*Map*
Máquina de escribir	*Typewriter*
Marca registrada	*Trademark*
Marcador	*Bookmark*
Marcador	*Marker*
Marketing	*Marketing*
Marrón	*Brown*
Más tarde	*Later*
Más temprano	*Earlier*
Matemáticas	*Mathematics*
Materiales	*Materials*
Máximo	*Maximum*
Mediar	*Mediate (to)*
Media	*Stocking*
Médico	*Doctor*
Medio	*Middle*
Medios	*Media*
Memoranda	*Memo*
Mensaje	*Message*
Mentor	*Mentor*
Menú	*Menu*
Mercado	*Market*
Mercancías	*Goods*
Merienda	*Snack*
Mes	*Month*
Mezquita	*Mosque*
Micrófono	*Microphone*
Mínimo	*Minimum*
Minuto	*Minute*
Mirar	*Look (to)*
Misión	*Mission*
Modelo	*Model*

Modem	*Modem*
Monitor	*Monitor*
Monitor de colores	*Color monitor*
Monitor de computadora	*Computer monitor* (in Latin America)
Monitor de ordenador	*Computer monitor* (in Spain)
Montar	*Set up (to)*
Morado	*Purple*
Mostrar	*Show (to)*
Motor de búsqueda	*Search engine*
Mover	*Move (to)*
Multimedia	*Multimedia*
Museo	*Museum*
Música	*Music*
Música clásica	*Classical music*

N

Naranja	*Orange*
Navegar	*Surf (to)*
Navegar por Internet	*Surf the Web*
Necesitar	*Need (to)*
Negociando	*Negotiating*
Negociar	*Negotiate (to)*
Negociar	*Transact (to)*
Negociar	*Bargain (to)*
Negocio	*Business*
Negocio	*Deal*
Negrita	*Bold*
Negro	*Black*
Nevoso	*Snowy*
Nieve	*Snow*
Niño	*Child*
Niños	*Children*

No	*No*
Noche	*Evening*
Noche	*Night*
Nombrar	*Name (to)*
Nombre	*Name*
Norteamericano	*American*
Nota	*Note*
Noticias	*News*
Nublado	*Cloudy*
Nueve	*Nine*
Nuevo	*New*
Número	*Number*
Número de teléfono	*Telephone number*

O

Objetivo	*Goal*
Objetivo	*Objective*
Objeto	*Object*
Obligación contractual	*Contractual obligation*
Obra musical	*Musical*
Ocupado	*Busy*
Ocho	*Eight*
Oficina	*Office*
Oficina central	*Central office*
Oficina de esquina	*Corner office*
Ofrecer	*Offer (to)*
Opción	*Option*
Opción sobre acciones	*Stock option*
Ópera	*Opera*
Operación	*Operation*
Operador	*Operator*
Operadora de teléfono	*Telephone operator*
Operar	*Operate (to)*
Orador	*Speaker*

Ordenador	*Computer* (in Spain)
Ordenador central	*Mainframe computer* (in Spain)
Ordenador portátil	*Laptop computer* (in Spain)
Organización	*Organization*
Organizar	*Organize (to)*
Orientación	*Orientation*
Origen	*Origin*
Orquesta	*Orchestra*
Otoño	*Fall*

P

Padre	*Parent*
Página	*Page*
Página inicial	*Home page*
Pago	*Payment*
Pago inicial	*Down payment*
País	*Country*
Palco	*Box*
Pantalla	*Screen*
Pantalla plana	*Flat-panel display*
Papel	*Handout*
Papel	*Paper*
Papelera	*Bin*
Paquete	*Package*
Parada	*Stop*
Parque	*Park*
Parque de atracciones	*Amusement park*
Parte	*Part*
Participante	*Participant*
Participar	*Participate*
Partido	*Play*
Pasaporte	*Passport*

Pasatiempo	*Hobby*
Pastel	*Pie*
Patente	*Patent*
Pausar	*Pause (to)*
Pedazo	*Slice*
Pedido por correo	*Mail order*
Película	*Film*
Película	*Movie*
Pensión	*Pension*
Perro	*Dog*
Personal	*Human resources*
Personal	*Personnel*
Perspicacia	*Insight*
Pescado	*Fish*
Pie	*Bottom*
Pieza	*Part*
Pila	*Stack*
Ping pong	*Ping-Pong*
Pizarra	*Blackboard*
Planificar	*Plan (to)*
Pleito	*Lawsuit*
Podio	*Podium*
Policía	*Policeman*
Polígono	*Polygon*
Póliza/pólizas/política(s)	*Policy/policies*
Pollo	*Chicken*
Poner una etiqueta	*Label (to)*
Por favor	*Please*
Porcentaje	*Percentage*
Portal	*Portal*
Portátil	*Portable*
Portero	*Porter*
Posición	*Location*
Posición	*Position*
Posponer	*Postpone (to)*

Precio	*Price*
Precio competitivo	*Competitive price*
Pregunta	*Query*
Pregunta	*Question*
Pregunta y Respuesta	*Q&A*
Preguntar	*Ask (to)*
Preguntar	*Question (to)*
Presentación	*Presentation*
Presentación PowerPoint	*PowerPoint presentation*
Presentar	*Present (to)*
Presentar	*Presenting*
Presidenta del consejo de dirección	*Chairwoman*
Presidente	*President*
Presidente del consejo de dirección	*Chairman*
Presidente/a del consejo de dirección	*Chairperson*
Primavera	*Spring*
Primero	*First*
Problema	*Problem*
Procedimiento	*Procedure*
Proceso	*Process*
Procurar	*Procure (to)*
Producción	*Production*
Producir	*Produce (to)*
Producto	*Product*
Programa	*Program*
Promoción	*Promotion*
Propiedad	*Property*
Proponer	*Propose (to)*
Propósito	*Purpose*
Propuesta	*Proposal*
Proveer	*Provide (to)*

Proyector de diapositivas	*Slide projector*
Pueblo	*Town*
Puerco	*Pork*
Puerta	*Door*
Puerta de embarque	*Gate*
Puesto de trabajo	*Work station*
Puro/Tabaco	*Cigar*

Q

Querer	*Want (to)*
Quizás	*Maybe*
Quiosco de periódicos	*Newsstand*

R

Raro	*Rare*
Reacción	*Feedback*
Reaccionar	*Feedback (to)*
Realidad virtual	*Virtual reality*
Reanudar	*Reboot*
Reanudar	*Resume (to)*
Recepción	*Reception*
Recepcionista	*Receptionist*
Recibir	*Receive (to)*
Recomendación	*Recommendation*
Recomendar	*Recommend (to)*
Reconocimiento de voz	*Voice recognition*
Reconsiderar	*Reconsider (to)*
Rechazar	*Reject (to)*
Rectángulo	*Rectangle*
Recursos humanos	*Human resources*
Red	*Network*
Red mundial	*World Wide Web*
Reducir	*Downsize (to)*

Reenviar	*Forward (to)*
Referencia	*Reference*
Referenciar	*Reference (to)*
Refrescos	*Refreshments*
Registrar	*Record (to)*
Registrar	*Register (to)*
Registrarse	*Check in (to)*
Registro	*Record*
Registro	*Recording*
Regresar	*Return (to)*
Regresión	*Regression*
Reloj de pared	*Clock*
Remisión	*Referral*
Rendimiento	*Yield*
Reorganizar	*Reorganize (to)*
Reserva	*Reservation*
Reservado	*Reserved*
Reservar	*Reserve (to)*
Resolver un problema	*Solve a problem (to)*
Responsabilidad	*Accountability*
Respuesta	*Answer*
Restaurante	*Restaurant*
Resultado	*Result*
Retroproyector	*Overhead projector*
Reunión	*Meeting*
Reunirse	*Meet (to)*
Revelar	*Reveal (to)*
Revisar	*Check (to)*
Revista	*Magazine*
Riesgo	*Risk*
Rojo	*Red*
Ropa	*Clothing*
Ropa interior	*Underwear*
Rugby	*Rugby*

Saber	*Know (to)*
Sala de espera	*Waiting room*
Salario	*Salary*
Salida	*Exit*
Salir	*Exit (to)*
Salón de clase	*Classroom*
Salón de conciertos	*Concert hall*
Salud	*Health*
Sastre	*Tailor*
Secretaria	*Secretary*
Segundo	*Second*
Seguro	*Insurance*
Seis	*Six*
Semana	*Week*
Seminario	*Seminar*
Servicial	*Helpful*
Servicio	*Service*
Servicio al cliente	*Customer service*
Servicio en línea	*Online service*
Servidor	*Server*
Sí	*Yes*
Siete	*Seven*
Silencio	*Quiet*
Silla	*Chair*
Símbolo de numeros	*Pound sign*
Sinagoga	*Synagogue*
Sindicato	*Union/Trade union*
Sistema de sonido	*Sound system*
Sistema	*System*
Sistema operativo	*Operating system*
Sitio	*Site*
Sobre	*Envelope*
Socio	*Partner*

Software	*Software*
Solicitar	*Request (to)*
Solución de problema	*Problem solving*
Sombra	*Shadow*
Sombreado	*Shaded*
Sombrero	*Hat*
Sombrilla/Paraguas	*Umbrella*
Someter	*Submit*
Souvenir	*Souvenir*
Subrayar	*Underline*
Subsidio	*Grant*
Suministrar	*Supply (to)*
Suministro	*Supply*
Superior	*Top*
Supervisor	*Supervisor*

T

Tabaco	*Tobacco*
Tabla	*Table*
Tablero	*Board*
Taller de trabajo	*Workshop*
Tarde	*Late*
Tarima	*Dais*
Tarjeta telefónica	*Calling card*
Tarjeta de presentación	*Business card*
Taxi	*Taxi*
Té	*Tea*
Teatro	*Theater*
Tecla	*Key*
Telefonear	*Phone (to)*
Teléfono	*Telephone*
Teléfono celular/móvil	*Cellular phone*
Teléfono de automóvil	*Car phone*

Teléfono portátil	*Portable phone*
Televisión	*Television*
Tema	*Subject*
Tema principal	*Key issue*
Temperatura	*Temperature*
Templado	*Warm*
Temprano	*Early*
Tensión	*Stress*
Teoría	*Theory*
Terminar la conexión	*Log off (to)*
Terminología	*Terminology*
Tesis	*Thesis*
Tesis central	*Central thesis*
Tesorero	*Treasurer*
Texto	*Text*
Tiempo	*Weather*
Tipo (de imprenta)	*Type*
Título	*Title*
Tiza	*Chalk*
Toma de decisión	*Decision making*
Torta	*Cake*
Trabajar	*Work (to)*
Trabajo	*Job*
Traje	*Suit*
Transferir	*Transfer (to)*
Transacción	*Transaction*
Transbordador	*Ferry*
Transparencia	*Transparency*
Transporte	*Transportation*
Trato	*Deal*
Tres	*Three*
Triángulo	*Triangle*

U

| Último | *Last* |
| Uno | *One* |

V

Valor	*Value*
Valor de mercado	*Market value*
Valorar	*Value (to)*
Vegetal	*Vegetable*
Vegetariano	*Vegetarian*
Vencido	*Due*
Vencido	*Past due*
Vender	*Sell (to)*
Vender	*Selling*
Venta	*Sales call*
Venta	*Sale*
Ventana	*Window*
Ver	*See (to)*
Verano	*Summer*
Verde	*Green*
Verdura	*Vegetable*
Vertical	*Vertical*
Vía	*Via*
Viajar	*Travel (to)*
Viaje	*Travel*
Vicepresidente	*Vice president*
Video	*Video*
Videoconferencia	*Video conferencing*
Vigilar	*Watch (to)*
Vino	*Wine*
Visión	*Vision*

Visita turística	*Sightseeing*
Volver a marcar	*Redial (to)*
Vuelo	*Flight*

W

Word	*Word software*
WordPerfect	*WordPerfect software*

Z

Zapato	*Shoe*
Zoológico	*Zoo*

INDEX

NOTES

NOTES

NOTES

NOTES

NOTES

NOTES